Becoming and Being Old
Sociological Approaches to Later Life

edited by

Bill Bytheway, Teresa Keil,

Patricia Allatt, Alan Bryman

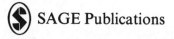

SAGE Publications

London • Newbury Park • New Delhi

published in association with the British Sociological Association

207969

SAGE Publications Ltd
28 Banner Street
London EC1Y 8QE

Sage Publications Inc
2111 West Hillcrest Drive
Newbury Park, California 91320

SAGE Publications India Pvt Ltd
32, M-Block Market
Greater Kailash – I
New Delhi 110 048

British Library Cataloguing in Publication data

Becoming and being old : sociological
    approaches to later life.
    1. Old age. Sociological perspectives
    I. Bytheway, W.R. (William R.)
    305.2'6

ISBN 0-8039-8170-8
ISBN 0-8039-8171-6 Pbk

Library of Congress catalog card number 88-062124

Typeset by Megaron, Cardiff.
Printed in Great Britain by J.W. Arrowsmith Ltd., Bristol

Becoming and Being Old

Contents

Preface

The chapters which appear in this book are based upon presentations at the British Sociological Association Conference, 'The Sociology of the Life Cycle', held at Loughborough University of Technology in March 1986. Two volumes of conference papers have already been published (Bryman *et al.*, 1987; and Allatt *et al.*, 1987). This third volume was prompted by the interest that was subsequently expressed in the papers that related to later life. We should like to thank all those who gave papers, the participants at the conference and those others who have contributed to the success of the conference. In particular we would like to thank the contributors to this volume, and Anne Dix and Mike Milotte of the British Sociological Association who have assisted and encouraged us in the completion of this third volume.

References

Allatt, P., Keil, T., Bryman, A. and Bytheway, B. (eds) (1987) *Women and the Life Cycle*. London: Macmillan.
Bryman, A., Bytheway, B., Allatt, P. and Keil, T. (eds) (1987) *Rethinking the Life Cycle*. London: Macmillan.

Introduction

When the British Sociological Association holds a conference on 'the life cycle', one should not be surprised when over a dozen of the 108 presented papers relate fairly directly to old age. Three of these have been included in the earlier volume of conference papers, *Rethinking the Life Cycle* (Williams, 1987; Finch, 1987; Cheal, 1987). They contributed to a comprehensive critique of the overly restricting concept of the life cycle. All three papers implied that a model which postulates a sequence of stages that concludes in 'old age' is no longer adequate. Finch, in particular, along with a number of other contributors, proposed the adoption of 'the life course' as a more appropriate concept, one that does not reduce life to a predetermined sequence abstracted from individual and corporate histories. This strategy, however, is also the subject of some sceptical comment, for example, by Stubbs in note 1 of her contribution to this volume (Chapter 1).

The problem, of course, is that it is not easy to reject convincingly the notion of old age as an invalid construction, in that the concept of old age has been central to popular accounts of the course of life over many centuries. Somehow or other sociologists have to promote the study of later life which relates to both 'the realities' and 'the ideologies' of the ageing experience. The contributions to this volume are primarily oriented to the former. This, we would suggest, is largely because the realities of old age have come to be seen within contemporary government policies in most countries as presenting problems that require study, understanding and solutions; and sociologists, among others, have responded.

In planning the structure of this book it was clear that the available material fell into two groups. In addition to those contributions focussed upon 'the elderly' there were others relating to various transitions in mid- and later life. Rather than reflect the life cycle model and have this latter group represent some 'pre-old-age' stage or indeed 'a period of transition', it seemed more appropriate to attempt a more direct linking between the two groups using a rather more sociological model.

It is the word 'old' that prompts this alternative. It is one of many adjectives in the English language that are directly associated with the social statuses that can be ascribed to individual people. Within contemporary literature on sexism and racism there are many discussions of the importance of language and the ways in which adjectives such as 'female' and 'coloured' can both reflect and induce stereotypical ways of thinking. There have been similar discussions about the implications of words such as 'geriatric' and 'elderly'. Strangely, much of this has skirted around the more simple and basic word, 'old'.

Let us suppose that we accept this word as applicable to certain people and that those to whom it is applied at any point in time are born before those to whom it is not applied. It would then follow that in the course of life people become old and thereafter remain old. Given this simple model, implicit as it is within the linguistic structure of popular speech (at least in the English language), the sociological student of age would be encouraged to distinguish between the process of becoming and the status of being old.

To date, gerontologists have tended towards a double standard, on occasions disputing the notion of 'becoming old' (for example, 'No one becomes old overnight') whilst simultaneously drawing heavily upon samples of 'elderly people'. The sociologist could argue that this confusion reflects popular ideologies that simultaneously segregate 'the elderly' and seek to deny the inevitability of the ageing process. A good if enigmatic example of such double-think is to be found in the opening paragraph of the foreword to the White Paper *Growing Older*: 'a large number of us can in future expect to live longer. There will be many more very old people' (Department of Health and Social Security, 1981: iii).

Concluding this volume are two chapters which critically examine the utility of the concept of old age. It is in the complex interplay between institutions, belief and personal experience that the sociologist has most to contribute to the interdisciplinary study of age and old age, and it is this idea that underlies the organisation of this volume.

Chapter 1 by Stubbs focusses upon the purchase of council houses in Sunderland during the 1970s and 1980s. Stubbs shows how this kind of change in housing tenure relates to the process of ageing and concludes from her fieldwork that those approaching pensionable age are seeking to secure a future for their families through the purchase of property. Change in housing tenure is a striking example of the need for the critical analysis of age relations to be grounded in 'meanings . . . for specific kinds of people in specific sets of social relations in specific locations at specific times'.

Laczko's (Chapter 2) is the first of three chapters largely focussed upon retirement. Laczko is concerned in particular with early retirement and the increasingly complex transition from work to retirement. Using data from the General Household Survey (the first of three chapters in this volume to do so), he demonstrates how the lower social classes are the more vulnerable to unemployment and ill health as they approach the end of their working lives. He shows that there is greater heterogeneity in income within the 'non-employed' 60- to 64-year-olds than within the retired 65- to 69-year-olds, suggesting a conclusion that early work-ending is leading towards 'two nations': one being those most dependent upon state benefits and having the lowest incomes, and the other retiring early on the basis of occupational pensions and continuing unearned and spouse's earnings.

Schuller's Chapter 3 neatly complements Laczko's. Drawing upon fieldwork in Greenwich, Schuller seeks to amplify the ambiguity of formal employment within working life. He argues that current shifts in the labour market are leading to a 'feminisation of employment' characterised by fragmentation, discontinuity, unpredictability, downward mobility, part-time work and marginal status. In conclusion, Schuller suggests that the knot which tied ending work to entering old age is being loosened. He predicts that a new vocabulary will develop regarding both state benefits and self-identity.

Long in Chapter 4 draws upon a study of men living in Edinburgh who retired 'normally' from full-time employment at the age of 65. He was interested to study how they coped with the negative connotations of retirement and what part leisure played in their response. Like Schuller, he draws our attention to the inherent ambiguity that exists, even when retirement is a sharply defined threshold. He sees leisure as a means of maintaining continuity over the transition and of retaining a sense of autonomy and choice over the course of life.

These four chapters indicate how the process of becoming old is characterised by ambiguity and heterogeneity. National policies and associated trends in housing regulation and employment directly affect the approach of individuals to their 'old age'. Ageing individuals variously endeavour to secure the future for themselves and their families both by successfully negotiating an end to their working lives, and by acquiring control over their dwellings and daily activities. Those with economic power are better able to exercise choice and increasingly benefit from recent social trends.

Turning now to 'being old', Arber and Gilbert in Chapter 5 use the 1980 General Household Survey to critically examine the composition of households that include people aged 65 or over. Focussing in particular upon the provision of care, they find that nearly three-quarters of all co-resident carers are spouses or siblings – themselves elderly people. Only an eighth are the married women who have typified 'the carer' in recent critical discussions of community care policies. Whilst it is clear from their analysis that major gender differences remain, particularly in regard to the process of selection, they provide a salutory reminder that there is more to being old than simply a slide from independence into dependency.

To substantiate this, Bytheway in Chapter 6 provides a case study that illustrates how care is produced within and between households. It also provides good evidence of the dramatic changes that have occurred over the last thirty years in the process of becoming old. In particular, whilst chronological age remains the most frequently used criterion for the exclusion of older people from employment and for the determination of their pension and welfare benefits, the actual regulations which are deployed have been totally transformed within the space of one generation. In regard to being old, however, the study suggests that, rather than the structured dependency resulting from state policies, it may be the passing of the older generation that has their children's generation feeling that they have now become old.

Returning again to the General Household Survey, Evandrou and Victor in Chapter 7 examine variation within the population aged 65 and over. In particular they are concerned to relate different life-styles in old age to social class. Following Bertaux they show that occupational measures of social class are predictive of variation in income, tenure, housing quality and consumer durables. However, recognising the limitations of occupation as an indicator of the social class of women, they advocate the use of tenure as an alternative axis of differentiation, and show that it too is an effective indicator of health status and income.

Wall's contribution (Chapter 8) extends this critical analysis of national statistics concerning the elderly population, by undertaking a comparison of European census data regarding the living arrangements of elderly people. Inevitably the potential of this level of analysis is almost completely frustrated by the lack of consistency between different countries. Nevertheless, he is able to demonstrate the trend towards solitary living, particularly in Western Europe, and argues that the 'considerable diversity' that still survives in living arrangements warrants more detailed examination. He might have added that his study also suggests that a comparative analysis would be useful of the priorities of the various census authorities, and of what this would imply about different national policies regarding the needs that arise from being old.

Featherstone and Hepworth in Chapter 9 open the concluding part of the book with a critical discussion of the utility of the concept of the life course and of the use of chronological age in its modern institutionalisation. They draw our attention to changes in popular culture and to postmodern theorising based upon emergent cultural tendencies. Gubrium's thesis that old age is a mask concealing a more youthful self is shown to be increasingly popular as evidenced by the importance of clothes in constructing age-specific images. In conclusion they propose that old age can only be understood in the context of (a) the accounts that are constructed of other stages of life, (b) the course of the individual's past life and (c) the relation of old people to younger generations.

In the final chapter (Chapter 10), Blakemore sets the experience of old age against that of minority ethnic status and asks the question: does age matter? He argues that the study of ageing should be engaged in other areas of sociological discourse, and in the study of ethnicity in particular. Like other contributors to this volume, he questions the presumption that age is 'the great leveller', and critically examines the double jeopardy hypothesis regarding age and race. He concentrates specifically upon (a) social relationships and (b) indicators of life-satisfaction in later life, among Afro-Caribbean and South Asian people living in Britain. He concludes with an open verdict regarding double jeopardy, and disputes the value of such court-room approaches to sociological inquiry. He suggests that a positive answer to the question in the title of his chapter may be found in comparisons not between different social groups but rather between generations or cohorts within particular groups.

References

Bryman, A., Bytheway, B., Allatt, P. and Keil, T. (eds) (1987) *Rethinking the Life Cycle*. London: Macmillan.

Cheal, D. (1987) 'Intergenerational transfers and life course management: towards a socio-economic perspective', in Bryman *et al.*, op. cit., pp. 141–54.

Department of Health and Social Security (1981) *Growing Older*. London: HMSO.

Finch, J. (1987) 'Family obligations and the life course', in Bryman *et al.*, op. cit., pp. 155–69.

Williams, R. (1987) 'Images of old age and generation among older Aberdonians', in Bryman *et al.*, op. cit., pp. 88–102.

PART ONE

BECOMING OLD

1

Property Rites? An Investigation of Tenure Change in Middle Age

Cherrie Stubbs

Mid-life seems a curiously empty stretch in most life cycle accounts of ageing. The middle aged are only seen as being sociologically interesting if they face problems such as those associated with employment (redundancy with little prospect of re-employment, or professional 'burn-out', for example), individual stress (the 'mid-life crisis') or coping with the biological exigencies of ageing (Fogarty, 1975). Of equal sociological importance, however, are the social relations between age-groups and generations and the social transitions that the 'middle aged' may face. Attempting to delineate precisely those in mid-life is a thankless task, since the experience will differ by gender and class, race and nationality. Consequently, a relational rather than categorical analysis is indicated. Moreover, the positive advantages that mid-life can bring also repay attention.

Becoming older means negotiating changing social roles, relations and expectations, as well as facing biological transitions, often with little positive ideological support in Western society (Phillipson, 1982). However, this process can involve acquiring new forms of power, influence and security, particularly in the context of the family (Fogarty, 1975).

In this chapter, I intend to demonstrate how one social transition, a change of housing tenure, relates to the process of ageing for a group of mid-life tenants who bought their council houses from a northern local authority. Their experiences are not universal: as will be demonstrated below, the former tenants constitute a restricted group, bound by the class, gender and age relations of their situation. The tenure shift they experienced was unique. Their histories, however, do serve to illustrate the importance of housing in age relations, and the role of ideology in personal life decisions.

Ageing and tenure

Ageing and age relations have received scant attention in the sociology of housing. The challenge, as Kemeny (1979) recognised, is to understand the interplay between the lifetime occupation of housing and the family life cycle, but few housing experts have taken up this challenge (Watson, 1986).

Housing is a very particular form of property. It relates in an immediate way to issues of birth, death and sexuality, and is one means by which they are socially regulated, largely by the enforcement of the link between housing provision and family-household living. The deferral of child-rearing in order to maximise mortgage repayments, the bearing of children in order to establish an independent (or rather state-benefit-dependent) household in the public sector or the patri-archal sexual dependency still implicit in many tenure relations are all examples of this (Watson, 1986). A moment's reflection on the powerful appeal of 'starter homes' for young couples, of 'family' housing or of the 'granny flat' would indicate that securing the normality of the nuclear family – an institutional arrangement now involving a minority of British households at any one time – is at issue here. The life cycle[1] into which households are slotted in such conceptualisations is of course a *family* life cycle.

In this ideologically acceptable family life cycle, domestic property clearly plays some material part. It also plays a symbolic role in the rituals legitimating transitions such as coming of age and marriage. For example, adult status is implied by the symbolic granting of 'the key of the door', and 'carrying over the threshold' has many of the features and connotations of the rituals that Bocock (1974) describes as characteristic of industrial societies. Home ownership has also been suggested as a key cultural signifier of responsibility and maturity – and indeed a significant rite of passage (Musgrove and Middleton, 1981). Conversely, to give up one's home or to remain within the household of the family of origin is to prejudice the right to adult status.

Housing, then, can exacerbate a problematic status, in a situation where domestic property is a cultural signifier of social relations and boundaries, as well as an indicator of material standing. If domestic property gives access to credit (both material and ideological), the lack of it can have de-valorising effects, as Watson (1986) has discussed in relation to single homeless women. At a time when council tenancy[2] is being marginalised (Forrest and Murie, 1986), the prospect of ageing without the security of domestic property ownership might be expected to be daunting for the middle-aged council tenant, particularly when significant others of the same age group have achieved the status of ownership.

It is, of course, members of the mid-life group who have made most gains from the spread of owner occupation. They have benefited in particular from the capital gains from domestic property engendered by the 'Barber boom' of the early 1970s, largely at the expense of other age groups. In one of the few discussions of this, Murie and Forrest note that 'the cohort of first generation owners whose purchase of housing between the wars marked the first significant growth of owner-occupation are now ageing outright owners' (1980: 11). They suggest that the inheritance of domestic property is most likely to occur when households are well on into a housing career, and highlight the importance of inter-generational transfers, and indeed transfers that skip a generation, in this inheritance.

In some ways, those who are now in their middle years approximate to what Abrams (1982) meant by a 'generation', a term that in his usage involves a cultural consciousness of time and place. Their experience of housing in general has cultural meaning which derives from the historical costs and benefits of those experiences, both material and non-material. Tenure relations in particular are historically and socially constructed;[3] and even within tenure groups the *meaning* of that tenure will be spatially and historically bounded, and will entail differing material and ideological realities for different kinds of people. This cohort, whose social consciousness was forged out of welfare and warfare, was responsible for establishing public housing as a majority tenure as part of the post-war settlement that was in some ways 'collectivist', involving a distinct sense of historic mission. Perhaps uniquely, the people who made individual housing decisions in the 1940s and 1950s did so at a time when public housing was seen as the progressive tenure, albeit in ways that were never secure – in part at least because of the social relations of the production and provision of that housing. The cohort of people that is now buying council housing is precisely the cohort for whom public tenures worked: they are buying at a time when that collective settlement is being threatened.

The purchase of council housing on Wearside

Details of the history of council house sales in Sunderland have been given elsewhere (Stubbs, 1985). Briefly, a short period of sales in the early 1970s was followed by a second period in the early 1980s. Given a relatively high degree of immobility in Sunderland, it was possible to select three adjoining estates and undertake a comparative study of two distinct groups of early and late buyers and a matched group of non-buyers. Consequently, a stratified sample survey was conducted with three groups of residents, all of whom had been resident at the same address since at least 1973. The three groups were obtained as follows:

1 a 50 per cent sample of households who had bought during the early round of sales and who were still resident at the same address at the time of the survey;
2 a 20 per cent sample of those buying under the 1980 Act, who had also been resident at the same address in 1973;
3 a 5 per cent sample of non-buyers, who had similarly been resident in 1973, but who had not registered any intention to buy under the Act.

The estates chosen reflected the middle range of Sunderland's housing stock, neither the most popular nor those that are the most 'difficult to let'. The household survey was conducted with any adult member of the household, and was complemented by taped interviews, the majority of which involved both partners where applicable. The distribution of households who took part in the household survey is shown in Table 1.1. Overall, 163 households (almost four-fifths of the 208 who were initially approached) took part in the study, with refusals or non-contacts being concentrated in the non-buyers category.

Table 1.1 *Household survey respondents*

	Early buyers	Late buyers	Non-buyers	Total
Estate 1				
Refusals	1	6	17	24
Interviewed	13	41	37	91
Estate 2				
Refusals	1	5	8	14
Interviewed	12	22	17	51
Estate 3				
Refusals	1	1	5	7
Interviewed	2	11	8	21
Total				
Refusals	3	12	30	45
Interviewed	27	74	62	163

It is important to note that this was not a random survey of all purchasing households, and does not enable claims to be made about all purchasers. It does, however, enable a comparison between three groups of people who had shared many housing experiences until the decision to buy.

Social background of respondents

The majority of households in the sample could roughly be designated
as 'middle aged'. Overall, the ages of the respondents spanned the late
thirties to the late sixties, over 80 per cent being in their forties or fifties.
The buying households were significantly younger than the non-
buyers, as Table 1.2 makes clear.

Table 1.2   *Age of respondent at time of survey*

	Early buyers %	Late buyers %	Non-buyers %
Under 40	7	8	7
41–50	41	44	16
51–60	48	40	37
Over 60	4	9	40
Total (= 100%)	27	74	62

The majority of buyers were still in the labour market at the time of
the survey. The employment experiences of the *men* in the early buyers'
households approximated very closely to the buyers studied by Murie
(1975) in Birmingham in the 1970s. At the time of purchase, the
majority of them were in skilled manual employment. None was
unemployed, sick or retired, and their job descriptions remind us of the
range of male employment opportunities that have to some extent been
lost during the current recession. However, their experience was very
similar to men in later buying households. These late buyers were
equally unlikely to have been 'economically inactive' in 1973, and if
anything were somewhat more likely to be in skilled, time-served jobs
in the mining, construction or shipbuilding industries than were the
men in early buying households.

Murie provided little information on the employment experiences of
women in the purchasing households that he studied, despite his
assertion of the importance of multiple wage packets in the purchase of
Birmingham council houses. In Sunderland, the majority of women in
households that bought in the 1970s certainly did contribute directly to
the household income at the time of purchase. They were employed in a
range of jobs, often part-time, which included office work, catering,
hospital and factory work. Much of this was on the twilight shift in the
local manufacturing concerns which have provided a traditional
source of female employment in the area.

Again, in this they were very similar to women in households that did
not buy in the 1970s, but bought later. Table 1.3 illustrates the distinct

similarity between the employment patterns of both men *and* women in both early and late buying households. It is the men and women in the eventual non-buying households who stand out as being less likely to have been in paid employment at that early stage. Some of them had already retired by 1973, but the high proportion of full-time women employees in the non-buying households also suggests that an age-related factor was at work. These full-timers would obviously have been contributing *more* to the household income than would many of the women in buying households. There is little here, then, to support the idea that women's earnings were central to the early decision to buy.

Table 1.3   *Employment status in 1973*

	Early buyers		Late buyers		Non-buyers	
	male %	female %	male %	female %	male %	female %
Full-time	89	22	77	15	63	24
Part-time	—	44	—	43	—	18
Sick	—	—	—	1	7	1
Unemployed	—	—	—	1	5	2
Retired	—	—	—	—	7	10
Houseworker	—	33	—	35	—	37
Not applicable	5	—	4	—	16	3
Not relevant	5	—	20	5	3	4

Women in non-buying households were more likely to be doing manual jobs, but the differences are not large enough to suggest that women's 'skill levels', any more than their wage packets, were crucial to the decision to buy. On the contrary, all of the interview material suggested that, for the buyers, it was 'his' wage that bought the house for 'her', and respondents were at pains to stress that she 'didn't *have* to work'.

Changing labour markets in Sunderland, and the crucial role increasingly being played by female part-time employment (see, for example, Stone and Stephens, 1986; Stubbs and Wheelock, 1986), make it improbable that women's full-time earnings are central to the calculation today, either. Available evidence would suggest that women's participation in the 'formal' economy in Sunderland is heavily overdetermined by family circumstance (Chaney, 1985), and the supplementary benefit earnings rule further ensures locally that full-time work for married women is not the norm. Not surprisingly, then, women's employment patterns in the 1980s again show a tendency for the buyers to be in part-time employment, and for such women to be in employed households.

By the time that the respondents were considering their options under the 'right to buy' legislation, many more people in non-buying households – both male and female – were describing themselves as retired, as Table 1.4 indicates.

Table 1.4   *Employment status in 1983*

| | Early buyers | | Late buyers | | Non-buyers | |
	male %	female %	male %	female %	male %	female %
Full-time	63	19	70	16	21	10
Part-time	—	41	1	41	2	13
Sick	4	—	3	1	3	2
Unemployed	19	8	15	4	21	8
Retired	—	4	7	11	24	19
Houseworker	—	30	—	26	—	39
Not applicable	15	—	4	1	29	10

Although the men in households that bought in the 1980s were less likely to be retired than men in non-buying households, they were almost as likely to be unemployed. By the 1980s, both women and men in all three groups had experienced the redundancy and unemployment that the current restructuring has brought to the town. The indications are, then, that age and/or life cycle stage are the most important social factors affecting the decision to buy.

Household structure

The connection between the purchase of council housing and life cycle stage is made clearer when we examine the household structures of the three groups. The buyers at both phases stand out as being more likely to have been at an earlier stage of the family life cycle, to have still been living as part of a couple and to have had dependent children living with them. This approximation to a nuclear family norm is partly a function of age, but it is more than this. All of the divorced or separated were found in the non-buyers category, for instance, as well as the overwhelming majority of people whose marriage had been split by death. Equally there were few cohabitees in the buyers category. Although the pattern of nuclear family household living was dominant across all three groups (for instance, 95 per cent of the sample had been married only once, and the vast majority of marriages had lasted over twenty years), and was in part a function of the study design, the differences that do occur are of significance. They tend to suggest that occupation of the kind of council housing that one might want to buy is likely to be an outcome of conformist family practices, but that it is necessary to be of the right age to take advantage of this. Maximum discounts, of course, were given to those settled households which had achieved a particular kind of housing through transfer or through continuous occupation, either of which is likely to involve similarly 'normal' family behaviour. The data are summarised in Table 1.5.

Table 1.5 *Family household situation in 1983*

	Early buyers %	Late buyers %	Non- buyers %
Single person	4	2	16
Couple	19	21	23
Single parent (plus dependent children)	—	3	—
Couple (plus dependent children)	26	37	15
Household with dependent adults	4	2	5
Household with non-dependent older children	38	4	12
Household with dependent older children	7	31	30

The single households in the non-buyers category are primarily older people. Over a quarter of the non-buyers were widowed, compared with less than 5 per cent of people in buying households. The relatively low number of households containing dependent children is also indicative of the age factor.

On the basis of this data, it would seem that council house purchase in the 1980s is, as Murie suggested in the 1970s, 'associated with the position of purchasers in the family cycle, with retirement and the prospect of children leaving home influencing decisions, alongside income and social class' (1975: 127). It is not legitimate to suggest a connection with children's wage-earning potential, however. The early buyers are *now* more likely to have adult children contributing to the household income, but these children were *not* earning at the time of purchase. Further doubt is cast on the idea that adult children's earnings might be taken into account in the decision to buy by comparing current non-buyers with current buyers. The late buyers are presently over three times *less* likely to have adult wage-earning

children living with them than non-buyers, as well as being significantly *more* likely to have dependent children living at home. Such
differences as there are in the contribution of children's wage packets
to the household finances, then, seem again to be an outcome of life
cycle stage rather than indications of material differences structuring a
decision to buy. There was no more evidence in the interview material
that children's earnings were taken into account in the purchase
decision than there was that wives' earnings were a determining factor.
Indeed, the very strong impression was that, at both phases, the male/
'family' wage was what mattered.

The early buyers, then, had tended to buy in early middle age, with
dependent school-children still at home, and with the woman either
working full-time in the house or combining domestic work with part-
time paid employment. The later buyers in the Sunderland sample,
however, seem to constitute two distinct groups: one that is very similar
in life cycle terms to the early buyers, catching up on what is seen as a
missed opportunity, and a younger cohort which is replicating the
experience of the early buyers, but in a very different ideological and
political climate, when the economics of purchase are constructed very
differently.

It is possible to agree to some extent that buyers in the 1970s, and
some of those in the 1980s, tended to be 'those tenants who can squeeze
in the necessary mortgage payments between the end of their family
rearing and the beginning of retirement . . . when the inducement of a
discount for length of residence is also highest' (Popplestone, 1980: 8).
However, this picture is *not* true of all of the buyers of the 1980s. Some
of them were younger than Popplestone suggests (this group no doubt
overlapping with the buyers who did not fulfil my criteria of residence),
whilst others were well into their sixties. Some of them had dependent
children still living at home and were far from the end of child-rearing;
others had already seen their children well settled into their own adult
lives.

Housing histories

The housing histories of the Sunderland households illustrate very
clearly the ways in which life cycles are lived out within particular
generational constraints, and the ways in which ideological and
material constraints at each period structure the 'choices' that are
available. What Abrams (1982: 240) calls 'the calender of the life cycle
of the individual and the calender of historical experience' are closely
related for these tenants.

Sunderland's housing stock, like that of any other local authority, reflects the balance of class and gender forces of the time of its construction, and both quantity and quality of dwellings available to households in housing need have varied (Dennis, 1970). The housing available in the 1950s was and still is preferred by most tenants to the housing – and particularly the flats – of the 1960s. Housing built at a time of very traditional gender relations is still popular. Many of the buyers and non-buyers alike had entered tenure in the 1940s and 1950s before the challenge to traditional nuclear family living was established and at a time when council tenancy was both respected and respectable. These particular households represent the generation for whom council house tenancy became a normal working-class tenure. In their own lives, many of them exemplify the tenure changes that have occurred nationally over the period, moving from private renting through council tenure to ownership. They have consequently been subject to the changing political evaluations of council tenure that have been apparent through that time.

As children, men and women in buying and non-buying households alike had been brought up in a variety of tenures, though the buyers at both phases had had more experience of owner occupation than had non-buyers, and more of the current non-buyers had spent their childhood in privately rented accommodation (75 per cent of women and 66 per cent of men, compared with figures of 44 and 40 per cent for early buyers). The experience of childhood ownership may have sensitised the early buyers to the possibility of purchase in the 1970s. Many couples in all three groups had started their married life in the rooms or flats in the central areas of Sunderland that were to be cleared in the 1960s. They still remembered vividly the physical conditions and insecurity that this tenure involved at that time. Almost without exception, they spoke of the housing need that only the building of council estates had alleviated. In other words, the real though partial gains that an imperfectly collectivised solution represented were recognised as such by those with lengthy experience of council tenancy. Particularly for the residents on the estates built in the early 1950s, the new housing was seen as a 'dream come true', and time wiped out any memory of the loneliness or social isolation that the community studies of the 1960s had commented on. This was true for buyers and non-buyers alike. Many of them, for instance, had been involved in the early days in establishing community associations or youth clubs, and a number of the women had worked in local shops, pubs or schools.

Early buyers had been more likely to come into the council sector through the waiting list than had households in the other categories, and were less likely to have been through the experience of slum clearance. Many of them had put their names down on the waiting list at marriage or on the birth of a first child, and had had to wait some time before securing a council house – see Table 1.6.

For those who had achieved desirable council housing in the 1950s through whatever channels – and about half of the early buyers reported that they were well pleased with their first and only house – council tenancy as such seems to have presented few problems in the early days. Though some referred to the resentment they felt at having to have permission to 'hang a nail on a wall', more reported being well satisfied. As one said: 'After the rooms, being a council tenant was paradise, absolute paradise'. It was the comparison with what had gone before that was so important. The facilities were better, the amount of space was better, and there was less grumbling about the council as a landlord than there had been about the private landlords. Furthermore, the relatively settled nature of council tenancy compared with private landlordism had allowed tenants either to change and 'improve' the house that they were allocated, or to arrange a transfer to better accommodation.

Table 1.6   *Access to council housing*

	Early buyers %	Late buyers %	Non-buyers %
Waiting list	59	46	42
Clearance	26	37	42
Homeless	4	8	5
Other	11	10	11

The decision to buy

When the opportunity to buy the house that the household was occupying arose in the early 1970s, by no means as much publicity and controversy surrounded the initiative as was to happen in the 1980s. Indeed, sizeable proportions of both late buyers (28.4 per cent) and eventual non-buyers (37.1 per cent) were not aware of the early option to buy, and others were simply not interested in buying at that time. However, those who were to go on to buy in the 1980s were both more knowledgeable about, and more interested in, the possibility of purchase at that earlier time. They had also shown more interest in property ownership in general than had the non-buyers, with more of them reporting that they had discussed the possibility at the time of marriage. This possibility, though, had remained a remote, generalised hope, rather than an option that was actively investigated. Indeed, only one or two households in any of the groups had looked at properties to buy before 1970, and similarly few had looked seriously before the 1980 Act came into force. The reasons given for not buying in the earlier round of sales are interesting: the one given most often (by 34 per cent of the late buyers and by 53 per cent of the eventual non-buyers) was low wages, but this was closely followed for the late buyers by attitudes such as: 'We weren't brought up to it. We thought it would be a millstone round our necks'. Dislike of the house or neighbours was the next most common reason given. In other words, quite strongly held views against ownership in general or against ownership of that particular house seem as important in explaining the early non-purchase as do material economic circumstances. By the early 1980s, both had changed.

Some indication of what was to change was foreshadowed in the reasons given by those who did buy in the 1970s. Many were already making judgements, vindicated in practice, that the material costs of remaining a council tenant would rise for households such as theirs: 'We got a shock at the way Washington New Town rents were going, and thought Sunderland's would go the same way'. Or: 'The wife got worried at the rumours of means-tested rents. Our repayments are at a fixed rate of interest, but the rents never go down'. Such households are well aware *now* that their current monthly mortgage repayments are on average only a quarter of their neighbours' rental costs. At the time, however, material calculations did not seem overwhelming. Only two of the early buyers talked in terms of seeing the house as a *bargain* at the 20 per cent discount then being offered. Most had had no intention of reselling at the time of purchase. The material issue was one of rents, not capital accumulation.

The other aspect that was to change was, of course, the socio-political dimension of remaining a tenant: the changing nature of council landlordism and the related stigmatisation of council tenancy. Much of this had to do with the notable worsening of physical conditions on the estates, but many of the early buyers had been critical of the council well before the deterioration of services in recent years.

It would be wrong, however, to see the early decision to buy as a straightforward escape from the constraints of tenancy. What became very clear from the interviews was that buying fitted into a pattern of securing a family life-style that the buyers perceived to be under threat from the changing nature of the local state. Purchase was as much a matter of securing family use values and status values as it was of enhancing market position or of securing freedoms.

The irony is that, on one level, the local state has operated with a model of nuclear family living that is very similar to that of its tenants, but one that is hardly sustainable today. For example, although informal observation in area housing offices suggests that 'better' housing is still going to 'better' families, the nature of housing relations at present means that few such family households are currently being housed in the council sector. Residualisation means that the council stock becomes a refuge for different kinds of households. Looking at this process in Sunderland, Campbell notes that 'Labourism has failed to produce a politics of private life which is not patriarchal; at best it pities the dole queue mothers, at worst it scorns them' (1984: 79). An authority which is profoundly patriarchal, then, finds itself administering a housing stock that is tenanted by a combination of elderly and non-nuclear families.

The Sunderland residents are, of course, aware of this connection between tenure form and family life, but not in any critical way. On the contrary, they currently see ownership as a welcome opportunity to *consolidate* family life. Both late and early buyers had largely restricted their discussions about purchase to other family members, and there was little evidence of joint action with neighbours to secure market values. It was the family that counted in the decision-making process, and family use values that were being secured by that decision. A number of both early and late buying parents saw their action as securing a resident (or more importantly a non-resident) son or daughter's future. This was a growing concern for the later buyers as they saw the deterioration of opportunities in the council sector. As one said: 'The daughter's dumped in a flat, and there's others get offered six or seven houses. At least there'll be something for her when I go.'

For the early buyers in particular, buying was an emotional and symbolic commitment to a family future that outweighed any motive of material gain: 'It's security for the future for them.' Or: 'The kids want to stay here.' Or even more directly: 'It's mine now. And I don't want anyone else to have the house even when I die. The family's been here since the house was built, and I want them to go on living here.'

The familism of the buying households was in tune with the familism of the local state (and vice versa). The double-edged paternalism of attitudes such as 'I bought it for her' was repeated quite frequently in discussions of the undertaking and financing of the *improvements* that are so much a feature of the transfer of tenure. This was how one early buyer expressed it: 'My main idea is that I like to think which way a woman should have her place, you know. To make it easy for her. A woman's job is hard, and these changes, I like to think, make it easier for her.' It is domination of the most benevolent kind. I think that it is possible to argue that domestic life was further privatised for this group of people at the same time as tenure was privatised. The home improvements and garden fences were just one side of it; as important was the withdrawal from a collective experience and an espousal of privatised responsibility for children's futures.

This was, of course, just one strand in a complex web of motivations and meanings. Particularly for the later buyers, the 'decision' *was* heavily overdetermined (1) by the material inducements being constructed by the central state, (2) by the experience of neighbours who just like themselves had bought earlier and who were benefiting financially from the purchase and (3) by the changing meaning and nature of council tenancy in the 1970s. But even so, it would still seem that the financial calculations were matched by a strong emotional appeal. When asked how they felt about the house just after they had bought it, for instance, the majority of buyers were prepared to say that after the change of tenure they *did* feel differently about the house which they had lived in for years. The tendency was even more marked for later buyers – see Table 1.7.

Table 1.7   *Reactions to house after purchase*

	Early buyers %	Late buyers %
Feel secure	4	13
Feel independent	15	7
'More mine, somehow'	19	37
More likely to improve or take care of it	22	31
See it as an investment now	7	6
No change	33	4

Tenure change as a rite of passage?

How are we to understand this? After all, the same people were occupying the same housing in the same place in the same family relations. The impact of the tenure change on their labour market position had been negligible. On any real assessment of dreams and realities, the housing that they will continue to occupy will be a compromise – difficult to be sure of selling; part of a housing market whose boundaries and functions are as yet indeterminate; in a peripheral spatial location in a town in which, Nissan notwithstanding, the labour force is being restructured into a reserve if not a surplus role.

Hardly a reality that is in any *real* sense part of a national property-owning popular democracy. Not even perhaps a very sound long-term individual bet, unless subsidies are maintained and repair grants made more widely available. Equally, there is still the barely submerged taint of the illegitimacy of council tenure to negotiate. 'Who'd buy a council house?' was a sentiment expressed by more than one buyer.

Even so, at this point in the restructuring of the social relations of tenure, most people *did* feel differently about their houses after purchase. This difference is not, I think, any response to a deep seated ontological need for security, as Saunders (1984) seems to suggest. Nor is it really to be understood as a growing up, a coming to maturity, as Musgrove and Middleton (1981) imply, when they suggest that in industrial society acquiring a mortgage constitutes the most significant rite of passage of all.[4]

Clearly the situation of the Sunderland tenants was shaped by their very *particular* experience of a change of tenure. However, it would do violation to their lives to suggest that becoming a mortgage holder constituted their most critical *rite de passage*. Such a formulation surely devalues the many years of adult responsibility that these people had experienced. Indeed, it is misleading to conceptualise it in such terms at all. The tenure change involved hardly negotiated a sacred/profane opposition, nor did it involve the rites of 'separation, transition or incorporation' that van Gennep implied in his original usage of the term (1960:11). Indeed, though one could at a stretch cite the building of porches as statements of separation, and the bowing of windows as an expression of changed status, the public affirmation of changed status is rather *uneasily* recognised as such by the inhabitants. These former tenants do not exemplify the dual link of changed public status and changed private identity: at most, they relate differently to their private dwelling space.

For example, many of the early buyers, though admitting that they personally regarded the house differently after purchase, did *not* want to be regarded differently by their neighbours. They were at pains to point out that they were still the same people, and for a number of them that meant that they were still working class. Similarly, there were no public ceremonies of a collective nature involved, little to suggest the insertion of residents into a different set of objective social relations. The significance remains personal, and is personally and privately celebrated. Consequently, generalised categories such as *rites de passage* that derive from the analysis of less diverse societies where this particular public/private distinction may be less often recognised seem particularly inappropriate in understanding tenure changes in Britain today.

Conclusion

The conclusions to be drawn from this study are threefold. First, it illustrates the *ideological* intervention being attempted in the sphere of tenure. The rhetoric may be of home ownership as a universal condition, but the reality is that any tenure experience is socially, spatially and historically contingent. The importance of this highly specific, one-off extension of owner occupation lies in its incorporative effects at an ideological level – incorporative, that is, in the hegemonic sense of an attempt to secure a particular social consciousness.

In this incorporation, familism is playing a major role. However, the study indicates that this process is neither secured nor unproblematic. It may be tempting to say that those who bought their council houses had been bought by the forces of capital and patriarchy: this would not do justice to the complexity and ambiguities surrounding their experience. Even though collectivism is weakened by this particular intervention, and patriarchy strengthened, most of the buyers are still aware of themselves as working-class men and women.

Secondly, then, it points to the importance of gender relations in the study of housing, and the contradictions that are emerging for the state in this area. An intensification of family life and female dependence had followed ownership, though of course tenure is just one of a whole set of experiences that structure individual beliefs and practices. The gender dominations inherent in this remained taken for granted by the women concerned, and the politics of gender did not emerge in discussion. There is still a lack of public feminist discourse in areas like Sunderland,[5] so such an absence is not surprising, but it contrasts strongly with the awareness of class issues and impacts on the part of the buyers.[6] The language of gender is not part of their everyday world views in the way that the language of class is. That does not, however, absolve or excuse neglect of the issues on the part of housing analysts.

Thirdly, the case study illustrates the fruitfulness of a generational account of housing experience. It shows the importance of securing family use values in people's housing decisions, and points to an inter-generational dynamic, as the later middle aged attempt to secure provision for their children.

It suggests that those approaching and passing pensionable age are concerned with securing a future for their children as much as for themselves. They are consolidating an autonomous private family life, and perhaps also preparing the ground for future reciprocation with the younger generation; in exchange for caring for our old age, you will benefit by inheriting our property.

In sum, the research casts doubt on any analysis of the social relations of tenure that ignores the meanings that tenure has for specific kinds of people in specific sets of social relations in specific locations at specific times. The life cycle stage of the buyers, the gender relations of their households and the generational experience of public housing occurred in a combination that is unlikely to be repeated. Fewer of the older tenants will buy, unless the terms of purchase are substantially altered. Few younger tenants will be in housing that they would want to buy. And the emerging difficulties of mortgage arrears and repair problems that some of the current purchasers are facing could well begin to deter those currently considering purchase. The 'right to buy' generation, then, have made their housing gain – if gain it turns out to be – at the expense of other age groups.

In future work on council house purchase, amongst the more interesting long-term questions will be those of property transfer and inter-generational inheritance. It is to be hoped that in such work the impact of ownership on household formation and the gender relations of the household will assume greater prominence. Perhaps by then, owner occupation will indeed be the 'normal' working-class tenure. The terms and conditions of that ownership and occupation, however, are likely to remain highly fragmented and socially differentiated.

Notes

1 There are difficulties with a life cycle conceptualisation of ageing. For instance, there is a tendency for such work to revert to an essentialist, biological, ahistorical and unidirectional mode of thought. At best, it is descriptive rather than analytic. However, I am not persuaded that alternatives, such as the idea of a life course (Hareven, 1978), circumvent all of these problems. Therefore the term 'life cycle' is used here as an ideological category to be inspected rather than as a predictive concept.

2 The very terms 'council housing' and 'council tenancy' are interesting when compared to the alternatives of 'home ownership', 'owner occupation' and 'private housing'. The identity bestowed on the owner by the label includes privacy, home-making and occupational rights. The 'council tenant' on the other hand has his or her relations of subordination to the local state made very clear. The situation of the owner *vis-à-vis* finance capital remains hidden. The dominance of financial institutions remains concealed, whilst the dominance of the local state is highlighted.

3 See Ball (1983), Gray (1982) and Hamnett (1984) for discussions of this.

4 Musgrove and Middleton (1981) suggest that acquiring a mortgage is a highly symbolic, emotionally charged event, representing a clear turning point in the lives of the groups that they studied, whatever their life cycle stage. It was 'the mortgage rather than marriage that marked the transition to adulthood and independence', denoting worth through debt, a 'real transition from youth to adult status', a 'mark of dignity and honour'. For one of their respondents, they suggest that 'a stately and dignified progression through life was marked by a series of mortgages of increasing magnitude' (Musgrove and Middleton, 1981: 46).

5 There is, for example, no women's committee of the local authority.

6 For many, the problem was to deny these impacts ('we're still the same people'); for others, particularly some of the younger recent buyers, the concern was to present the

shift as a step towards social mobility. They recognised the saliency of domestic property in this, for their children if not for themselves. Such buyers are hoping to sell, though most are well aware of how unlikely they are ever to be able to afford their dream house along the north-easterly coastal fringe of the town.

References

Abrams, P. (1982) *Historical Sociology*. Shepton Mallet: Open Books.

Anderson, M. (1985) 'The emergence of the modern life cycle in Britain', *Social History*, 10 (1): 69–87.

Ball, M. (1983) *Housing Policy and Economic Power*. London: Methuen.

Bocock, R. (1974) *Ritual in Industrial Society*. London: Allen & Unwin.

Campbell, B. (1984) *Wigan Pier Revisited*. London: Virago.

Chaney, J. (1985) 'Returning to work', in P. Close and R. Collins (eds), *Family and Economy in Modern Society*. London: Macmillan. pp. 162–73.

Dennis, N. (1970) *People and Planning*. London: Faber.

Fogarty, M. (1975) *Forty to Sixty*. London: Bedford Square Press.

Forrest, R. and Murie, A. (1986) 'Marginalisation and subsidised individualism', *Journal of Urban and Regional Research*, 10 (2): 46--66.

Gray, F. (1982) 'Owner occupation and social relations', in S. Merrett (ed.), *Owner Occupation in Britain*. London: Routledge & Kegan Paul. pp. 267–89.

Hamnett, C. (1984) 'Housing the two nations', *Urban Studies*, 32: 389–405.

Hareven, T. (1978) 'Family time and historical time', in A. Rossi *et al.* (eds), *The Family*. New York: Norton.

Kemeny, J. (1979) *Home Ownership and the Family Life Cycle*. Birmingham: Centre for Urban and Regional Studies, Working Paper No. 13.

Murie, A. (1975) *The Sale of Council Houses*. Birmingham: Centre for Urban and Regional Studies, Occasional Paper No. 35.

Murie, A. and Forrest, R. (1980) 'Wealth, inheritance and housing policy', *Policy and Politics*, 8 (1):1–20.

Musgrove, F. and Middleton, R. (1981) 'Rites of passage and the meaning of age in three contrasted social groups', *British Journal of Sociology*, 32 (1):39–55.

Phillipson, C. (1982) *Capitalism and the Construction of Old Age*. London: Macmillan.

Popplestone, G. (1980) 'Why some won't buy', *Housing and Planning Review*, 36 (3).

Saunders, P. (1984) 'Beyond housing classes,' *International Journal of Urban and Regional Research*, 8 (2):202–27.

Stone, I. and Stephens, J. (1986) *Economic Restructuring and Employment Change on Wearside*. Sunderland: External Development Unit, Contextual Report for the EEC and the Borough of Sunderland.

Stubbs, C. (1985) *An Interest in the Kingdom*. Sunderland: Sunderland Polytechnic Working Paper.

Stubbs, C. and Wheelock, J. (1986) *Women's Work: Gender and the Wearside Local Economy*. Sunderland: External Development Unit, Report for the EEC and the Borough of Sunderland.

van Gennep, A. (1960) *The Rites of Passage*. London: Routledge & Kegan Paul.

Watson, S. (1986) 'The marginalisation of non-family households in Britain', *International Journal of Urban and Regional Research*, 10 (2):8–28.

2

Between Work and Retirement: Becoming 'Old' in the 1980s

Frank Laczko

The spread of retirement, and the transformation of old age into a social category to which one gains access by virtue of reaching a specified age, is a relatively recent phenomenon, one which is associated with the establishment of a set of age-based income entitlements administered by the state – the public pension. Throughout the nineteenth century and well into the twentieth, the majority of old people did not retire (Myles, 1984: 1).

In recent years, with the considerable fall in the number of older workers in employment in the years preceding state pensionable age (in particular males), it would seem that we have entered a new period in the history of retirement where 'retirement' commences well before old age and the receipt of a state pension. However, although more older workers may be considered to be retired in terms of the accepted common-sense meaning of 'giving up work' (Parker, 1980), there are different types of retirement and different routes out of the labour market. For many older men and women the period spent out of the labour market is increasing, but not necessarily the period spent in retirement. Thus the life span is being socially redefined in a more complex fashion than is often suggested.

In this chapter I outline how the patterns of early exit from the labour force vary. What has emerged in the 1980s is an increase both in the range of pre-retirement categories and statuses and in the numbers of older people in them. The evidence suggests that the transition between work and retirement is becoming increasingly complex and that it is becoming more difficult to classify older people according to their attachment to the labour force. Substantial numbers of older men and women who are not in paid work no longer fit easily into conventionally defined categories such as 'unemployed', 'retired' and 'sick'. Another change is that more older workers enter retirement involuntarily, and after a period of long-term sickness or long-term unemployment, than directly from gainful employment. Moreover, the meaning of retirement has changed as receipt of pre-retirement benefit becomes increasingly associated with complete economic inactivity.

This change in the transition between work and retirement has implications for the economic well-being of the elderly and for understanding how retirement is experienced. An individual's experience of retirement is likely to be influenced by the nature of the transition into it. If this is negative as a consequence of the retirement being enforced or premature, the subsequent experience of retirement may be negative too, particularly if it is associated with a low income. These changes also have important implications for the income of the elderly. While the proportion of the elderly in poverty in Britain remains high, especially compared to some other European countries (see Hedstrom and Ringen, 1987), the overall position of old people has been very gradually improving (Child Poverty Action Group, 1987). But what will be the effect of the growth in early retirement on poverty among the elderly?

Towards the end of this chapter I discuss some of the likely long term income consequences for older people, particularly those from manual occupations, of the growth in early exit from the labour force. In Laczko *et al.* (1988) we investigated the extent of poverty among those who left the labour force early. In this chapter I take up the question of how far the growing dis-employment of older workers will have the effect of feeding through a cohort of less-well-off-than-average elderly people, thereby decreasing the relative average income of the elderly and increasing inequality amongst them. The incomes of retired married couples where the husband is aged 65 to 69 are compared to the incomes of married couples where the husband is aged 60 to 64 and is not in gainful employment.

The evidence used is based on analyses of the General Household Surveys for 1980 – 2 and the Labour Force Surveys for 1981 and 1983. These surveys permit me to consider how older people define their own status in later life irrespective of administrative categories based on the kind of benefits that they are receiving, their main sources of income and their age.

Data and definitions

The General Household Survey (GHS) is a nationally representative sample of the general population resident in private (that is, non-institutional) households (Office of Population Censuses and Surveys, 1984). The sample size is approximately 11,000 households. Because this is too small for the analysis of the sub-group consisting of those aged 60 to 64, it has been necessary to aggregate data over the three years 1980 to 1982. The Labour Force Survey (LFS) is a representative sample survey of people aged over 16 who are living in private households in Great Britain (77,000 in 1983). The survey was conducted in alternate years from 1973 to 1983 but is now carried out annually. In 1983 the response rate was 82 per cent (Office of Population Censuses and Surveys, 1986).

There are many ways of defining retirement and early retirement, and no single definition can be unambiguously applied. As Bond notes:

> Many studies utilise administrative definitions such as time of retirement or age at retirement; others construct normative definitions based on the researcher's perceptions of retirement such as the number of hours worked per week or the number of years of employment; and some studies use the individual's own perception of whether they were retired or not. (1986:221)

The GHS uses self-definition to categorise the early retired; respondents who are not doing any paid work are asked to select the first reason which applies to them from the following list: permanently unable to work, retired, keeping house, unemployed, doing something else. While this definition excludes those working part-time (about 2 per cent of employed men aged 60 to 64 work part-time), it does allow us to see to what extent those who have left the workforce early actually define themselves as retired. We can establish comparison categories of the 'early retired', 'unemployed' and 'long-term sick' that are based upon respondents' own perceptions of their status. We can also explore the factors associated with self-definition according to these categories and the relative importance of different routes to retirement at normal pensionable age.

Patterns of exit from the labour market

In 1985 only 66.7 per cent of men aged 55 to 64 were economically active, compared to 91.3 per cent in 1970 (OECD, 1986). These figures include the unemployed, many of whom are not looking for work and consider themselves to be 'retired' or 'sick/disabled' or fall into the 'discouraged worker' category (Laczko, 1987). In 1984, for example, LFS data show that over half of the unemployed men aged 55 and above in the United Kingdom had not looked for work in the four weeks prior to the survey. By 1985 only 57.5 per cent of men aged 55 to 64 were employed compared to a figure of 86.7 per cent in 1970 (*Employment Gazette*, 1985).

Class
If we disaggregate these figures we find that manual workers, particularly the semi-skilled and unskilled, have an even lower employment rate – see Table 2.1. For example, data from the GHS for

1980–82 show that the employment rate of men aged 60 to 64 in social classes 5 and 6 (semi- and unskilled) was only 57 per cent, whereas that of men in social classes 1 and 2 was 67 per cent – Table 2.1. However, it is not the case that more manual workers retire early; their low employment rate results chiefly from their greater vulnerability to sickness/disability and unemployment. For example, whilst 23 per cent of men in social classes 1 and 2 describe themselves as retired, the figure for men in social classes 5 and 6 is only 13 per cent. Conversely, only 6 per cent of managers and employers were permanently sick and only 4 per cent unemployed, whereas the corresponding figures for semi-skilled and unskilled men were 18 per cent and 12 per cent respectively. Thus it is clear that the pattern of exit from the labour market varies substantially according to social class, and that it is men in lower social classes that have been disproportionately affected by the decline in older workers' employment opportunities. It should also be added that the importance of the unemployment route out of the labour market is much greater than Table 2.1 suggests, because the unemployed category does not include those receiving unemployment benefit but not actively searching for work.

Table 2.1 *Self-defined activity status of men aged 60 to 64 by socio-economic group, 1980–2 (percentages)*

	Non-manual		Manual		
	Employers/ managers	Intermediate junior non-manual	Skilled	Semi- and unskilled	All
Employed	67	63	61	57	61
Retired	23	19	14	13	16
Unemployed	4	7	8	12	8
Permanently sick or disabled	6	11	17	18	15
Total (= 100%)	435	334	829	557	2,155

Source: GHS, 1980–2; own calculations

These class differences in the importance of exit routes reflect the fact that, in general, workers in lower social classes are more vulnerable to unemployment and are more likely to have poor health, but they also reflect the fact that non-manual workers have greater opportunities to retire early. They are more likely to have a good occupational pension and are more likely to be employed in occupations with a lower retirement age (see Laczko *et al.*, 1988).

Women

It is well established that women's activity rates have been more stable. In 1971 the economic activity rate of women aged 55 to 59 was 51.1 per cent compared to 51.8 per cent in 1985 (*Employment Gazette*, May 1985). These figures conceal the fact that the participation rate of unmarried older women has been declining quite sharply: for example, from 67.2 per cent in 1971 to 53 per cent in 1983 (ibid.). It makes less sense to consider the employment rate of older women over time, since it is well known that a high proportion of unemployed women fail to register for work because they are not eligible for benefits.

Age

A breakdown of the statistics by single-year age groups reveals further the extent of the fall in older men's participation rates, and the wide differences between different age groups. Table 2.2 provides a cross-sectional 'snapshot' of the economic status in 1983 of older male respondents aged 50 to 65 by single-year age groups. There is a particularly sharp fall in the proportion of older men in employment after age 62. At age 62, over 50 per cent of men are in work, but at ages 63 and 64 the figure falls to 40 per cent. Thus already by 1983 the majority of men aged 63 and 64 were not in work. However, only about half of those not in work in this age group consider themselves to be retired. It is not until age 65 that the majority of men (77.9 per cent) see themselves as having retired. Thus although the *de facto* normal age at which the majority of men cease working may no longer be 65, most older men do not appear to consider themselves to be 'retired' until 65. Those who are most likely to describe themselves as retired are men in social classes 1 and 2. Two-thirds of non-employed men aged 60 to 64 in social classes 1 and 2 decribe themselves as retired, but less than a third of non-employed men in social classes 5 and 6 do so – see Table 2.1.

Advocates of early retirement often claim that it is preferable for older workers to take early retirement, since this reduces the risk of others being made unemployed who do not have an alternative status, that of 'retiree', open to them (Kuhlewind, 1985). But the data from the LFS and GHS suggest that the status of those who leave work early is somewhat more ambiguous than is often presumed, and that it varies substantially according to social class. This diversity is further illustrated in Table 2.2, which distinguishes between the unemployed and 'discouraged workers'.

As retirement age approaches, the proportion of older men who are unemployed and actively seeking work declines markedly from 7.7 per cent at age 61 to 3.2 per cent at age 64. Conversely Table 2.2 shows that

Table 2.2 *Economic status of men aged 50 to 64, 1983 (percentages)*

									Age							
	50	51	52	53	54	55	56	57	58	59	60	61	62	63	64	65
Self-employed	7	12	13	12	11	11	13	11	10	8	9	9	8	8	8	5
Full-time employed	69	71	69	71	68	65	62	65	59	60	51	47	43	30	30	7
Part-time employed	0	1	1	1	1	0	1	1	1	2	2	2	2	2	2	5
Unemployed[1]	6	7	7	6	8	8	9	7	8	7	7	8	6	5	3	1
Retired	0	0	1	0	0	1	1	2	3	4	10	12	18	25	29	78
Long-term sick or disabled	4	4	4	4	6	7	9	8	10	12	13	14	15	16	18	0
Doesn't want a job	0	0	0	0	1	1	1	1	1	1	1	2	1	2	3	0
'Discouraged'[2]	1	1	1	2	1	1	1	1	3	2	3	3	3	5	4	0
Others[3]	4	4	4	4	4	4	4	4	6	4	4	4	4	7	3	4
Total (= 100%)	1,206	1,102	1,275	1,163	1,165	1,171	1,185	1,206	1,132	1,180	1,102	1,117	1,334	1,259	881	818

[1] Actively seeking work in reference week.
[2] Believes no jobs are available.
[3] Includes those on 'a government scheme', 'temporarily sick', 'on holiday' and 'waiting to start a job'.

Source: LFS, 1983; own calculations

those closer to state pensionable age are more likely to fall into the 'discouraged worker' category. In the LFS, people who are not in work or seeking work are asked the reasons why they were not looking for work in the week before the survey. People who spontaneously say that the *main* reason why they did not look for work was because they 'believe no jobs are available' are conventionally described as 'discouraged workers'. At age 63 the proportion of older men who are unemployed is roughly the same as the proportion who are 'discouraged': 4.9 per cent compared to 4.6 per cent; and by age 64 more men are 'discouraged' than unemployed: 4.3 per cent compared to 3.2 per cent.

The picture for women is very different. Table 2.3 provides a breakdown of the economic status of women aged 50 to 74 by single years. One of the most striking points to emerge is that the majority of women do not retire at 60, or at least they do not consider that they have retired. At age 60 only a third of women describe themselves as 'retirees'. The majority, 35 per cent, fall into the 'looking after the home' category. Retirement seems to be associated with previous labour force participation. Those women who have not been in paid employment do not consider that they have retired from 'looking after the home'. It is not in fact until age 65 that the majority of women describe themselves as 'retired', but even at age 74 only 56 per cent of women say they have retired. Thus reaching state pensionable age has much more symbolic importance for men than for women.

Between the ages of 55 and 59 the proportion of women in full-time employment falls sharply from 25.7 per cent to 18.7 per cent. It is interesting to note that not only does the proportion of 'retired' women increase from 2.7 per cent to 10.0 per cent between 55 and 59, but there is also an increase in the proportion of women 'looking after the home' from 30.8 per cent to 34.6 per cent. The latter women may be still interested in working but not eligible for unemployment benefit, or they may be ineligible for an occupational pension unlike some of the 'early retired' women.

Unemployment and economic inactivity

Self-defined status may not correspond with benefit status. If we consider how self-defined economic inactivity categories relate to receipt of unemployment benefit or supplementary benefit in respect of unemployment, we find that there is a fair amount of overlap between different non-employment categories. A number of people who describe themselves in Tables 2.1, 2.2 and 2.3 as 'retired' or 'sick' or who fall into the 'discouraged' category are actually unemployed and

Table 2.3 *Economic status of women aged 50 to 74, 1983 (percentages)*

	Age																								
	50	51	52	53	54	55	56	57	58	59	60	61	62	63	64	65	66	67	68	69	70	71	72	73	74
Self-employed	4	5	3	4	4	3	3	3	3	3	2	2	3	4	1	1	1	1	1	1	1	0	0	0	1
Full-time employed	28	28	26	25	24	26	22	22	19	18	9	6	5	4	4	2	1	1	1	1	1	0	0	0	0
Part-time employed	28	28	29	27	27	21	23	22	20	18	12	14	11	10	9	5	5	4	4	3	2	2	1	1	1
Unemployed[1]	4	4	2	3	3	3	3	3	2	2	1	1	0	0	0	0	1	0	0	0	0	0	0	0	0
Looking after home	24	25	26	27	27	30	31	32	34	35	35	32	33	32	34	32	37	36	35	34	38	34	37	37	39
Retired	0	0	1	2	2	3	4	5	6	10	33	39	41	45	46	54	52	53	56	56	54	57	57	56	56
Long term sick or disabled	3	3	4	3	4	5	5	5	6	6	6	0	0	0	0	0	0	0	0	0	0	0	0	0	0
Doesn't want a job	3	2	3	3	3	4	4	4	4	3	3	3	3	3	3	3	2	2	2	3	2	3	3	4	0
'Discouraged'[1,2]	1	1	1	2	2	1	1	1	2	1	1	1	0	0	0	0	0	0	0	0	0	0	0	0	2
Others[3]	6	4	4	5	3	4	4	4	4	3	4	3	4	4	3	2	1	2	2	2	3	3	1	3	1
Total (= 100%)	1291	1121	1249	1167	1223	1167	1217	1236	1178	1235	1381	1269	1395	1352	1002	1062	1075	1008	1169	1173	1176	960	1053	980	971

[1] Actively seeking work in reference week.
[2] Believe no jobs are available.
[3] Includes those on 'a government scheme', 'temporarily sick', on 'holiday' and 'waiting to start a job'.

Source: LFS, 1983; own calculations

receiving unemployment benefit – see Table 2.4. For example, 16.5 per cent of men aged 60 to 64 who were 'retired' in the LFS in 1983 and 10.1 per cent who were 'sick' were receiving unemployment benefit or supplementary benefit in respect of unemployment. Between 1981 and 1983 there was a substantial increase in the proportion of older men aged 50 to 64 who were economically inactive, according to the LFS (that is, they were not actively seeking work), but who were receiving unemployment benefit – see Table 2.5.

Table 2.4 *Percentage of older economically inactive males receiving unemployment benefit (including supplementary benefit in respect to unemployment) in 1981 and 1983*

	1981	1983
50–9	13	36
Population base	(1,308)	(1,461)
60–4	9	22
Population base	(1,763)	(2,391)

Source: LFS, 1981 and 1983; own calculations

Table 2.5 *Percentage of older unemployed receiving unemployment benefit and not actively looking for work in the last week*

	1981	1983
Men 50–9	19	34
Population base	(406)	(1,337)
Men 60–4	31	42
Population base	(467)	(835)
Women 50–9	30	42
Population base	(114)	(356)

Source: LFS, 1981 and 1983; own calculations

As unemployment has become increasingly prolonged, more and more unemployed older workers have ceased looking for work or at least have become less active job-seekers. Table 2.5 shows that the percentage of older unemployed men and women receiving unemployment benefit and not seeking work rose sharply between 1981 and 1983. As unemployment nearly doubled between 1981 and 1983, the percentage of older unemployed claimants not looking for work increased from 31 to 42 per cent among men aged 60 to 64 and from 30 to 42 per cent among women aged 50 to 59. The sharpest increase was among men aged 50 to 59, where the proportion rose from 19 to 34 per cent. As I have shown elsewhere (Laczko, 1987), a substantial proportion of older men and women receiving unemployment benefit, around a third in the case of men aged 60 to 64 and women aged 50 to 59, say they are not looking for work because they are 'retired', 'sick' or 'discouraged' or, in the case of women, 'looking after the home'.

These trends illustrate that a rising proportion of older men and women do not fit easily into conventional categories such as 'unemployed', 'retired', 'sick' or 'housewives', and that the differences between these categories are becoming increasingly blurred. The meaning of the economically inactive categories is changing, particularly for men, as an increasing proportion of the 'sick' and 'retired' receive unemployment benefit and the meaning of unemployment is changing as more and more older unemployed workers give up the search for work (Laczko, 1987: 248).

Reasons for leaving work early

High unemployment is also changing both the way in which people enter retirement and their reasons for retiring. A substantial proportion of older workers are now retiring after a period of long-term unemployment or long-term sickness. Moreover, an increasing proportion of older workers is entering retirement involuntarily. Retirement and old age are increasingly defined by the requirements of the labour market. The passage from work to inactivity has become much more sudden (Guillemard, 1986: 287). Most older men can no longer expect to stop working at age 65 and make their plans for retirement with this age in mind.

Unlike people who retire at state pensionable age, those who retire early are often denied the opportunity to work. For example, under the Job Release Scheme,[1] beneficiaries effectively have no right to work, because they lose benefit if earning more than £4 per week. This is not the case for the elderly receiving a state pension. Many more older men have effectively retired early on the long-term rate of supplementary benefit, where similar restrictions on earnings apply.[2] In addition to the sharp increases in long-term unemployment among older men in recent years, there has also been an increase in long-term sickness and in the proportion of older men receiving invalidity benefit (Piachaud, 1986).

It has been demonstrated that part of the increase in disability is attributable to the general rise in unemployment (Piachaud, 1986). Unlike in many other countries, an individual in the UK does not have to have a fixed level of disability before he or she can receive invalidity benefit. It is usually left to a person's doctor to judge whether they are incapable of working and to provide the relevant medical certificate.

Such judgements may vary according to changing labour market conditions, but this does not necessarily imply that more older workers with poor job prospects have been able to choose to leave the labour market early on invalidity benefit. What seems more likely, from a consideration of current trends in invalidity benefit, is that once an older man becomes sick he is more likely to remain sick for longer than before because it is increasingly difficult to re-enter the labour market. In recent years there has been a significant increase in the duration of invalidity among older men, and this accounts for a greater part of the increase in invalidity than do increases in the 'flow' of older men able to receive invalidity benefit (Department of Health and Social Security, 1987, personal communication).

There is also evidence from the LFS of 1983 which casts some doubt on the voluntary nature of much early retirement (Laczko *et al.*, 1988). Among early retired men aged 60 to 64, the main reason given for leaving their last job was that their employer had introduced an early retirement scheme in order to cut back on staff. Men from manual occupations were more likely than men from non-manual occupations to give this reason (62 per cent compared to 47 per cent). The manual early retired men were also more likely than the non-manual early retired men to have left their last job because of redundancy or dismissal (14 per cent compared with 3 per cent). Unlike earlier studies (for example, Parker, 1980), Laczko *et al.*, (1988) did not find that ill health was a major reason for early retirement.

Income in old age

What are the likely consequences for the incomes of the elderly of recent changes in the transition between work and retirement, and the fall in the age of exit from the labour force? Below I compare the incomes of non-employed married men aged 60 to 64 with the incomes of retired married men aged 65 to 69, using the GHS data for 1980–82. The data are restricted to men and couples because of the small proportions in the survey of non-employed women below age 60 and of single older non-employed men.

I have chosen to confine my analyses to elderly men aged 65 to 69 in order to try to restrict cohort effects. It is well established that the young elderly are generally better off than the older elderly, who are often poorer because they have benefited less from changes such as the growth in occupational pension provision. My aim is to compare the incomes of those who left work early with the incomes of the recently retired who left work at 65, but it should be pointed out that some retired men aged 65 to 69 will have stopped working before 65. Table

2.6 shows that about a quarter of retired men aged 65 to 69 who left work in the three years before the 1983 LFS did not retire from their last job at the normal retirement age for their occupation.

Table 2.6 *Reason for leaving last job: retired men aged 65 to 69 (percentages)*

	Manual	Non-manual
Dismissed, made redundant	11	5
Retired early when employer cut back on staff	8	8
Ill health	4	5
Retired at normal age for occupation	73	77
Other (including family/ personal reasons; temporary work)	4	5
Total (= 100%)	(722)	(409)

Source: LFS, 1983; own calculations

It should also be recalled that we are unable to examine income from earnings, as the definition of retirement in the GHS refers only to men who are not in paid work. In the case of the non-employed, the numbers involved are very small (Laczko *et al.*, 1988), but earnings are an important, although declining, source of income for elderly couples aged 65 to 69. In 1982 it was estimated that 26 per cent of married pensioner couples aged 65 to 69 received income from employment or self-employment (Department of Health and Social Security, 1984). However, I have been able to include wives' earnings in my calculations.

Poverty

I have chosen to compare the incomes of the early retired and retired in relation to a measure of income poverty. The approach adopted is that of comparing income in relation to the supplementary benefit (SB) scale rate which is the 'benchmark' usually taken in poverty studies in the UK.

It must be stressed, however, that the results are limited in a number of respects. First, the data provide no information on housing benefits. Another difficulty is that the GHS provides only gross income data for those not in paid employment, and in this respect the data under-represent to a limited extent the proportion of couples on low incomes.

In most studies concerned with assessing pensioner poverty, incomes are measured in relation to the SB long-term rate, since this is the rate payable to the elderly (Hemming, 1984). In order to allow for the fact that I am comparing incomes over a three-year period, I have taken the scale rate for 1981 as my 'benchmark', because this figure approximates to the median rate for these three years.

I have divided the results into four categories: (1) those with incomes on or below SB, (2) those with incomes up to 140 per cent of SB, conventionally regarded as those being close to poverty, (3) those with incomes greater than 140 per cent but not more than 200 per cent and (4) those with incomes over 200 per cent of SB. In 1981 the long-term rate of SB for a couple was £47.35 per week, and those with incomes up to 40 per cent above this level were receiving between £47.36 and £66.26 per week. Table 2.7 shows how the total gross income per week of non-employed and retired couples compares to these levels. The data are presented according to whether or not the man was previously employed in a non-manual or manual occupation.

The results of Table 2.7 show that the highest proportion of people who are well off are the non-manual non-employed, and the highest proportion of people who are poor (that is, with incomes at or below SB level) are the manual non-employed. There is therefore greater inequality of income within the older non-employed population than within the retired population. The majority (54 per cent) of the non-manual non-employed have incomes more than 200 per cent of SB, whereas the majority (54 per cent) of the manual non-employed have incomes on or near the poverty line (that is, on or below 140 per cent of SB). The retired are more likely to have incomes between the two extremes of the SB level and 200 per cent of SB (72 per cent in the case of the manual retired and 52 per cent of the non-manual retired). It has long been established that there are 'two nations in old age' (Titmuss, 1963: 74), and this is reflected in Table 2.7, where it can be seen that the median income of the non-manual retired is £74 per week, whereas the median income of the manual retired is only £59 per week. However, the difference in median income between the manual and non-manual non-employed is even sharper: £143 and £63 per week respectively.

However, there is also greater inequality within the manual non-employed group than among the manual retired. A quarter of the manual non-employed have incomes on or below SB, compared to 19 per cent of the manual retired; and 21 per cent of the manual non-employed have incomes greater than 200 per cent of SB, compared to 9 per cent of the manual retired.

In general, the social class backgrounds of the non-employed and retired are very similar – see Table 2.8 – but within the non-employed population there are sharp class differences. Manual workers are much more likely to leave the labour market via unemployment or sickness,

Table 2.7 *Distribution of weekly income of retired couples where husband is aged 65 to 69, and of 'non-employed' couples where husband is aged 60 to 64 (percentages)*

	Median	Below or on SB	Up to 140% of SB	Over 140% and up to 200%	Over 200%	Total (= 100%)
Manual:						
non-empl.	£63	25	29	25	21	(260)
retired	£59	19	48	24	9	(629)
Non-manual:						
non-empl.	£143	13	12	20	54	(143)
retired	£74	16	25	27	32	(351)

Source: GHS, 1980–2; own calculations

whilst non-manual workers are more likely to retire early. The greater degree of inequality within the manual non-employed than within the retired population probably reflects the differences of income between the unemployed and early retired. Laczko *et al.* (1988) have shown that the older unemployed have the lowest incomes among the non-employed.

Table 2.8 *Socio-economic group of the male according to retirement/employment status (percentages)*

Age	60–4 Early retired	Unemployed	Sick	All non-employed	65–9 Retired
Employers, managers	28	10	9	17	17
Intermediate, junior non-manual	18	13	12	15	16
Skilled manual	33	40	46	39	38
Semi- and unskilled	21	37	33	29	28
Total (= 100%)	(350)	(177)	(302)	(829)	(1608)

Source: GHS, 1980–2; own calculations

The greater degree of inequality within the non-employed population as a whole compared to the retired probably reflects the fact that the non-employed population includes at one extreme long-term unemployed men who are chiefly reliant on state benefits, and at the other non-manual workers who are able to retire early on other, more adequate, sources of income.

Table 2.9 provides an indication of the importance of different sources of income for the retired and non-employed on different levels of income. It can be seen that those who are most dependent on state benefits have the lowest income. More than 80 per cent of the income of the retired and non-employed who have incomes on or below SB, comes from state benefits, whereas this is the case for less than half of the retired and non-employed with incomes greater than 140 per cent of SB. Those who are better off are more likely to receive more of their income from an occupational pension, unearned income and spouse's earnings. However, unlike income from an occupational pension, income from a spouse's earnings is likely to be a more temporary source of income, and in later years the full effects of leaving the labour force early and accepting retirement on a reduced pension are likely to be felt.

Table 2.9   *Source of average gross income per week: 'non-employed' couples with husband aged 60 to 64, and retired couples with husband aged 65 to 69 (percentages)*

Income	On or below SB		Up to 140% of SB		More than 140% of SB	
Age	60–4	65–9	60–4	65–9	60–4	65–9
Occupational pension	7	4	19	10	33	28
State benefits	82	94	68	83	29	44
Unearned income	3	0.2	7	5	12	13
Wife's earnings	3	2	5	1	18	10
Other[1]	5	—	1	2	8	5
Total (= 100%)	(55)	(131)	(70)	(268)	(148)	(231)

[1]Other income includes private pensions or annuities, income from friends or relatives from outside the household.

Source: GHS, 1980–2; own calculations

Table 2.9 also highlights important differences between the retired and non-employed. The retired in general tend to receive a greater part of their income from state benefits, whereas the non-employed are more reliant on occupational pensions. The non-employed, particularly those with incomes greater than 140 per cent of SB, are more likely to receive a greater part of their income from the market than are the retired. For example, of those with incomes greater than 140 per cent of SB, 18 per cent of the income of the non-employed comes from spouse's earnings, compared to 10 per cent of that of the retired. Greater reliance on income from the market and from occupational pensions also has its disadvantages. As we saw above, the non-employed are somewhat more likely than the retired to have incomes on or below SB, and Table 2.9 suggests that this may be because they are less likely to be receiving state benefits – which at least provide a guaranteed minimum level of income. In all, 94 per cent of the income of the retired with incomes on or below SB comes from state benefits, compared to a figure of 82 per cent for the corresponding non-employed.

Concluding comments

What are the implications of the above comparison of the incomes of the non-employed and retired for the future incomes of the elderly? First, it would seem that the increase in non-employment is likely to contribute to greater inequality in old age in so far as there is a much wider dispersion of incomes within the non-employed group than within the retired group. However, it is not the case that the non-employed are generally poorer than the retired, although it should be remembered that we have not been able to compare the incomes of the non-employed with the elderly as a whole, because those who receive earnings are excluded. But it also has to be remembered that the non-employed will have to live on a low income for a longer period than the retired. In later years, financial problems can arise as savings dwindle, spouses stop working, houses fall into disrepair and, unless fully indexed, the purchasing value of pensions decreases. Furthermore, we have seen that within the non-employed population there are a minority of people who currently have incomes lower than the retired. For these people, mostly manual workers, earlier retirement means simply more years in poverty.

Notes

I would like to thank the Office of Population Censuses and Surveys, which carried out the Labour Force Survey, for allowing me to use it. I would also like to thank the Economic and Social Research Council Data Archive at the University of Essex for preparing and distributing the data. This research was carried out under an Economic and Social Research Council grant. Finally, I would like to thank Sara Arber, Angela Dale, Nigel Gilbert and especially Michael O'Higgins for valuable comments on an earlier version of this chapter.

1 See Laczko *et al.* (1988) for a description of this scheme, which is due to close in 1988.

2 Between April and August 1983, 162,000 men aged 60 to 64 were affected by this measure.

References

Bond, J. (1986) 'Retirement: causes and consequences', *Ageing and Society*, 61: 219–39.
Child Poverty Action Group (1987) *Poverty: the Facts*. London: CPAG.
Department of Health and Social Security (1984) *Population, Pension Costs and Pensioners' Incomes*. London: HMSO.
Employment Gazette (1985) 'Unemployment: estimates from the Labour Force Survey compared with the monthly claimant count', October: 393–6.
Guillemard, A. (1986) *Le Déclin du Social*. Paris: Presses Universitaires de France.
Hedstrom, P. and Ringen, S., (1987) 'Age and income in contemporary society: a research note', *Journal of Social Policy*, 16 (2): 227–39.
Hemming, R. (1984) *Poverty and Incentives*. Oxford: Oxford University Press.
Kuhlewind, G. (1985) 'How efficient and effective is early retirement as a policy for redistributing work?' Paper given to the International Symposium on Distributing the Rewards of Economic Activity: Alternative Transfer and Employment Policies towards Economically Active and Non-Active Groups, Augsburg, October (*mimeo*).
Laczko, F. (1987) 'Older workers, unemployment and the discouraged worker effect', in S. di Gregorio (ed.), *Social Gerontology: New Directions*. London: Croom Helm.
Laczko, F., Dale, A., Arber, S. and Gilbert, N. (1988) 'Early retirement in a period of high unemployment', *Journal of Social Policy*, 17 (2): 313–34.
Myles, J. (1984) *Old Age in the Welfare State*. Boston: Little, Brown.
Organisation for Economic Co-operation and Development (1986) *Labour Force Statistics*. Paris: OECD.
Office of Population Censuses and Surveys (1984) *The General Household Survey 1982*. London: HMSO.
Office of Population Censuses and Surveys (1986) *The Labour Force Survey 1983 and 1984*. London: HMSO.
Parker, S. (1980) *Older Workers and Retirement*. London: HMSO.
Piachaud, D. (1986) 'Disability, retirement and unemployment of older men', *Journal of Social Policy*, 5 (2): 145–62.
Titmuss, R.M. (1963) *Essays on the Welfare State*, 2nd edn. London: Allen & Unwin.

3

Work-Ending: Employment and Ambiguity in Later Life

Tom Schuller

Society, like a bicycle, needs parts of itself to go round and round if it is to sustain itself. Repetition, with its sibling predictability, is an essential element of the identity of any social being, from the individual upwards. Without it we cannot define or even recognise behaviour and character. Unlike a bicycle, however, there must also be deviation from the perfect circle if momentum is to be maintained. Even the most conservative society cannot reproduce itself exactly; even the most conservative person cannot behave or think in exactly the same way year in year out. Life cycle analysis requires a closer examination of the recurrences and repetitions that constitute patterns of social and institutional behaviour, but also of the irregularities and breaks with tradition that form a counterpoint to them.

In *The Constitution of Society*, Giddens identifies three levels of temporal analysis: the *durée* of day-to-day existence, the life span of the individual and the *longue durée* of institutions (1984: 35). He further differentiates these types according to whether they are 'reversible' or not:

> Whether or not time 'as such' (whatever that would be) is reversible, the events and routines of daily life do not have a one-way flow to them. . . Daily life has a duration, a flow, but it does not lead anywhere; the very adjective 'day-to-day' and its synonyms indicate that time here is constituted only in repetition. The life of the individual, by contrast, is not only finite but irreversible, 'being towards death' . . . Time in this case is time of the body, a frontier of presence quite different from the evaporation of time-space inherent in the duration of day-to-day activity. Our lives 'pass away' in irreversible time with the passing away of the organism. The fact that we speak of the 'life cycle' implies that there are elements of repetition here too. But the life cycle is really a concept that belongs to the succession of generations and thus to the third dimension of temporality indicated above. This is the 'supra-individual' *durée* of the long-term existence of institutions, the *longue durée* of institutional time.

Giddens' use of the term 'reversible' is open to question, in that it implies a retracing of steps rather than the repetition, in greater or lesser degrees of exactitude, of an established pattern. It also ignores the problem of change: on the one hand the extent to which the performance of a routine can differ from its predecessor without losing its identity as a reproduced pattern, and on the other the mechanisms which rupture the pattern and initiate new practices (see Archer, 1985, for a critique). But if supplemented in these respects a framework such as his can be used to analyse specific practices. In particular, we can examine the notion of the life cycle and the relationship between the experiences of succeeding generations over time.

The specific practice which I shall address in this chapter is that of retirement, loosely understood as the final termination of formal employment. I shall examine how far changes in employment patterns should cause us to modify our conception of retirement and the implications this has for our picture of the life cycle. Secondly, I shall consider how these changes affect the norms which shape our view of later life. I shall argue that the fragmentation of the labour market for older workers brings to the fore the ambiguity of the majority's position in relation to formal employment, and that the overall experience of employment should therefore be characterised in terms of this ambiguity rather than of continuity and security.

The study on which this chapter is based dealt with a specific group of people. Geographically they were located in the London borough of Greenwich, and they were all in the age range 50 to 65. The main purpose of the study was to explore the effect of leaving full-time employment on the temporal structure of their lives. The concern of this chapter, however, is not with the day-to-day routines but with the implications of changes in the pattern of employment for the picture we have of the life cycle. The primary focus is therefore on the institutional level as defined above by Giddens.

The extension and resegmentation of the life cycle

It is said that only the Eskimo seems to view life as an unbroken continuum to be lived out as it comes (Smith, 1961: 109). In every other society, the life of an individual is divided into a series of segments, marked off more or less clearly by events or rituals which are more or less socially recognised. In most cases both the entry into employment and the exit from it are major events which signal the end of one stage and the beginning of the next. Variation at once becomes apparent. Inevitably, social class influences the timing of the experience and its nature. If we look only at duration, a middle-class person with a university education may enter employment at around 22 and leave it at 60, whereas her male working-class contemporary gets a job (if he is lucky) at 16 and carries on to 65 – perhaps even later if an inadequate pension forces him to continue working beyond the recognised age of retirement. The gender differentiation, as we shall explore later, is highly significant, with the complexity of the interaction between formal employment and other activities in women's careers underrated in much of the literature on the life cycle (Dex, 1985). Women will have experienced more interruptions than men in their working lives in a range of different ways. Nevertheless the ending of employment has been an event of acknowledged significance in the pattern of individual lives for both sexes.

The way in which this has been accomplished has varied over the ages. The history of retirement is a muddled one (Thane, 1978), and the title of Leslie Hannah's recent book, *Inventing Retirement* (1986), is suggestive of the way in which withdrawal from the labour force has depended on a range of economic and social considerations. The title may, in fact, impute too purposive a flavour to the process, for Hannah's account shows clearly the incoherence and irrationality which has characterised the evolution of pensions and retirement policy over the last hundred years. Be that as it may, retirement has often been considered the penultimate *rite de passage*: after the gold watch only the funeral procession remains.[1] Accounts of the life cycle make this the final stage – if, indeed, they judge it worthwhile to include it at all. For many accounts are 'developmental', and there are inhibitions about including what is commonly seen as a period of decline as a stage of development.

Increasingly, though, these inhibitions are being challenged. Demography is one of the major forces here. As the balance of the population shifts and the average age and longevity increase, so a whole variety of concerns comes into play. Crude material calculations assume mounting importance, as the costs of pensions and of medical care for the elderly rise exponentially. Considerations of social justice are still strong enough to force discussion, however sporadic, of the rights of older people. And these people themselves, panther-like or not, are more and more capable of making their voices heard, neither shrill nor subservient but asserting their right to participate fully in the life of society (Bornat *et al.*, 1985).

One consequence has been the division of old age into two: the third and the fourth ages. The third age covers the period after retirement but before dependency; the fourth age is that of dependency leading up to death (see Frankenberg, 1988, for some discussion of the notion of 'lifedeath'). The numbering sits uneasily within life cycle analyses, since it compresses all previous stages into two portmanteau categories. Our concern, however, is with the transition from the previous stage, whatever numerical label is attached. Individuals do not themselves repeat the sequence of events and stages that make up a life. At this level, unlike their daily or annual routines, time is linear. So much is obvious. But ending employment remains a key event for the majority of the population, and in that sense this generation is repeating the experience of its forebears – the template, as it has been suitably termed (Seltzer and Troll, 1986). It is imaginable that this should not be the case. If income and status were no longer derived so predominantly from formal employment, and if people moved freely throughout their lives between periods of paid and unpaid work, leisure and education, the significance of retirement might evaporate and new markers be found for the segmentation of the life cycle. For the time being, however, the final transition out of paid work remains a major marker in the cycle.

Against this there are substantial changes in the character and significance of this transition. It is increasingly a process which extends over time, rather than a clear-cut event, and this process involves a much higher level of ambiguity than previously (Schuller, 1987). It is experienced very differently by different social groups. This of course has always been the case, but requires detailed analysis in the light of changing circumstances. Above all, it occupies a different temporal location in the life cycle, as the average age at which it takes place moves down. This is closely related to trends in the labour market for the age group.

There have been periodic dramatic changes in the economic activity rates of older workers. Historically those at the upper end of the age spectrum have often been particularly vulnerable to cyclical movements in the economy, sucked into employment at times of labour shortage and expelled, often unceremoniously, when unemployment rises (Phillipson, 1983). Current employent trends are graphically represented in the figures for this group, especially in the differential effects on men and women – see Table 3.1. For men, the national trend over the last decade shows a very sharp fall in economic activity rates, from 83 per cent in 1971 to 54 per cent in 1985 for those aged 60 to 64, the period immediately preceding the official retirement age. By contrast, women in the equivalent age group, 55 to 59, have actually raised their level of participation over the same period from 51 per cent to 52 per cent.

Contrast this picture with projections made in 1966 by the Ministry of Labour, as it was then known – Table 3.2. The projections were based on trends up to 1965 and reached forward from 1966 to 1981. The expectation was that economic activity rates for males would continue exactly as they were, at 98 per cent for men aged 50 to 54, 96 per cent for those aged 55 to 59 and 90 per cent for 60- to 64-year-olds. A slight dip, from 38 per cent in 1966 to 30.5 per cent in 1981, was envisaged for those aged 65 and over. For women the rates were seen as holding steady for those not married, at 62 per cent for 55- to 59-year-olds and 29 per cent for 60- to 64-year-olds, and increasing for married women, from 39 to 52 per cent and 21 to 26 per cent for the respective age groups.

Table 3.1 *Economic activity rates of the civilian labour force by age and sex, Great Britain, 1986 (percentages)*

	Age	1971	1981	1985
Males				
	45–59	94.8	93.0	88.9
	60–4	82.9	69.3	54.4
	65+	19.2	10.3	8.2
	Age	1971	1981	1985
Females				
	45–54	62.0	68.0	69.4
	55–9	50.8	53.4	51.8
	60+	12.4	8.3	6.8

Source: Social Trends, 17, 1986

Table 3.2 *1966 forecasts of the economic activity rates of the working population, for 1966–81 (percentages)*

Age	Males		Unmarried females		Married females	
	1966	1981	1966	1981	1966	1981
50–4	98	98	71	75	47	58
55–9	96	96	62	62	39	52
60–4	90	90	29	29	21	26
65–9	38	30.5	5	4.5	8	9.5

Source: Ministry of Labour Gazette, November 1966

That the projections were well wide of the mark for the male rates is evident. What is more striking is the assumption made then of *constancy* in the pattern of labour force participation. The rates for men of all ages up to 65 were seen as straightforwardly remaining for fifteen years at the levels of the first half of the 1960s. Had the projections been accurate, the current generation of men would indeed have been repeating the pattern of their predecessors. To point to the inaccuracy is not to exploit hindsight unfairly; it is simply to underline the difficulty of anticipating changes in the pattern of institutional time. And even if such changes are anticipated, they may not be catered for.

Evidence from the Greenwich survey confirms the current position.

An initial questionnaire was sent to 3,161 men and women aged 50 to 65 on the registers of five medical practices. An overall response rate of 76 per cent was achieved, with the aid of two reminders; 149 people who had left full-time employment within the last two years – whom we christened 'work-enders' – were then interviewed. Almost half (46 per cent) of the initial population were not in work, of whom only 32 had never had a job. Allowing for the fact that some of the women were past the official pensionable age of 60, *almost exactly one-third* (456 out of 1,392) *of those over 50 but below 'normal' retirement age were not employed, even in part-time jobs.*

Some of this population may get jobs again. The departure from the labour market can be a prolonged process which does not even necessarily come to an end at formal retirement age. The fact that over 20 per cent of the women and 9 per cent of the men were still working past 60 and 65 respectively is itself a significant comment on the 'normality' of retirement ages. A small number of those identified as work-enders in the screening survey had found work by the time they were approached for an interview. Quite apart from the imperative of material need, the habit of work – perhaps an apter phrase than the work ethic to describe people's attitude to employment – dies hard. Nevertheless the chances of anyone within striking distance of retirement age finding work once they are out of a job is low, always assuming they want to in the first place.

In the longer term, the implication for our picture of the life cycle is that we are approaching the time when the average person will live for as long after the age at which they finish work as they spent in work before it. The template of previous generations – long work, short retirement – is dissolving. The trend pointed to in these results is one of three factors which combine to suggest this forcibly. Complementing the lowering of the age of retirement are the increase in life expectancy and the raising of the average age of entry into employment. The combination of the three brings the durations of working life and life after work closer to parity. On average, both are coming markedly closer to three decades. If we uncurl the life cycle into a life course (linear) and discard the pre-maturity years, the fulcrum on which it balances is the ending of work.

However, the issue cannot be treated in this simple arithmetic fashion, in terms of quantitative time only. The shift is recent and rapid, and social attitudes are far from adjusting to it. There are examples from our interviews of individuals who give a striking freshness to the phrase 'a new lease of life', finding themselves busier than ever before and enjoying new horizons. The extra years afforded by an early release from work, even where this was not a voluntary move, are treated as a gift of time, an additional phase which was not accorded to their parents' generation. But the shift in the overall balance of the life cycle has yet to be translated into a major change in the time horizons of this cohort.

Arguably there are four key dimensions along which progress through the life course is measured. There is the biological, referring to the person as a physical organism; the psychological, referring to the development of the personality; the social, which deals with the individual as member of a family or other social unit; and the economic, which refers to his or her position as a producer. For some time 'becoming old' has been more or less tightly defined as the point at which at least two of these dimensions – physical condition and labour market status – mesh together at a specific age to produce a decisive moment when the individual moves on to a subsequent stage.

Such an understanding has always exhibited a gender bias, being based overwhelmingly on the male experience. This point is the focus of the next section. For the moment we need to note that this supposed interlocking is anyway to a large extent a socially constructed phenomenon. Peter Townsend stresses the arbitrariness of the relationship between retirement and personal circumstances: 'Neither does the history of the adoption of new retirement or pension schemes show much correspondence with trends in the distribution of individual health, skills and preferences' (1986: 26; see Dex and Phillipson, 1986, in the same volume for an elaborated account of the socially constructed nature of retirement). External events have now combined to dislocate what has in any case always been a socially engineered as much as an intrinsic connection between physical condition and labour market position. People who retire at the 'normal' age do so rarely because that is the moment when they are ready to do so in any natural physiological sense, but because in a rather crude way society has found it convenient to impose a more or less standardised moment of transition. Now jobs are physically less demanding, and most people maintain physical health longer, and yet the age at which they finish work is coming down. The congruence of factors which give some degree of common identity to a generation at the point of retirement has been significantly loosened.

Ambiguity and impermanence: the feminisation of employment in later life

Employment and the sequence of occupational positions that individuals follow are only one dimension of the life cycle. This must be firmly borne in mind in relation to the argument I shall put forward in this section. Changes in family status, for example, arguably constitute a more important component of the individual's overall development. Given that limitation, however, I shall argue that the shifts in the labour market discussed in the preceding section provide further ammunition against a model of the life cycle which takes as the norm a single prolonged stretch of continuous employment. Expressed at its simplest, this male paradigm is being replaced by one which makes the experience of most women the norm. Characterising this as the feminisation of employment involves reference to the following features: the fragmentation and discontinuity of employment; the absence of a predictable occupational future; a high incidence of downward occupational mobility; involvement in part-time work; marginal employment status; and a high level of ambiguity in the status of those not in formal employment. There are, of course, other significant features which are recognised as characterising female employment, but those listed have particular implications for the temporal structure of people's lives. They refer on the one hand to the nature of people's occupational biographies, past, present and future, and on the other to the varying categories of time use. The overall picture is one of a complex and volatile mix of paid employment, overt and covert unemployment, leisure and domestic activity.[2]

Most of these features require little further explanation. Some have already been discussed in the previous section. Although in general people still expect to work to the appointed retirement age, the trend is towards a greater diversity in the age at which they finish employment. Nor is the boundary so often crossed in one definitive step; instead withdrawal from the labour market can be a prolonged and sometimes painful process, perhaps involving several downward steps on the occupational ladder. Once a worker has left a job, voluntarily or not, it is difficult for him or her to be sure what their working future is. In short, older workers, like women of all ages, have a relatively low degree of assurance about how long they will be working for and at what level they will be able to resume work should they leave their current post.

In one sense it is legitimate and useful to distinguish between 'core' and 'peripheral' or 'marginal' workers. Core workers are predominantly prime age, white, male and educated. They enjoy not only higher pay but above all a degree of security – a future with the organisation. The marginals have no future, other than in the very short term. The polarisation is becoming sharper, and deserves emphasis. But in another sense it is misleading to refer to marginal groups, for they are by now distinctly a majority, wherever the precise lines are drawn between the different categories. It has always been wrong to base policies and attitudes on the assumption that the male model of full-time and continuous employment is the only one that deserves serious recognition; it is even less justifiable now that the model applies only to a diminishing minority of the working population.

The question of part-time employment requires some elaboration. The upsurge of part-time jobs and the fact that the vast majority of these are taken by women are well known. The proportion of all employees who are part-timers rose from about one in seven in 1971 to almost one in four in 1986; nearly 90 per cent of the part-timers are women (Institute for Employment Research, 1987: 25). Is there a parallel trend amongst older workers which would support the idea of a predominantly part-time economy? Official data give little support. The practice of graduated retirement – moving to working part-time within the same company as a lead-in to retirement – seems not to have gained much ground. There is no evidence of a major trend for older workers to leave a full-time job and take a part-time one elsewhere. Nevertheless the members of this age group habitually express a clear preference for the opportunity of working part-time, and 20 per cent of all males in part-time employment in 1981 were to be found in the 65 to 69 age group (*Labour Market Quarterly*, May 1985). It would not be surprising if it became more common for employers to use older employees on a part-time basis as part of their general move to more flexible workforces.

The feature which requires most elaboration is that of *status ambiguity*. Women have more uncertainty as a group about how to define themselves in relation to the labour market. How temporary is the interruption to a career caused by child-bearing and child-rearing? And once one has got beyond the apologetic 'I'm just a housewife', how far is status to be defined in terms of employment? As Dex remarks: 'there are clearly a variety of women's experiences of not working and a variety of ways in which they arrive in such situations' (1985: 63). Exactly the same is true of many older workers, male or female.

The gap pointed to above, between the trend to a lower male economic activity rate and the acceptance of a reshaped life cycle, has caused many men to experience a high degree of ambiguity in assessing or even describing their current circumstances. Victor Turner has drawn on van Gennep's definition of the structure of rites of passage to explore the notion of liminality (Turner, 1978). The three stages in a rite of passage are separation, margin and aggregation. During the middle phase the passenger, or liminar, is in an ambiguous state, betwixt and between all familiar lines of classification, before he or she returns to a role in society with clearly defined rights and obligations. Turner applies this to pilgrimage, which he analyses in relation to religious experience and the way this has crossed the boundary between the spheres of work and leisure. Work-ending, arguably, has similar features, especially since it is located at the interface between work and leisure at a point where the boundaries are less and less clearly defined. Redundancy, (early) retirement, ill health and unemployment overlap and intermingle confusingly.

Summarily, there are two major sources of ambiguity which affect the work-ender. At the level of formally defined social status there is considerable confusion. For the most part, the state continues to pay its pension only to men and women who have reached the ages of 65 and 60 respectively. Over the last few years there has been a whole series of initiatives designed to remove older workers from the active labour force, as a statistical device or in practice. The measures have exhibited varying degrees of generosity, but whatever the material effects on the individuals involved they have done little to establish a new status for them. Society widely regards those who are out of work and over 55 as 'unemployable', but without changing its policies and practices accordingly. The nettle of what should be done with formal retirement ages which have a diminishing link to the labour market has yet to be grasped. State pensionable age is not the only important marker. The receipt of a disability allowance is a crucial feature of many people's income, and this has to be officially approved. We are witnessing a bureaucratically induced increase in the level of ill health and disability, since the transition from work is often wrapped up as retirement on health grounds (Piachaud, 1986). Classifying people as sick rather than making them redundant may be a genuinely humane device. It may often be used unconsciously rather than deliberately, but a good number of those who leave on the grounds of ill health are at least partly aware that the decision to allow or compel their release is based on judgements which are not purely medical.

Complementing this blurring of official categories is a high degree of personal or subjective ambiguity. The downward shift in the age at which employment ends has left many men, in particular, in a state of uncertainty over their status and role in society. This occurs even where at company level the transition has been managed quite explicitly, formally and humanely. One example from Greenwich will serve to illustrate the point. Mr L. had worked in the energy business. The generating plant at which he had spent the last twelve years had been scheduled for closure some two years before. All employees had been informed of this, and offered the choice of early retirement or a new job in one of a number of other plants. They had been given the opportunity of visiting the plants, during working time, to see whether they liked the idea of transferring. In Mr L.'s case the journey time involved in any of the new jobs had been decisive in causing him to opt for early retirement. (It is worth noting that for this age group the time spent travelling was often a crucial influence on the quality of their working lives; the stress of unpredictable traffic or transport was qualitatively different from the manageable strain of routine work.) The date for Mr L.'s departure was fixed well in advance, and the redundancy payment reasonably generous. He had no material worries. Why then was he thoroughly discontent? In part it was because of a lack of occupation. A gardener and a handyman, Mr L. could not fill his time with these activities, and attempts to serve as a volunteer worker for a charity dealing with the handicapped had not been successful; he and his friend Mrs E. had felt exploited by the professionals involved, who had allowed them to work whilst they themselves gossiped and drank coffee in their own little clique. These experiences could happen to anyone (which is not to downgrade their importance for Mr L.). The particular source of Mr L.'s unhappiness was his uncertainty about his own place in society. Being about the same age, 60, Mrs E. had at least passed the official age of retirement, and although she too was dissatisfied with the lack of outlet for her energy she had her own part-time business as a reflexologist (foot masseur). Mr L. had no such structuring component to his daily or weekly round. As he saw it he was in a complete limbo, from which he would not escape until he reached formal retirement age. This was symbolised by his yen for a free bus pass. It was not the money to be saved on the fares that mattered, nor was he particularly keen to be classified as a pensioner. But the mere fact of having a bus pass would have let him know where he stood in society's eyes and released him from his liminal state.

Conclusion

The collapse of the labour market for older workers, combined with the trend to greater longevity, has changed our picture of the life cycle. The generation of men currently finishing their working lives may be the last – at least for a while, until the demand for labour changes again – to exhibit the pattern which has been regarded as the norm: several decades of full-time employment ('full-time' being fuller in the past than it is now, with many jobs leaving room for little else other than rest and recuperation) followed by a few years or even months of retirement, the two phases being sharply distinguished. The duration of the cycle has been extended, and one of the major markers in it – retirement as the formal ending of employment – has been loosened from its established post-war position. Loosened, but not completley dislodged: like a wobbly tooth it is still in place, but the ceaseless probing of economic events is winkling it out.

In fact, of course, the preceding generation had to cope with all the unpredictability and misery of the Depression, reminding us of the newness and ephemerality even of apparently established practices. The pattern of the post-war decades is being replaced by a more diverse and unpredictable combination of formal employment and other activities. This, I have suggested, resembles in many repects the employment experience and careers of many women – in particular in the ambiguity surrounding the boundaries which separate paid employment from the several forms of unwaged activity. One consequence is that (relative) impermanence and uncertainty may now be taken to be the norm in employment, and the male paradigm of permanent and full-time employment may be regarded instead as the deviant case.

This brings us back to the interrelationship between different temporal levels. As long as employment was organised on the basis of work as a full-time activity continuing through adult life without interruption up to a clear-cut and predictable terminus, it allowed a more comfortable mesh between conventional masculine routines at the daily level and regular reproduction of career patterns for men than existed on the female side. The fragmentation and unpredictability of employment raise questions that we are poorly equipped to answer on how both men and women cope with irregular and unfamiliar patterns of activity, either on a daily basis or within longer time frames. As Luscher pointed out (1974), we know very little about the differences in ability to relate time perspectives to plans of action or careers; we know even less about how those abilities are shaped, and how they are affected by changes in the pattern of institutional time.

What, in sum, does this imply for our understanding of 'becoming old'? It is as well, in the first place, to remind ourselves that the trends identified in this chapter, and particularly in the first part of it, could perfectly well be reversed. The haemorrhage of older people from the labour market could cease, as employers become aware of the resources that they are jettisoning and policy-makers of the costs of a socially created dependency. The installation of what would in my view be more sensible and just policies at organisational and national level would see the expansion of choice to older workers, enabling them to leave work, gradually or abruptly, at the time when they felt physically, financially, or psychologically ready to do so. Such an approach would certainly see more people working later. Even without enlightenment of this kind it is perfectly possible that another turn of the economic wheel will see demand for labour increase and a further revision of the value of older people's labour power.

The second trend, that of the erosion of the dominance of the traditional male career paradigm, is less likely to be reversed, given social as well as economic pressures. But the consequences of this erosion are not easy to foresee. Put simply, there are two alternatives: a further growth in temporary, marginal and part-time work, with all its attendant insecurities; or the spread of flexible working patterns, with an acceptable convergence between men and women.

That said, the implications of the analysis can be summarily stated. It is less and less plausible to define the process of becoming old by reference to conventional labour market positions. The loosening of the knot which tied together ending work and entering old age affects both the previous and the subsequent stages of the life course. At some point a new vocabulary will begin to emerge, both for official use – for example in the payment of state benefits – and for the individuals concerned to be able to express their identity. Some will be able to exploit the ambiguities to define a satisfactory position for themselves, socially and psychologically; others will suffer from the lack of a clearly recognised set of markers. It is not always an advantage to be only as old as you feel.

Notes

The study on which this chapter is based was funded by the Leverhulme Trust and was carried out with Johnston Birchall and Michael Young at the Institute of Community Studies in Bethnal Green. Thanks to Terry Lovell and Paul Marginson for helpful comments.

1 See Musgrove and Middleton (1981) for an exploration of the links between chronological age, rites of passage and position in the social structure.

2 'Norm' should not be taken to imply that this pattern is an inevitable or a desirable one. Whether it is 'chosen' or 'imposed' is another area for discussion (though it is worth remarking here that some fairly grotesque verbal combinations have been invented to give a gloss on events – 'compulsory voluntary early retirement' being one such usage coined in an Institute of Manpower Studies report). 'Norm' is used here in the analytical sense to describe the broad pattern followed by most of the population, to be distinguished from the kind of norm which is imposed by a minority group, reflecting their power to shape thinking and policy.

References

Archer, M. (1985) 'Structuration versus morphogenesis', in S.N. Eisenstadt and H.J. Helle (eds), *Macro-Sociological Theory: Perspectives on Sociological Theory*, Vol. 1. London: Sage.
Bakke, E. (1933) *The Unemployed Worker*. London: Nesbit.
Bornat, J., Phillipson, C. and Ward, S. (1985) *A Manifesto for Old Age*. London: Pluto Press.

Dex, S. (1985) *The Sexual Division of Labour*. London: Allen & Unwin.
Dex, S. and Phillipson, C. (1986) 'Social policy and the older worker', in C. Phillipson and A. Walker (eds), *Ageing and Social Policy: a Critical Assessment*. Aldershot: Gower.
Frankenberg, R. (1988) 'Your time or mine?', in M. Young and T. Schuller (eds), *The Rhythms of Society*. London: Routledge & Kegan Paul.
Giddens, A. (1984) *The Constitution of Society*. Cambridge: Polity Press.
Hannah, L. (1986) *Inventing Retirement*. Cambridge: Cambridge University Press.
Institute for Employment Research (1987) *Review of the Economy and Employment*. Warwick: University of Warwick.
Jahoda, M., Lazarsfeld, P., and Ziesel, H. (1933/1972) *Marienthal: The Sociography of an Unemployed Community*. London: Tavistock.
Luscher, K. (1974) 'Time: a much neglected dimension in social theory and research', *Sociological Analysis and Theory*, 4 (3).
Musgrove, F. and Middleton, R. (1981), 'Rites of passage and the meaning of age', *British Journal of Sociology*, 32 (1): 39–55.
Phillipson, C. (1983) *Capitalism and the Construction of Old Age*. London: Macmillan.
Piachaud, D. (1986) 'Disability, retirement and unemployment of older men', *Journal of Social Policy*, 15 (2): 145–62.
Schuller, T. (1987) 'Second adolescence? The transition from paid employment', *Work, Employment and Society*, 1 (3): 352–70.
Seltzer, M. and Troll, L. (1986), 'Expected life history: a model in non-linear time', *American Behavioural Scientist*, 29 (6).
Smith, R. (1961) 'Cultural differences and the concept of time', in R. Kleemeier (ed.), *Aging and Leisure*. New York: Oxford University Press.
Thane, P. (1978) 'The muddled history of retiring at 60 and 65', *New Society*, 826: 234–6.
Thompson, E.P. (1967) 'Time, work-discipline and industrial capitalism', *Past and Present*, 38: 56–97.
Townsend, P. (1986) 'Ageism and social policy', in C. Phillipson and A. Walker (eds), *Ageing and Social Policy: a Critical Assessment*. Aldershot: Gower.
Turner, V. (1978) *Image and Pilgrimage in Christian Culture*. New York: Columbia University Press.

4

A Part to Play: Men Experiencing Leisure through Retirement

Jonathan Long

Although retirement is essentially about relinquishing paid employment it has often been problematised in terms of growing old. Certainly many of those approaching retirement resent it because they see it as assigning the stamp of old age.

While, for the most part, talk of death within a year of retirement has been discounted, negative views of retirement seem to persist. Perhaps the majority retiring now recognise that they are embarking on what may be another substantial phase of their life. In 1985 Schuller observed: 'It is indeed difficult to discern why a sudden expansion of free time is a blessing for some and a tragic gift for others'.

This incomprehension reflects the work-centredness that still persists among academic interpretations of retirement. To understand this conundrum requires an examination of that complex popularly termed 'leisure'. This is not to deny the significance of work. After all, for most of those currently retiring, work has been a characteristic of daily life for forty years or more. But most of us are not one-dimensional people (Marcuse, 1964). Nor is leisure one dimensional (see, for example, Roberts, 1978; Kelly, 1983; Stockdale, 1987); and in the absence of work (at least in the sense of paid employment) one simplistic definition of leisure is denied us – it can no longer simply be 'not work'. Moreover, it is no longer adequate to think of leisure purely in terms of an amalgam of leisure activities. In trying to understand social processes it is more fruitful to think of leisure in terms of values and associated roles. Unfortunately for social researchers these are not intrinsic, but are ascribed by the individual.

For our own project,[1] we assumed that those characteristics most closely associated with leisure were autonomy and choice. That 'point of departure' led us to examine the roles of leisure, and explore how these shifted during the transition from full employment to retirement. This led us to define empirically a set of leisure-related roles analogous to the 'categories of experience' that Jahoda (1979, 1982) has identified as being derived from work. These leisure-related experiences or roles appeared to be:

(a) mixing socially;
(b) helping others, feeling needed, being committed;
(c) being creative;
(d) filling time;
(e) relaxing;
(f) getting out and away;
(g) exercise and keeping fit;
(h) learning and keeping mentally active.

It would be easy enough to provide alternative or additional labels for such roles. However, to understand the transition experienced in the period around retirement, the important thing is not to counterpose work and leisure as monolithic entities, but to recognise that people's lives comprise a number of different roles. It is the balancing of such roles rather than individual activities that is important in negotiating a transition such as retirement.

For the vast majority, retirement still *appears* to be a sharply defined threshold (one day in employment, the next not) with all its attendant symbolism. There can be little doubting the significance of that threshold as a *rite de passage* (Crawford, 1973), yet there is also a more extended transition. While still in work, people start to 'wind down' psychologically, even if not in formal working practices – reducing to two or three days a week in the last few months is still rare. Moreover, some manage to continue some work commitment long into retirement, whether through consultancy for a few professionals or through a part-time job for others. Even the change in finance is not as abrupt as at first appears. Whether or not they have the cushion of savings accumulated over the years, many have a home, a car and consumer durables that represent an extension of their working lives into retirement; the real crunch may well come later when these need to be repaired or replaced.

Whether retirement does in fact represent a transition or a threshold, its symbolic position in the ageing process remains. People's ability to negotiate it successfully and construct a positive retirement depends in no small part on the extent to which the amalgam of leisure can satisfy the requirements of these roles. That this is possible was demonstrated by the majority of our respondents, and the potential exists for it to apply to others. To expect some magical transformation at the touch of a button upon retirement is, however, unreasonable. Circumstances may change quickly, but people do not. If people's leisure lives are not well developed prior to retirement it is likely that in only a minority of cases will they suddenly blossom afterwards. Quite simply, a long-standing diversity of interests heightens the chances that satisfying roles will continue into retirement.

The expected disjunctures associated with retirement and encroaching old age are:

(a) having nothing to do;
(b) a fall in income;
(c) declining health;
(d) losing a sense of purpose;
(e) reduced social contact.

It is largely because of these that retirement has been seen to be such a threshold. The contribution that leisure can make in these regards must necessarily vary from one to the other, and from one individual to another.

Something to do

Whatever else the debate might revolve round, leisure can certainly provide something to do in the time previously occupied by employment. Table 4.1 demonstrates that the main increase in the use of time after retirement was in leisure at home, with a slightly smaller increase in domestic responsibilities and personal care. Apocryphal stories abound about how people do not know how they ever had time to work, and some respondents cast themselves in this image. Those who have always appeared busy because of their work need not change once they retire, unless they wish to – busyness remains a possible lifestyle. For others, not all was purposive activity, and many leisure pursuits were used simply as a means of filling time.

Table 4.1 *Use of time before and after retirement: percentage of time by type of activity*

	Before	After
Work	23	2
Domestic	18	25
Leisure at home	14	23
Leisure away from home	8	10
Sleep	33	36
Other (including travel)	4	4

Source: Long and Wimbush, 1985

Leisure provides the opportunity for the constructive use of time, but not all know how to use it. Certainly it was not uncommon for respondents to agree that they did have spare time in retirement (though still a minority). But having spare time meant very different things to different people. Some who agreed that they had spare time observed that it was no different from when they had been in employment. Some who appeared to be very busy insisted that they had plenty of spare time – it was just that they occupied it with activities that they chose – while others who appeared to do very little apart from watching television maintained there was always something to do just pottering around the house.

Thus, it was not spare time that was a problem. Indeed, having more time to spend on activities that had previously been starved of this resource was given as one of the advantages of retirement by a third of respondents. It was 'time on your hands' that was seen to be the enemy. Those who felt that they had time on their hands did tend to report fewer activities and were also more likely to have had a worse experience of retirement than they had expected (or had their fears confirmed).

Yet only a third took up a new activity other than domestic chores – see Table 4.2. The norm was to spend more time doing the same kind of things as they had previously been involved in. Although they were not identified as new activities, there were some that were mentioned much more frequently in retirement. Some of these had already been popular before retirement – watching television, reading, social activities (mainly visits to and from family and friends), walking, trips, holidays and DIY. But others had previously been mentioned only rarely, like listening to the radio, going to the library, chatting, helping family and friends, playing with children and looking after pets. It is not likely that these were new, but they now had a greater significance. Table 4.3 presents information from the respondents' time diaries to show the areas in which the main increases occurred in the allocation of time.

Table 4.2 *Leisure pursuits taken up since retirement (percentages)*

None	58
Domestic	8
Bowls (outdoor and indoor)	7
Committee/political meetings	5
DIY/repair/maintenance	4
Educational activities	4
Photography	3
Other sport	3
Miscellany	13

Source: Long and Wimbush, 1985

Many intentions to take up new activities just did not materialise. Some no longer felt the need for additional interests when they tasted the reality of retirement, and others confessed to laziness. In fact it was the fear of laziness that drove many to make sure they did as much as possible.

Table 4.3   *Main increases in use of time after retirement*

	Percentage of waking hours	
	before retirement	after retirement
Watching television	12.4	19.2
Meals/tea/coffee, etc.	9.5	13.2
Reading	3.6	8.9
Visits to and from friends and relatives	3.3	5.8
Shopping	2.5	4.9
DIY/decorating/repairs	0.7	4.7
Walking	1.1	3.1

Source: Long and Wimbush, 1985

Those who still felt the need for a routine were normally able to restructure schedules around domestic commitments and leisure interests. In the absence of the imposed disciplines of work, this emphasised the individual's powers of self-discipline in deploying events generally characterised by greater flexibility and choice. Others, however, felt that the very idea of routine was anathema to retirement and were wary of the ease with which they might slip into 'a rut'. While being in 'a rut' is seen as being unfulfilling, 45 per cent of the sample sought the security of a familiar routine. Others (31 per cent) felt comfortable if they had a basic schedule within and around which they could accommodate more spontaneous activities. Being able to do what you want when you want to do it was the most commonly cited advantage of retirement – 59 per cent reported this after retirement – and yet only a quarter (24 per cent) said they had a varied daily pattern.

Clearly it is important to avoid the error of confusing activity with fulfilment, but there did tend to be a fairly clear general relationship between the two in the eyes of the retired. Hence, it was observed that the timing of retirement was important – for example, it was felt that retiring in summer made the transition easier because there was more to do than in winter.

Income

One of the major problems associated with retirement is the fall in income that results from giving up paid employment. Leisure is likely to do little to ease this particular problem and, indeed, may exacerbate it. It is not unnatural to feel resentment if, at the end of a long working life, the financial resources do not exist to allow the enjoyment of the leisure of retirement. While the time available during retirement may represent opportunities, these are commonly constrained by lack of finance. For example, one man was well aware of the opportunity he now had to follow his passion for national hunt racing by going to Perth and Kelso but he was unable to make this a reality because he could not afford to run a car. Instead, he went to the local bookie to place his 10p bet and then returned home to shout at the television.

In a consumer society, the lack of money (or even having less money than one is used to) can undermine status and jeopardise social links. For example, not being able to go out as much, being unable to buy a round of drinks and being limited in the extent of travel were all mentioned frequently and serve to limit the ability to mix socially. Conspicuous consumption, which secures status, is not possible for the majority of the retired.

However, only a small minority indicated that their financial position was worse than they had expected, and 5 per cent even maintained that they were no worse off than before. Being able to make ends meet in retirement was a matter of pride, especially for wives who had long had the task of balancing the household budget. Most of those retiring had accepted that they would have to 'cut the cloth accordingly', a thriftiness familiar to many of that generation. Even some of those who maintained that they had no financial problems were only able to say this because they had already practised restraint by cutting their expenditure. Managing on a reduced income normally entailed budgeting carefully for the essential household expenses such as rent, rates, food, electricity and gas bills. Only if there was any left could it be used for less essential items. Consumer-oriented leisure fell into this category of what might previously have been regular items of expenditure, but which were now regarded as luxuries. They were engaged in either less often or in a cheaper form.

Some now saw their leisure interests more in terms of productivity – as a way of saving money – as in the case of home brewing and car maintenance. The need for greater thrift was common to most respondents, but clearly there was a differential impact, with the working class being hardest hit. There can be little doubt that the consequences of having little money to spend on leisure, especially sociable leisure activities, had an adverse effect on the quality of life:

> You've got to have a little bit of money in your bank, because there is no good in retiring, having time on your hands, and not a bob or two in your pocket because it just means that you wander around lost. I reckon that the biggest bugbear for ordinary working-class people is a slight shortage of money. (Retired respondent)

Despite the financial difficulties experienced by many, only 15 per cent said they no longer took holidays. This suggests a high level of holiday taking, but for some this was because they were having a fling after retirement, visiting places they had been unable to make time for while at work and in particular making lengthy visits to sons and daughters who had emigrated. Others acknowledged that their holidays were now either shorter or of a cheaper form.

Health

Just as the opportunity to work tends to be associated with being fit and able-bodied, so retirement is associated with being unfit and unhealthy. Although there does tend to be a relationship between old age and declining health, the relationship with retirement is less clear-cut. The earlier view of retirement inducing ill health and a gallop towards death (Sheldon, 1950; Anderson and Cowan, 1956; Townsend, 1959) now seems very much mistaken. If there is an association it would seem more likely that ill health precipitates retirement rather than the reverse.

It seems at least as likely that retirement is associated with improved physical health as the burden of labour is lifted. However, on the basis of our interviews prior to retirement, it seemed possible that some might suffer declining mental health following retirement, with the loss of the stimulation, satisfaction, purpose and self-esteem provided by employment. But at the same time there were clearly some who expected their well-being to be enhanced simply through the removal of the worry, stress and dissatisfaction that had become associated with work.

Among our respondents there was indeed a slight improvement in self-reported health after retirement. Moreover, if life-satisfaction is an indicator of psychological well-being, it would seem that that had also increased. There was no doubt that many did miss some of the satisfactions they had derived from their work, but there were also the benefits of lower levels of stress and pressure, and much in their retired life-styles provided its own satisfactions.

When asked what were the most important aspects of their lives after retirement, health was mentioned twice as often as before and, indeed, became the most frequently cited factor. The identification of health as an important aspect appeared to bear only a limited relationship to either their standard of health or personal mobility. This increased awareness of the significance and value of good health did not, however, mean that they used their leisure pursuits instrumentally to advance good health. There were exceptions, of course, like the man who swam three times a week with the specific aim of keeping fit, but for the most part this was not the case. However, many more did recognise the value of 'keeping active', and more still were enthusiastic about getting out of the house for a walk. In general, respondents were more likely to do things designed to get fresh air after retirement, partly with the assistance of pensioner bus passes.

There was a small minority for whom health and fitness had always been important in contributing to their life-satisfaction, and who actively sought to maintain their physical fitness through continued exercise and sporting activity. In such cases there was a reciprocal relationship in that they were able to maintain their level of physical activity largely through their enjoyment of continued good health.

For a few, exercise before retirement had been linked to their work (for example, walking to and from work, swimming with workmates at lunchtimes, hillwalking with colleagues). Although retirement normally brought an end to these activities, respondents usually managed to transfer their enjoyment of physical activity to other pursuits even if the level of involvement sometimes declined. The general lack of a direct, active programme for personal fitness among the retired is perhaps only because it is something that is conventionally associated with participation in active sport and other activities requiring physical exertion, which most of this age group have long since given up in favour of gentler sports, a spectator role or walking. Such transitions were not attributable to retirement, but were the outcome of a more gradual ageing process, often over a period of decades.

Although the study served generally to reveal positive models of retirement, the links between health and leisure were most clearly identified when poor health acted as a constraint. It is not just things like sport and hillwalking that are affected – other leisure pursuits like gardening, DIY and singing, anything that involves moving away from the home, may all be limited. Such restrictions on the range of possible pursuits normally cause some frustration and disappointment, especially if the health problem is recent and there has not yet been sufficient time to adjust to or accept the position. Indeed, people in this position were more likely to have had a worse experience of retirement than they had hoped for. For them life in retirement tended to become even more centred around the home and its immediate environs than for the rest of the retired. In these circumstances walking locally was the most popular form of regular outdoor activity, since it allows exercise while taking things at one's own pace and resting when necessary. Even this reduced range of activity is constrained by bad weather, (strong winds, cold, damp) which exacerbates many illnesses.

For many affected by ill health, the loss of the socialising aspects of work proves particularly crucial as their restricted mobility limits their ability to make new contacts. Reliance on the family then commonly increases, and may be accompanied by worries about being dependent on others and becoming isolated.

It is not only personal ill health that may curtail leisure activities, for so too can having responsibility for a dependent spouse or relative. This situation may cause resentment, but can also offer fulfilment through caring for others, feeling needed and giving support.

Social networks

Although for the most part far from disengaging, respondents were generally aware of a lengthy process of 'settling down':

> We used to go to a lot of parties, but I think a lot of people have given it up too. It is a sort of age group that has drifted apart. I am a bit old for football now – I used to like football. I would have taken up golf in a big way, but I never got round to it . . . After we settled down, I thought, 'It doesn't seem worthwhile bothering about now.' I take the kids [grandchildren] around a bit. (Retired respondent)

Many respondents recognised that a less expansive life-style was developing for them with the departure of friends and relatives (through either removal or death), or because of a lack of money which limits visits to clubs and other social arenas as well as restricting the amount of entertaining that can be done in the home.

It was the social contact that people said they missed most about their work. This had been valued less in terms of making lasting friendships than in the social stimulus derived from interacting with others with a common interest. Yet despite this, almost three-quarters said they had made no new friends since retirement a year or more earlier. However, this did not necessarily mean social isolation (although for some it did). Some felt they had no need to add to an already extensive network, and others who had made plenty of new social contacts were very selective in how they applied the term 'friend'. One referred to the people he had met as 'just cronies, just contacts, people who go up there [the pub] and have the same interests as myself – playing darts. They are not friends by any means. You're friendly enough with them on the night, but the friends you pick up in a pub you can pick up any time' (retired respondent).

But this is not very different from how most regarded the social contact derived from work; only one in five considered their work-mates to be friends beyond work. For most people, maintaining satisfying levels of interaction when denied the everyday social contact provided at work required the conscious and active development of previous or new relationships. Such considerations became particularly significant when deciding whether or not to move house on retirement. Neighbours would seem an obvious and immediate source of friendships, yet only half our respondents felt they saw more of the people living locally once they had retired than they had previously. Many kept neighbours at arm's length even if they shared several years of living in the same neighbourhood.

Some sought continuity in the level of their social interaction through the familiar channel of having a job, albeit a part-time one, and using that as a way to explore new contacts in retirement. Many sought such continuity through family ties, though only a minority (38 per cent) saw any more of their family. Much of this interaction, especially with grandchildren, was evidenced in leisure-related activities; much was also in the form of providing help and support to family members. For some this meant fulfilment and satisfaction, but for a few it was very much a mixed blessing. The few felt that the family was taking advantage of them, assuming that their time was at the family's disposal, while they wanted to use this time to develop their own interests.

Table 4.4 shows with whom people spent their time once they were no longer working. It reveals an emphasis on wife, family and self. Diaries completed by respondents identified an even greater emphasis on being alone. That is likely to be the case because the psychological significance of contact with others is much greater than the proportion of time spent with them.

Table 4.4   *Company in retirement*

Percentage of respondents spending time with:	
Wife	76
Family	45
Self	33
Friends	26
Club members	26
Other	6

Source: Long and Wimbush, 1985

The role of leisure in helping to secure these more extensive links was recognised by many: 'I don't think it would be a good thing to let that drop. You've got to have something to keep you a wee bit in with the rest of your friends. If I gave up golf I would give up a lot of my friends' (retired respondent). Many forms of leisure offer the opportunity for contact with others, but the pursuits most commonly mentioned in this light had been a part of the respondents' lives before their retirement, though perhaps on a less frequent or less committed basis. Popular among these socially oriented leisure pursuits was going to pubs, social clubs and sports clubs (most notably for bowls or golf). By limiting the frequency of involvement, the amount of money left over from household budgeting often influenced how far these leisure activities could play such a role.

Purpose

Shamefully, the retired are often made to feel like parasites, a drain on the welfare state (Elder, 1977; Phillipson, 1982). This contributes to feelings of worthlessness and worry about a lack of purpose or relevance.

A sense of helping others, feeling needed or being committed appears to be one of the most important aspects of leisure in retirement, though it has to be admitted that it was more often talked about than acted upon. It is not that this need had been absent before they retired, but that there had previously been alternative avenues for satisfying it through employment; as a role for leisure it gained increasing significance in retirement. As already shown, those with established family-based social networks had a ready outlet for such roles. They valued being able to share or facilitate family leisure and use their own 'leisure' time to help other members of the family play their part in the production process. This was usually welcomed (though not always) as a means of contributing to the family and society – a legitimate 'work' role.

Leisure commitments such as voluntary work undertaken for organisations such as the scouts, the church, committees and welfare groups were seen to provide not only valued social contacts with people of varying ages, but also a sense of purpose. As such they replace the function of breadwinner. A few, however, who had long been involved in such activity sought to rearrange their contribution so that it might fit more comfortably into what they saw as their newly leisured lifestyle.

Leisure outlets for creativity or productivity were described by some respondents as job substitutes in retirement, especially when they applied their work skills, like tradesmen who retained their image of being a handyman by taking on more DIY tasks in retirement. The extra time available to respondents after retirement was regarded by those with creative interests as a delight because they were able to devote periods of concentrated labour or thought to the benefit of skilled, dextrous and time-consuming activities.

When asked what advice they would give to others encountering retirement, 28 per cent stressed the importance of keeping mentally active. In keeping with this, learning was one of the roles of leisure that did tend to become more prominent in retirement, sometimes as just one aspect of pursuits more directly related to creativity or relaxation. While some chose formal routes to learning through classes, lectures and other organised activities, many more operated much more informally. They might either learn new skills from others around them or else teach themselves from books, television programmes or other opportunities. For example, reading or television viewing became a means of expanding their knowlege and skills.

This provides one of the many examples of restructuring the meaning and significance of what appears to be the same activity. It would, of course, be wrong to associate all mental activity with learning in this sense. It also entailed crosswords, puzzles, games and betting. But this, like people's creative activities, tended not to be newly acquired. Instead it represented the attribution of new meaning and significance to existing hobbies and interests. Those who did try to get involved in new activities tended to be those who already had some experience of volunteering, learning or being creative.

Retirement strategies

The eight different roles of leisure identified at the beginning of this chapter are vital in allowing people to adapt to their own view of retirement. The advice that retirees were prepared to offer to others – see Table 4.5 clearly indicates that there is no single recipe for a successful retirement. Interestingly though, this list is not so very

Table 4.5   *Advice to others about the key to a successful retirement(percentages)*

Keep physically active	33
Keep mentally active	28
Don't worry—enjoy it	23
Financial planning	22
Take up recreational activity	20
Take it as it comes—live a normal life	16
Get a job—don't retire	10
Adjust your life-style to income	7
Stay fit	6
Don't be lazy or lie in	5
Other	14
No advice to give	9
Total (= 100%)	96

Source: Long and Wimbush, 1985

different from the standard advice given in pre-retirement courses. This emphasises remaining both physically and mentally active, supported by taking up a recreational activity, keeping fit and avoiding being lazy. There was also an awareness of the value of financial planning prior to retirement and careful budgeting in retirement.

Although there was a general consensus regarding the desirability of keeping an interest and staying active, views about the desirable level of activity varied greatly. Some were intent on using leisure to maintain the momentum of life in employment, while others felt that if they had not achieved their goals by this stage in life they were unlikely to do so, and so decided to slow down and adopt a more relaxed, leisurely approach to being active.

A straightforward interpretation of the interviews (rather than any formal multivariate statistical technique) suggested that our respondents adopted a number of different strategies to allow them to adapt to retirement:

1 active leisure-based;
2 active work-like;
3 passive, take it easy;
4 part-time jobber;
5 passive, stay at home;
6 continued employment delaying retirement.

Generally it seemed that the first two approaches (1 and 2) allowed people to adapt well, whereas the last two suggested poor adaptations (5 and 6). The following listing summarises the relationship between these strategies and the way in which respondents coped (or failed to cope) with different areas of adjustment:

(a) nature of activities;
(b) level of activities;
(c) sources of life-satisfactions;
(d) attitudes in retirement;
(e) sources of sociability;
(f) status and self-image.

The adaptations necessary to deal with both deteriorating health and reduced finance have been omitted because they are of a different order, overarching other considerations. The adaptations sifted out and presented here are therefore independent of health and income, in so far as that is possible.

1   Active leisure-based:

(a) more time devoted to previous leisure interests; may have taken on more activities;

(b) busy, little spare time; many and varied commitments
(c) satisfactions generally transferred to leisure and home;
(d) enjoys retired life; happy to stop work; making the most of it;
(e) varied outlets for sociability;
(f) not concerned with status except wants to be seen to be active and fit.

2 Active work-like:

(a) intensification of previous or new jobs to compensate for loss of full-time employment;
(b) busy; little spare time; routines based on previous working day; wary of losing work discipline;
(c) work still important in life-satisfaction but gained through non-employment activities;
(d) enjoys retired life but would go back to employment if possible; happy as long as busy;
(e) sociability predominantly based on interests; quite extensive networks;
(f) wants to be seen to be productive; doesn't want to be just a pensioner.

3 Passive, take it easy:

(a) wife- and family-centred activities; little outside family;
(b) usually has spare time; takes life easy; relaxed;
(c) misses some aspects of work; satisfactions transferred to family life;
(d) low expectations; enjoys more relaxed pace of life but some dissatisfactions;
(e) largely family-centred sociability;
(f) good family man; helping others.

4 Part-time jobber:

(a) part-time work; more time for previous activities; self-created gradual retirement scheme;
(b) still active but more relaxed; routines centred on job;
(c) work-based satisfactions; leisure not regarded as compensation;
(d) quite happy; still has to cope with full retirement;
(e) mostly family-centred but some outside social contacts through work;
(f) self-image as at work but usually lower status.

5 Passive, stay at home:

(a) activities often restricted to home due to poor health and mobility; lack of variety;

(b) time hangs heavy; bored; much unstructured time;

(c) misses work; restricted opportunities to develop other sources of satisfaction;

(d) not enjoying retirement; largely negative attitudes;

(e) largely dependent on family for social contact; otherwise isolated;

(f) denuded status; no replacement identity.

6 Continued employment:

(a) work-centred activities; little time for other things; leisure poorly developed;

(b) very busy; little spare time;

(c) work is central source of satisfaction; plans to extend this into retirement;

(d) negative attitude to retirement; worries about finance and time use;

(e) largely private social networks beyond work;

(f) status and self-image remaining the same but now threatened.

Like leisure, work was evident in different forms. Those who had continued in full employment (category 6), despite their original intention to retire, still had to prepare a strategy to cope with retirement (unless they managed to die in harness). Not all those working part-time would be placed in category 4, because these jobs were no longer the most important aspects of their lives, nor indeed central to their coping strategies. Part-time work served to secure for them a gradual transition to retirement. 'Work' was central to the adaptation of many to retirement in category 2 in the shape of activities like gardening, doing up the house, voluntary work and assorted committee responsibilities. However, the loss of the breadwinner role *per se* did not seem to constitute a real problem in adapting to retirement unless it brought with it dependence.

Managing the transition to retirement commonly involved strengthening continuities while adjusting to and incorporating change to formulate gradually a new pattern of life. Continuities were evident in roles, social networks, activities and satisfactions, at the same time as changes occurred in the nature and level of activities, sources of satisfaction and sociability, income and routines. Making adjustments to the changes precipitated by retirement was eased if it was possible to find continuity and support in other aspects of life.

To understand the role of leisure in retirement it is necessary not just to see it in terms of activities, but also to recognise the satisfactions and meanings that are to be derived from them (for example, creativity, relaxation and sociability, as indicated above). Someone retiring might retain basically the same pattern of leisure yet find its importance and associated satisfactions changing. This applies particularly to family and domestic activities and other leisure and sport interests such as gardening and golf. On the other hand a minority did find new interests and activities (such as part-time employment, voluntary work and DIY) to compensate for satisfactions and roles previously obtained through their jobs.

Conclusions

Does leisure keep you young? A question of that kind would be hard to answer, but many respondents felt that such interests were essential to stop retired people just fading away in their favourite armchairs. Hence emphasis was given to keeping mentally and physically active, supported by recreational activity.

It would, of course, be wrong to equate either leisure or a successful retirement with activity – others enjoy different outlooks and life-styles. Nevertheless, those who did more activity-based things tended to fare better when assessing their satisfaction with life. Moreover, such activity helps to counter images of decrepit old age that might otherwise persist among the elderly as well as the population at large. Contentment for some, however, clearly lay in being able to take things easy.

It would also be wrong to elevate leisure to an undue level of significance. The significance of leisure depends upon the meanings constructed by the people themselves, in this case those who are retiring. It is the people who hold the key in their own abilities and orientations, not activities or some abstract concept.

Some aspects of life in retirement are what the retirees make of them (for example, levels of socialising, activity and routine), but our respondents demonstrated that leisure can play an important part in empowering people to derive satisfaction from the kind of retirement they have created or had imposed upon them. While leisure was used by some instrumentally to secure a change, it more commonly provided a sense of continuity. This continuity might come either through the continuance of the leisure interest itself, or through some leisure pursuit which allows a person to continue to derive satisfaction and meaning previously derived from some other aspect of life. The changes associated with the loss of work were not entirely negative, and the value of some aspects of leisure were their very constancy and familiarity.

Note

1 The project on which this chapter is based was commissioned by the Sports Council/Economic and Social Research Council Joint Panel on Recreation and Leisure Research, and was conducted first at the Tourism and Recreation Research Unit at the University of Edinburgh, and latterly at the Centre for Leisure Research at Dunfermline College of Physical Education in Edinburgh. As such, the chapter owes much to my various colleagues of those years. Both the findings of the project and the methodology adopted are reported elsewhere in more detail (Long and Wimbush, 1985; Long, 1985).

The project was a longitudinal study of the role that leisure played in the transition from an essentially work-oriented life-style to one that might be more oriented around leisure. Our sample comprised men in full-time employment, living in Edinburgh and about to retire at the 'statutory' age of retirement. When they were first interviewed within six months of their expected retirement, there were 129 of them (plus those in the pilot). They were interviewed again just over a year after their date of retirement, when there were 109 in the sample. Respondents came from an extremely wide range of backgrounds, almost evenly divided between manual and non-manual occupations.

Each interview was semi-structured, based on a checklist of issues, but also collected basic socio-demographic data, and respondents completed general life-satisfaction scales. In addition to the interviews, respondents also kept time diaries for a week at each stage.

References

Anderson, W.F. and Cowan, N.R. (1956) 'Work and retirement: influences on the health of older men', *The Lancet*, 2: 1344–7.

Crawford, M.P. (1973) 'Retirement: a *rite de passage*', *Sociological Review*, 21 (3): 447–61.

Elder, G. (1977) *The Alienated: Growing Old Today*. London: Writers & Readers.

Jahoda, M. (1979) 'The impact of unemployment in the 1930s and 1970s', *Bulletin of the British Psychological Society*, 32: 309–24.

Jahoda, M. (1982) *Work, Employment and Unemployment: A Social Psychological Analysis*. London: Cambridge University Press.

Kelly, J. (1983) *Leisure Identities and Interactions*. London: Allen & Unwin.

Long, J. (1985) *Leisure around Retirement: A Report of the Methodology Adopted for a Longitudinal Study*. Edinburgh: Centre for Leisure Research.

Long, J. and Wimbush, E. (1985) *Continuity and Change: Leisure around Retirement*. London: Sports Council/Economic and Social Research Concil.

Marcuse, H. (1964) *One Dimensional Man: The Ideology of Industrial Society*. London: Routledge & Kegan Paul.

Phillipson, C. (1982). *Capitalism and the Construction of Old Age*. London: Macmillan.

Roberts, K. (1978) *Contemporary Society and the Growth of Leisure*. London: Longman.

Schuller, T. (1985) 'Workending', *Work and Society*, 10.

Sheldon, J.H. (1950) 'The role of the aged in modern society', *British Medical Journal*, 11 February: 319–25.

Stockdale, J. (1987) *Methodological Techniques in Leisure Research*. London: Sports Council/Economic and Social Research Council.

Townsend, P. (1959) *The Family Life of Old People: An Inquiry in East London*. London: Routledge & Kegan Paul.

PART TWO

BEING OLD

5

Transitions in Caring: Gender, Life Course and the Care of the Elderly

Sara Arber and G. Nigel Gilbert

It is hardly new to argue that one implication of community care is that care falls primarily on the family. The unequal sexual division of caring which burdens women who care for the elderly and other dependent groups is widely recognised (Walker, 1981, 1982; Finch, 1984; Finch and Groves, 1980, 1983; Phillipson and Walker, 1986). The words of Walker are echoed by many writers: 'the implicit assumption of policies promoting community care is that such care will be provided, within the family, by women . . . Community and family in this context therefore can often serve as euphemisms for women' (Walker, 1981: 550).

An emphasis on the impact of community care policies on women leads to the danger of neglecting men as carers. This chapter will examine the ways in which the biographies of the elderly person and the carer are intertwined, resulting in differences in the nature of the caring relationship, and will show that women predominate only in certain types of caring biographies.

Using nationally representative data from the 1980 General Household Survey (GHS) we examine the gender of co-resident carers and explore the contradiction that, while men are assumed not to care, data from the GHS and other studies demonstrate that at least a third of carers are men. We suggest that men carers challenge dominant norms and values that caring is inherently feminine, a fundamental part of the identity of women. Men carers have been invisible to researchers, their experience denied or ignored because their unpaid domestic labour contradicts gender norms.

In order to understand why men have been neglected as carers, we examine how gender influences the trajectory of the elderly–carer relationship, and how the reasons for caring differ between men and women. A man is more likely to take on the caring role gradually because he has shared a household over a lifetime with his spouse or as an unmarried son living with his widowed parent. Women are more likely to enter a caring relationship because of moral obligations resulting in an elderly parent moving in to share the daughter's household, or less frequently to live with her daughter-in-law. Finally, the reasons why men carers have remained invisible will be explored with reference to the conflicts between caring and other public and private roles of the carer. It is suggested that the conflicts faced by married women carers have drawn greater attention to the plight of caring daughters, with the result that the burdens of care are commonly, but wrongly, assumed to fall primarily on daughters.

Gender and caring

The burdens of care faced by women carers have been well documented, notably by the Equal Opportunities Commission (1980, 1982; Charlesworth *et al.*, 1984). The influential study by Nissel and Bonnerjea (1982; see also Nissel, 1984) calculated the financial and social costs of married women caring for an elderly relative in their own home, including the costs of giving up or reducing paid employment.

The few studies which have systematically examined the sex ratio of carers have shown that between a quarter and two-fifths of carers are men, but that men carers differ from women carers in their age and the types of household in which they live. In 1978 an Equal Opportunities Commission study found that 25 per cent of carers were men (Equal Opportunities Commission, 1980). *Equal* numbers of men and women were found to be caring for their spouse, and examples are presented of men doing all the domestic and personal care tasks for their wives. A later Equal Opportunities Commission study was based on 157 elderly people with informal carers who had been referred to specialist services (geriatrics, psychiatry, psychogeriatrics, social services) in the North-west (Charlesworth *et al.*, 1984). Forty-one per cent of the carers were male, with equal numbers of men and women caring for a spouse. The authors remark that 'men constitute a substantial proportion of carers. This finding suggests the need for caution in the use of simple stereotypes of carers which may understate the role of men in caring for the elderly' (Charlesworth *et al.*, 1984: 10).

A small survey of one locality by Briggs (1983) found that 23 per cent of the 93 carers identified were men but that only 10 per cent of the male carers were under 65. Levin *et al.* (1983) studied the supporters of 150 elderly mentally infirm people; 37 per cent of the carers were men, the majority of whom were either spouses or unmarried sons. Forty-one per cent of the elderly confused were cared for by their spouse, with nearly as many husbands caring for their wives as vice versa. Similarly, where a single child lived with a confused elderly person, this was equally likely to be a son as a daughter. However, in Wright's (1983) study of 58 single carers, 38 per cent were sons and 62 per cent were daughters.

Research on the burdens of caring has been based mainly on relatively small unrepresentative samples often obtained from general practitioners, from referrals to specialist services or from some kind of snowball sampling. Many of these studies have only contained a small number of male carers (for example, Ungerson, 1987), and the focus of the analysis and interpretation has been on female carers. Some studies have specifically selected only *families* caring for an elderly relative, for example Nissel and Bonnerjea (1982), and not surprisingly have demonstrated that in these families the burden of care falls almost entirely on married women. Bytheway's recent work (1987) is an exception; his interest in male carers arose from an earlier study of a cross-section of older men made redundant from the Port Talbot steel works.

Despite the evidence noted above, most contemporary writing on caring for the frail elderly assumes that caring is done by women, with most of the burden falling on married daughters, many of whom have their own children to look after as well (Finch, 1987; Phillipson and Walker, 1986). A recent textbook on the family exemplifies this:

> Just as the bulk of housework and childcare is undertaken by mothers, so too by far the largest portion of the routine tending for the elderly is provided by daughters, and occasionally daughters-in-law . . . The support at a daily level is almost wholly given by women and is defined as a development of their routine domestic role. This responsibility for providing care for the infirm elderly has major repercussions on their own social activities at a stage in their life cycle when they might be looking forward to greater freedom as other claims on their time decline. (Allan, 1985: 130)

The stereotype embedded in Allan's work and other contemporary writing, that women and particularly married daughters bear the brunt of caring for the frail elderly, will be examined using a representative national sample.

Data and methods

The General Household Survey provides a nationally representative sample of over 4,500 elderly people living in private households. In the

1980 sample people aged 65 and over were asked questions about their ability to carry out various tasks, the nature and extent of help provided by informal carers and their receipt of statutory health and welfare services (Office of Population Censuses and Surveys, 1982). The large sample size, high response rate (82 per cent) and representative nature of the sample make the GHS a valuable data source to complement, extend and systematically test findings and theoretical ideas derived from small, qualitative and localised studies. The GHS is not representative of all the frail elderly because of the exclusion of those in institutional care. However, since the purpose of this chapter is to examine the gender of supporters of the elderly living in the community, the lack of representation of all elderly disabled people is no disadvantage.

In the GHS the extent of help required by an elderly person can be assessed from a series of questions relating to activities of daily living, mobility and capacity for self-care. Capacity to perform each of six tasks – bathing/washing all over, cutting toenails, walking outside, getting around the house, getting up and down stairs and getting in and out of bed – has been categorised into those able to do the task easily (code 0), those doing it with difficulty (code 1) and those who cannot manage at all except with help (code 2). These items form a Guttman Scale as described in Arber *et al.* (1988). The resulting measure of functional ability is very similar to one developed by Townsend and Wedderburn (1965), and used by Bebbington and Davies (1983).

This chapter focuses on the 10.7 per cent of elderly people in the 1980 GHS who are 'severely disabled', defined as those with a disability score of 6 or more. They are unable to walk outside without help, and most cannot manage to have a bath or wash all over unaided. They therefore require assistance from carers on a daily basis. Although the chapter is mainly concerned with this group, it is important to remember that half (49 per cent) of people over age 65 have no disability, and a quarter (26 per cent) have only slight disability (scores 1–2). The latter generally have difficulty cutting their toenails and may have difficulty climbing up and down stairs. Thus, three-quarters of the elderly are *not* in need of any help in carrying out the six tasks, or need only very minimal help from carers.

Gender and caring in shared households

The sexual division of caring is to a large extent determined by who else lives in the elderly person's household. Table 5.1 shows that a third of elderly people live alone and nearly half (45 per cent) live as one of a married couple. Among elderly people who are 'severely disabled' nearly two-fifths (38 per cent) live alone and 31 per cent live with only their spouse. The proportion who live with elderly people other than their spouse is small, 4.1 per cent; but nearly twice as many of the 'severely disabled', 7.5 per cent, live in these households, generally living with elderly siblings. A tenth of elderly people share a household with younger members only, which increases to 17 per cent of the elderly who require assistance on a day-to-day basis. Over half of these 'severely disabled' elderly people live with a younger person who is unmarried (9.0 per cent), 5.1 per cent with a younger married couple and 3.0 per cent with a couple and their dependent children or with a single parent. The proportion of elderly people who share their household with a younger couple without children rises five-fold with increasing frailty, from under one per cent to 5.1 per cent.

Table 5.1   *Type of household of elderly people (age 65 and over) by level of disability (column percentages)*

	Level of Disability				
	None (0)	Some (1–2)	Moderate (3–5)	Severe (6+)	All elderly people
Elderly living alone	28.5	36.8	43.8	38.3	33.9
Other elderly in household:					55.7
(a) Married couple only	52.0	44.6	34.9	31.3	45.4
(b) Other all elderly household[1]	3.5	4.4	2.8	7.5	4.1
(c) Elderly couple and unmarried adult(s)	7.8	4.2	4.4	5.8	6.2
Only non-elderly in household:					10.4
(d) Unmarried elderly and unmarried adult(s)	5.4	6.4	8.5	9.0	6.5
(e) Elderly and non-elderly couple[1]	0.9	1.5	3.3	5.1	1.9
(f) Elderly and non-elderly couple and children[1]	1.4	1.4	1.9	1.7	1.5
(g) Elderly and lone parent	0.4	0.6	0.3	1.3	0.5
Total (= 100%)	2,147	1,127	633	467	4,374

[1] A small number of married elderly are in each of these categories.

Source: GHS, 1980

Gender divisions among carers of the elderly who live alone are likely to differ from where the elderly live in the same household as the carer (Levin *et al.*, 1983). However, the 1980 GHS only provides a broad indication of the category of person who helps an elderly person living alone, and does not distinguish their gender. For example, 'sons and/or daughters' are the main source of informal support for elderly people living alone (Evandrou *et al.*, 1986). Because of this lack of information on carers' gender, the following analysis of carers excludes the 38 per cent of 'severely disabled' elderly people who live alone. The implications of restricting our focus to the two-thirds of frail elderly who share their home with others need to be borne in mind when interpreting the data presented in this chapter.

We have assumed that, in these households, the primary carer of the frail elderly person is another member of the same household. This assumption is not always valid. There is anecdotal evidence of, for example, a daughter living locally who provides a great deal of care for an elderly parent despite the presence of an able-bodied elderly husband or a co-resident brother (Henderson, personal communication). However, these cases are remarked upon because they are exceptions. The norm is that household members provide the vast bulk of care for the disabled elderly. Evandrou *et al.* (1986) show that over 90 per cent of married elderly people were helped with domestic and personal self-care tasks by their spouse; and where an unmarried elderly person was living with younger household members, under 5 per cent received any help with activities of daily living from people living outside the household. Rossiter and Wicks (1982), Parker (1985), Levin *et al.* (1983) and Hunt (1978) also show that where there are other household members only very limited support is provided by informal sources outside the household.

The household structure and gender of the carer of disabled elderly people in the 1980 GHS are shown in Table 5.2. Over half the 'severely disabled' elderly are living only with their spouse. This is higher, 57 per cent, among the elderly who have difficulty in the home (disability scale 6–7) and falls to 39 per cent of the elderly who require 'constant care' (disability scale 11 – 12). Irrespective of the degree of support required, half the spouses caring for an elderly disabled partner are men and half are women – Table 5.2(a). This confirms evidence from studies cited earlier (Equal Opportunities Commission, 1980; Charlesworth *et al.*, 1984; Briggs, 1983; Levin *et al.*, 1983) that equal numbers of men and women care for a 'severely disabled' spouse.

An additional 9 per cent of the frail elderly live with their spouse and younger unmarried adults, usually their children. Table 5.2(c) only indicates the gender of carer where the spouse and younger adult(s) are the same sex – for the remainder the gender of carer is not known ('DK'). Evandrou *et al.* (1986) show that in these types of household about two-thirds of care is provided by the spouse.

Twelve per cent of the elderly disabled share a household with one or more other elderly people (this category includes a small proportion of elderly couples living with another elderly person) – Table 5.2(b). Two-thirds of these elderly carers are women, many of whom are caring for their siblings. Only a tenth of carers are elderly men. In a quarter of these households, the GHS does not allow an assessment of the gender of carer (where there are three or more elderly people and the household contains both men and women).

Table 5.2 *Gender of carers sharing household with frail elderly people by degree of disability (column percentages)*

Type of household in which the elderly person is living	Degree of disability			
	(6–7) Difficulty in house	(8–10) Cannot bath/use stairs	(11–12) Constant care	All with 'severe' disability (6+)
(a) Elderly married couple only:				
Female carer	27	25	20	25
Male carer	30	26	19	26
(b) Other all elderly households:				
Female carer	4	12	8	8
Male carer	3	—	—	1
DK sex of carer	3	2	7	3
(c) Elderly couple and unmarried non-elderly adult(s):				
Female carers	3	—	2	1
Male carers	2	3	3	2
DK sex of carers	6	6	3	6
(d) Unmarried elderly and unmarried non-elderly adult(s):				
Female carer(s)	9	5	12	8
Male carer(s)	5	4	10	6
DK sex of carer(s)	—	3	—	1
(e,f,g) Two- /three generational household:				
(e) Married woman (no dependent children)	5	11	10	8
(f) Married woman (dependent children)	1	5	2	3
(g) Lone mother	3	—	3	2
Total (= 100%)	116	113	59	288

Source: GHS, 1980

The remaining 27 per cent of frail elderly people share their home only with members of the younger generation, generally their adult children. The majority, 15 per cent, are cared for by unmarried adult(s) – Table 5.2(d) – and a somewhat smaller proportion, 13 per cent, are cared for by a married child or a lone parent. There are significant differences between these two types of filial caring which influence the nature of the caring relationship. In households where an unmarried child cares for an elderly parent, nearly as many men as women are carers, 6 and 8 per cent respectively, a fact which has often been overlooked in previous studies of carers. However, where a frail elderly person is co-resident with a younger married couple, we have assumed that the principal carer is the wife. This may be an invalid assumption in a small minority of cases.

This analysis of carers of the frail elderly shows that the majority of co-resident carers are women, at least 55 per cent, but that a substantial minority, over a third (35 per cent), are men (it was not possible to distinguish the gender in 10 per cent of cases). Where the elderly person has difficulty in the house (disability scale 6–7), 40 per cent of carers are men. This falls to 33 per cent where the elderly person requires 'constant attention' (disability scale 11–12).

Table 5.3 *Main types of relationship between co-resident carer and 'severely disabled' elderly person and gender of carer*

	Percentage of all co-resident carers	Percentage of male carers[1]
(a) Married—spouse carer only	51	50
Spouse + adult children	9	
(b) Siblings + other elderly in household	12	10–30
(c) Filial—unmarried child (only younger adult in household)	15	40–45
(d) Filial—married child (younger married couple in household)	13	0–5
Percentage of co-resident carers who are men		35–40
Total (= 100%)	288	

[1]The percentage of male carers in each category is shown as a range, since some of those assigned 'don't know sex of carer' in Table 5.2 may be men.

We will argue that the nature of the caring relationship, the potential problems and the likely needs for support differ according to four main types of caring situation. These are shown in Table 5.3: whether the carer is in (a) a marital relationship, (b) a sibling relationship, (c) a filial relationship involving an unmarried carer or (d) a filial relationship involving a married carer. Men and women are equally likely to be caring for an elderly spouse (situation (a)), and slightly fewer unmarried sons than unmarried daughters are caring for an elderly parent (situation (c)). In the other two situations, men are unlikely to be carers. In order to understand the implications of feminist critiques of community care it is necessary to be aware of these gender differences in caring according to the nature of the kin relationship and the implications these differences have for the stresses and problems associated with caring.

Three-quarters of male carers are caring for their spouse, a relationship which is likely to be based on long-term co-residence, reciprocity and mutual support. The majority of other male carers are unmarried men caring for an elderly parent, probably having lived in the parental home for most of their life. Among younger male carers conflicts between caring and the man's primary responsibility to paid employment may be high, but these conflicts are likely to be acknowledged by statutory service providers.

Over a quarter of women carers are married daughters or lone parents. These younger married women carers are likely to have conflicting caring responsibilities. Caring for the elderly person may conflict with meeting her husband's needs, and for half these women there may be conflicts with the needs of their dependent children. Thus, married women carers may be subject to particular stresses which are not faced by men carers or by unmarried women.

The nature of caring

Our finding that over a third of carers of the frail elderly are men supports other research, yet there is very little acknowledgement of the role of male carers or of the difficulties men carers face. Their caring is hidden from public view and has not been the subject of critical scrutiny by researchers, pressure groups or policy-makers, mainly because of the assumption that the same unequal domestic division of labour is found in caring for the infirm elderly as in caring for children and for the young mentally and physically handicapped. Research has consistently demonstrated the minimal involvement of men in the latter private spheres.

Although at least a third of carers of the frail elderly are men, caring conflicts with norms of masculinity and appears to break fundamental gender roles. One way in which the literature has addressed this problem has been to ignore it, and another has been to suggest that men carers are not really doing much caring because they obtain much more support than women from voluntary and statutory services and from informal carers living outside the household. This argument dismisses male carers as an artefact; men are not considered 'real' carers who suffer the same social, emotional and physical consequences which women carers have been demonstrated to suffer.

The GHS data show that men carers cannot be dismissed because they receive a great deal more support than women carers. Discrimination in the provision of domiciliary health and welfare services is not based on gender *per se*, but is determined primarily by the household structure of the elderly person and the marital status of the carer (Arber *et al.*, 1988). Younger married women caring for an elderly person in their home receive least support. Younger unmarried male carers receive a similar level of support to unmarried women who care.

Table 5.4 *Who helps elderly person with activities of daily living by type of household and gender of carer (column percentages)*

	(a) Elderly couple		(c) Elderly couple		(d) Single elderly		(e,f) Elderly
	Male carer	Female carer	+ Young male(s)	+ Young female(s)	+ Young male(s)	+ Young female(s)	+ Younger married couple
Help with shopping:							
Spouse	79	84	57	47	—	—	—
Other in household	—	—	30	41	70	91	100
Son/daughter[1]	9	5	13	—	18	—	—
Other informal	10	9	—	12	12	6	—
Home help	2	2	—	—	—	2	—
Total (= 100%)	128	127	30	17	40	47	69
Help with bathing:							
Spouse	80	92	(78)[2]	(80)	—	—	—
Other in household	—	—	(22)	(20)	(22)	68	87
Son/daughter[1]	4	1	—	—	(11)	5	—
Other informal	5	—	—	—	(11)	—	—
Health service	11	7	—	—	(55)	26	13
Total (= 100%)	76	155	9	5	9	19	31
Help with cutting toenails:							
Spouse	27	41	43	7	—	—	—
Other in household	1	1	5	21	20	36	40
Son/daughter[1]	2	5	3	7	9	5	—
Other informal	3	1	3	—	4	—	3
Chiropodist	67	51	46	64	67	60	57
Total (= 100%)	235	208	37	14	45	42	60

[1] Not living with elderly person.
[2] Where base number is < 10, percentages are in brackets.

Source: GHS, 1980

In relation to support provided by informal carers living outside the household, Table 5.4 shows who helps where a frail elderly person is unable to perform three activities of daily living: shopping, bathing/

washing all over and cutting their toenails. (The analyses are based on self-perceived inability to do tasks, and do not control for any objective measure of disability.) Carers living in the same household provide the vast majority of help in relation to shopping and bathing. Among the elderly living with a younger married couple, there is *no* help provided by informal carers outside the household. This confirms other findings (for example, Nissel and Bonnerjea, 1982) that where a married daughter lives in the same household, the degree of help from other sources is minimal.

Men carers in most types of household receive somewhat more help than women. However, the difference is very small for elderly married couples; for example, 9 per cent of husbands caring for their wife receive help with shopping from children living outside the household, compared with 5 per cent where the wife is caring for her husband. Where a younger unmarried man is caring for an elderly parent, slightly more support is given by 'sons/daughters' living outside the household than where an unmarried woman is the carer, but even unmarried sons provide nearly three-quarters of the shopping for their frail elderly parent. Thus, both male and female carers living in the same household as an elderly infirm person provide the majority of help. Only in the case of cutting toenails is the role of household members less than that provided by statutory services, but even here a substantial proportion of assistance is given by co-resident carers.

Somewhat more help is provided by informal carers outside the household to male co-resident carers than to equivalent women carers, and the least help is provided where the elderly person lives with a younger married couple. These findings provide only limited support for Ungerson's (1983) thesis that men will not undertake personal caring tasks because of gender-related taboos. From the GHS data, men carers receive only slightly more help from informal carers than women. Therefore, men cannot be dismissed as not being 'real' carers.

History of the caring relationship

In order to understand differences between men and women who care it is necessary to locate the caring relationship within a time perspective. We will argue that the caring 'trajectory' differs between types of household and that this is one factor which differentiates male from female carers. The dynamics and history of the relationship influences attitudes towards caring and the extent to which caring can be considered 'natural' or is taken on because of kinship obligations.

The balance between 'natural' caring and 'obligated' caring will be influenced by a number of factors: first, whether caring is part of a marital, filial or sibling relationship; second, the length of co-residence; and third, the history of reciprocity versus dependency between the carer and the elderly person in the present relationship and in the recent past.

Marital versus filial caring

Literature on the reasons why people perform the often very arduous work of caring for the elderly focusses on the way in which normative rules about obligations to various categories of kin are differentially enforced and interpreted for men and women (see Finch, 1987; Qureshi and Simons, 1987). However, caring by spouses falls outside considerations of kin obligations. Indeed, Ungerson (1987a) does not discuss the motivations of wives to care for their husbands – 'on the grounds that, given that I am positing a choice to care, the marriage relationship contains so many coercive elements as to largely exclude options, at least in the short run' (p.191). There are parallels between mothers caring for young children and spouses caring for each other. Mothers care for their young children not because of obligations or duty. They do so because not to do so would be unthinkable. It is natural and assumed. Feminist debates have centred on the extent to which men are *also* engaged in caring for children, and have not questioned the 'naturalness' of mothers caring for their children.

Similarly, if a marriage partner is ill, it is 'natural' for the other partner to take over the physical and emotional care of their spouse and to perform domestic duties. This natural assumption will only be broken where there are other more compelling obligations, such as keeping the family financially viable – that is, carrying on in paid work. In these circumstances the spouse's 'natural' caring may be taken over by other kin, particularly the wife's mother. The GHS shows that two-thirds of male carers are caring for an elderly spouse and so are likely to be of retirement age and no longer 'required' to be in paid employment. In Ungerson's (1987a; 1987b) small sample, all four male carers were retired. Most elderly couples would not question the rightness of caring for each other. Thus, caring based on a marital relationship involves an unspoken, natural and unquestioned assumption of care.

Norms of autonomy and self-sufficiency of the married couple and the family unit were found by McKee (1987) in her study of family strategies when coping with long-term male unemployment. Family norms of self-sufficiency are one reason why support is provided from within the household first, irrespective of the gender of other household residents. This suggests that where a marital partner can care there will be little support from others outside the household.

Only where the elderly person is widowed, or the elderly spouse is also very frail, do children become potential carers, as illustrated in

Qureshi and Simons' (1987) hierarchy of normative expectations about who would give assistance. They suggest that, apart from the elderly person's spouse, the order of expectations for help from outside the household would be daughter, daughter-in-law, son, other relatives and non-relatives. Finch (1987) 'suggests that these normative rules together with implicit or explicit negotiations between kin generally result in a daughter doing the day-to-day care. Thus, there is a crucial distinction between carers who are married to the elderly person for whom the caring role develops 'naturally' and carers from the younger generation who are more likely to have made a decision to begin caring, based on kinship obligations.

Length of co-residence

The length of co-residence and history of the relationship between a carer and an elderly infirm person also influences the 'naturalness' of caring. Elderly married couples may have been married for forty years or more; indeed, the length of marriage and of co-residence often becomes a source of pride, instilling a sense of achievement. Similarly, an adult unmarried child who shares the elderly parent's household may have had lifelong co-residence. The greater the length of co-residence the greater the likelihood that caring will be seen as 'natural', and not to provide care would be unthinkable.

Although the GHS is a cross-sectional survey and does not provide any information about the history of the caring relationship, we can get some idea of how this history differs according to the gender of the carer by examining, first, the length of co-residence of the elderly person with other members of their household and, second, who owns the property or is responsible for the rent – that is, who has been classified as the 'head of household'.

From information on the length of time each person has lived in their present home, we calculated the minimum time any person has lived in the same house. Table 5.5 shows that over a third of 'severely disabled' elderly people have shared their home with the same people for over twenty years. Less than one-fifth (18 per cent) have all lived in their present home for under three years (however, many of these people may have shared the same household for a longer period but have moved home in the last three years).

The GHS data suggest that long-term co-residence is the norm for carers of the 'severely disabled' elderly, and one would therefore expect adoption of the caring role to be a 'natural' consequence of co-residence in these households. Younger married carers are less likely to have been co-resident for a long period; only 29 per cent have been co-resident for more than ten years, and 34 per cent have lived together in their current home for under three years. Among unmarried filial carers and sibling carers, a high proportion, 60 per cent, have been co-resident for more than ten years, and a relatively high proportion have been co-resident in the same home for only a short period. Some of the latter households will have been formed by the elderly person 'moving in' to join the carer in the recent past.

Where the filial relationship has been one of long-standing co-residence, such as an unmarried child who has always lived with his or her parent, the relationship may have gradually passed from the parent primarily providing services to the child, to one of reciprocity, and finally to one in which the elderly person is highly dependent and can provide little in return to the child except perhaps companionship. The classic example is an adult son who has never left home, or returned home after a broken marriage to receive domestic services from his mother. Gradually the mother becomes more disabled, and the balance of the relationship changes towards dependency. The role of unmarried sons in caring is illustrated by Qureshi and Simons (1987): 'If a relative, such as a son, lived in the household with the elderly person . . . the son would probably help in preference to any local daughters. Most households of this type were lifelong: usually sons still living in their mother's home' (pp. 129–30).

Table 5.5 *Shortest length of residence of any member of 'severely disabled' elderly person's household by type of household (column percentages)*

No. of years	(a) Elderly married couple	(b) Other all elderly households	(c) Elderly married couple + unmarried adults	(d) Unmarried elderly + unmarried adults	(e,f,g) Elderly + younger married couple[1]	All
0–2	14	21	12	17	34	18
3–5	8	12	4	17	18	11
6–10	14	6	24	10	18	14
11–20	27	24	24	12	18	23
21+	37	38	36	45	11	35
Total (=100%)	146	34	25	42	38	285

[1] Elderly living with younger married couples with and without dependent children and living with lone parents.

Source: GHS, 1980

Filial relationships in which the carer is married are likely to be quite different from those where an unmarried adult child is living with an elderly parent. Married women who care for an elderly person in their own home are much less likely to have been co-resident with their elderly parent for a long period. Table 5.5 illustrates that over half had become co-resident in the last five years, and in under a third of cases the parent had been co-resident for a considerable period of time (more than ten years). During lengthy co-residence, the parent may have provided services to the couple and their children, with possibly a gradual change from reciprocity to dependency. The gradualness of the transition may have made the onset of caring unidentifiable. Where co-residence occurred because of a sudden event such as the elderly person's severe illness or the death of the elderly person's spouse, the co-resident relationship is likely to have been characterised primarily by dependency. Thus, the shifting bounds between 'natural' caring and obligation are likely to be tempered by length of co-residence and the recent history of reciprocity.

A crucial factor in determining the nature of the caring relationship is therefore whether the elderly person and carer have been co-resident for a long period or whether the elderly person has moved in to live with the carer. In the latter cases, the motivation to care and form an extended household will be based on kinship obligations which are likely to be gendered.

The household the elderly person lives in

It is very rare for elderly married couples to move to live with unmarried younger people in the latter's home. Table 5.6(c) shows that an elderly married person is almost always the head of household or his spouse, when there are younger adults in the household. Three-quarters of the unmarried elderly who live only with an unmarried younger person are the head of the household – Table 5.6(d). But where the elderly person lives with a younger married couple three-quarters are the parent or the parent-in-law of the head of household. This suggests that the majority of elderly people living with married couples have moved in to live with the younger generation. About half are the parent of the wife, and a quarter are the parent of the husband. Where there are also dependent children in the household the elderly person is even less likely to be the head. The reverse is the case for lone mothers: over 90 per cent of lone mothers are living with elderly parents who are heads of household. Thus, elderly people move in to join the households of younger married couples, but in only a small minority of cases do they join the households of unmarried children or of lone parents.

There are more unmarried men, 153, living in an elderly person's home than unmarried women, 102 – Table 5.7. Men tend to remain in the parental home for longer both because of their older age at marriage and because they are less likely than women to form independent households unrelated to marriage or co-habitation

Table 5.6 *Relationship of elderly person to 'head of household' by type of household (column percentages)*[1]

| | (a) Married couple only | (b) Other all elderly households | (c) Elderly couple + adult(s) | (d) Unmarried elderly + adults | (e,f) Elderly + married couple | | (g) Elderly + lone parent |
					(e) no children	(f) dep. children	
Head of household[1]	57	44	64	74	23	14	75
Spouse of head of household	43	6	32	—	1	1	17
Parent	—	3	3	17	17	29	—
Parent-in-law	—	3	—	—	44	49	8
Sibling	—	27	—	4	2	—	—
Other relative	—	7	—	2	9	6	—
Non-relative)	—	10	—	2	3	1	—
Total (= 100%)	2,066	196	292	298	90	70	24

[1] The GHS defines the head of household as (in order of precedence) either the husband of the person or the person who owns the household accommodation or is legally responsible for the rent.

Source: GHS, 1980

Table 5.7 *Relationship of unmarried elderly person to 'head of household' by gender of carer and level of disability (unmarried elderly co-resident with younger unmarried person, category (d)) (column percentages)*

| | Male carer | | | | Female carer | | | |
| | Degree of disability | | | | Degree of disability | | | |
Elderly person is:	None (0)	Some (1 – 5)	Severe (6+)	All	None (0)	Some (1–5)	Severe (6+)	All
Head of household	76	86	75	80	86	69	61	72
Parent of head of household	17	9	12	13	4	27	26	21
Other (sibling, other relative, non-relative.)	7	5	12	7	11	4	13	8
Total (= 100%)	72	65	16	153	28	51	23	102
Row %	47	42	10		27	50	23	

Source: GHS, 1980

(Jones, 1986). Gender has an impact on the likelihood of living with a *severely disabled* elderly person. Nearly a quarter of unmarried women are living with a 'severely disabled' parent compared with only 10 per cent of unmarried men. This inequality results in a situation in which somewhat more unmarried women than unmarried men are caring for a 'severely disabled' elderly parent. Although most infirm elderly people have remained heads of household, suggesting that the caring relationship has been one of long standing, in cases where they have moved in to their unmarried child's home, they are more likely to join their daughter than their son.

Extended households may be formed to provide care for an infirm elderly relative, as well as for economic and housing reasons (Buckland and Hardey, 1987). The elderly disabled are more likely to live in a household with a younger married couple without children than in an extended household with grandchildren – Table 5.8. Nearly half the elderly living in a three-generation household have no disability, and only 12 per cent are 'severely disabled', whereas nearly a third of the elderly living with married couples without children are 'severely disabled' and an additional half have some disability. The lower disability level in households containing grandchildren might suggest a more reciprocal relationship, with the elderly person providing help, such as babysitting.

Table 5.8   *Relationship of elderly person to 'head of household' for elderly living with younger married couples by presence of children and level of disability (categories (e) and (f)) (column percentages)*

	Without children (e)				With children (f)			
	Degree of disability				Degree of disability			
Elderly person is:	None (0)	Some (1 – 5)	Severe (6 +)	All	None (0)	Some (1–5)	Severe (6 +)	All
Head of household or spouse	37	18	25	25	17	21	—	17
Parent	16	24	12	19	23	21	(50)[1]	26
Parent-in-law	26	39	62	43	50	54	(50)	52
Other (sibling, other relative, non-relative)	21	18	—	14	10	4	—	6
Total (= 100%)	19	38	24	81	30	28	8	66
Row %	23	47	30		45	42	12	

[1]Where base number is < 10, percentages are shown in brackets

Source: GHS, 1980

Where a disabled elderly person is co-resident with a married couple or lone parent, the history of the relationship is likely to influence the balance between 'natural' and 'obligated' motives for caring, and between reciprocity and dependency. Length of co-residence and the circumstances surrounding the initiation of co-residence are likely to be crucial factors. The GHS data suggest that co-residence is of recent origin for a high proportion of the elderly who live with married couples without dependent children, and that co-residence has been initiated at later stages of the elderly person's dependency.

Table 5.9 illustrates two ideal types of caring relationship based on whether co-residence has been 'lifelong' or the elderly person has moved in to live with the carer because of disability. In the former, caring can be considered 'natural' – the carer has 'no choice' whether to care. In the latter, the initiation of caring is motivated and is the result of kinship obligations which are influenced by gender norms. Where co-residence has been 'lifelong', the history of the relationship will have shifted gradually from reciprocity to dependency, and there will often be mutual support, especially where the other carer is elderly. 'Caring for' may be a natural extension of 'caring about', with caring based on mutual support over a long period of time. Where the elderly person moves in to the carer's household this is likely to be at a time of increased disability, with the result that the relationship is characterised by dependency and there is little recent history of reciprocity or mutual support. In 'lifelong' caring relationships, between 40 and 50 per cent of carers are likely to be men; but where the elderly person joins the carer's household, only a small proportion of carers, under 5 per cent, will be men. Over 80 per cent of all 'severely disabled' elderly are in 'lifelong' caring relationships.

Table 5.9   *Ideal types of caring trajectories*

'Lifelong' co-residence	Elderly person joins carer's household
'No choice': 'natural' caring	'Choice'—kin obligations to care, influenced by gender norms
Long co-residence	Short period of co-residence
Reciprocity—gradual change to dependency: mutual support	Abrupt entry of elderly person into household, elderly person is already dependent
Less conflict with other roles and obligations	More conflict with other roles and kin obligations
Nearly as many men as women are co-resident carers	Very few men are. co-resident carers

Conclusion: the conflicts of caring

The burdens of caring are well documented, and encompass physical, emotional, social and financial costs (Nissel and Bonnerjea, 1982; Parker, 1985; Levin *et al.*, 1983; Equal Opportunities Commission, 1980). Although these burdens are likely to be faced to a greater or lesser degree by all carers, irrespective of gender and type of household, the conflicts of caring may differ according to household composition, and role norms for age and gender. Men who care face role conflict because caring is in opposition to dominant gender norms about masculinity. Male carers are less likely than women to get support and status from their male peers for undertaking the 'feminine' activity of caring. Indeed, male carers may become more isolated from their friendship networks because of the incompatibility of caring with other aspects of male identity. However, male carers may receive more praise and status from health professionals, and they obtain marginally more support from state health sevices (Arber *et al.*, 1988).

An elderly person caring for their spouse or a sibling represents nearly three-quarters of all co-resident carers. The nature of the caring relationship is more likely to be based on mutual caring rather than on moral obligation and duty. These are often 'fragile caring units' of mutual support, which may break down because of physical strain or deterioration in the health of the other elderly person. However, there will be relatively few conflicts between caring and other roles, because there are no conflicts with paid work, and few conflicts with norms of social activity outside the home, or with obligations to other primary kin.

Restrictions on paid employment and social activities because of the constraints of caring may be felt in some types of caring relationship more than others. Unmarried sons and daughters who care are unlikely to face conflicting demands from other primary kin, but there may be severe conflicts between the demands of caring and the carer's paid employment and social activities. Younger unmarried carers may expect and be provided with a good deal of statutory service support where the demands of caring conflict with the carer's life in the public domain. Married women's paid employment may also be restricted, but this is less likely to be regarded sympathetically by the providers of statutory services than is the case for unmarried carers (Arber *et al.*, 1988).

The conflicts between married women's caring responsibilites and their obligations to their own family make the situation of married carers crucially different from that of unmarried carers. Households consisting of a frail elderly person and a younger married couple have been the subject of much research, perhaps because they are the ones in which there are most likely to be conflicts and problems. It is the caring situation in which the carer, whom we have assumed to be the wife, is most likely to perceive herself as being 'exploited', with little support from either formal or informal carers, and little acknowledgement of the sacrifices she is undergoing. Caring may restrict her involvement in paid employment, leisure and social activities, and the burden of caring is in addition to her 'normal' burdens of housework and child care. Married women carers therefore exemplify the sexist and exploitative elements within policies of community care, but it is important to recognise that carers who live in this type of household represent only an eighth of all co-resident carers of the disabled elderly.

Note

We would like to thank the Office of Population Censuses and Surveys for permission to use the General Household Survey, and the Economic and Social Research Council Data Archive for supplying the GHS data. The research was supported by the ESRC (grant no. G0125003) as part of the Ageing Initiative. In addition, the ESRC provided support for the preparation of the 1980 GHS into SPSS and SIR files. We are particularly grateful for the help of Maria Evandrou, who did much of the early work on which this chapter is based, and to Angela Dale, who developed the household structure classification.

References

Allan, G. (1985) *Family Life: Domestic Roles and Social Organisation*. Oxford: Blackwell.

Arber, S., Gilbert, G.N. and Evandrou, M. (1988) 'Gender, household composition and receipt of domiciliary services by the elderly disabled people', *Journal of Social Policy*, 17(2): 153–75.

Bebbington, A.C. and Davies B. (1983) 'Equity and efficiency in the allocation of personal social services', *Journal of Social Policy*, 12 (3): 309–30.

Briggs, A. (1983) *Who Cares?* Chatham, Kent: Association of Carers.

Buckland, S. and Hardey, M. (1987) 'The "extended household": low income households in affluent villages'. University of Surrey, (*mimeo*).

Bytheway, W.R. (1987) *Informal Care Systems: An Exploratory Study of Older Steel Workers in South Wales*. Report to Joseph Rowntree Memorial Trust, University College of Swansea.

Charlesworth, A., Wilkin, D. and Durie, A. (1984) *Carers and Services: A Comparison of Men and Women Caring for Dependent Elderly People*. Manchester: Equal Opportunities Commission.

Equal Opportunities Commission (1980) *The Experience of Caring for Elderly and Handicapped Dependants: Survey Report*. Manchester: EOC.

Equal Opportunities Commission (1982) *Who Cares for the Carers? Opportunities for Those Caring for the Elderly and Handicapped*. Manchester: EOC.

Evandrou, M., Arber, S., Dale, A. and Gilbert, G.N. (1986) 'Who cares for the elderly? Family care provision and receipt of statutory services', in C. Phillipson, M. Bernard and P. Strang (eds), *Dependency and Interdependency in Old Age – Theoretical Perspectives and Policy Alternatives*. London: Croom Helm. pp. 150–66.

Finch, J. (1984) 'Community care: developing non-sexist alternatives', *Critical Social Policy*, 9: 6–19.

Finch, J. (1987) 'Family obligations and the life course', in A. Bryman, W.R. Bytheway, P. Allatt and T. Keil (eds), *Rethinking the Life Cycle*. London: Macmillan. pp. 155–69.

Finch, J. and Groves, D. (1980) 'Community care and the family: a case for equal opportunities', *Journal of Social Policy*, 9 (4): 487–511.

Finch, J. and Groves, D. (eds) (1983) *A Labour of Love: Women, Work and Caring*. London: Routledge & Kegan Paul.

Hunt, A. (1978) *The Elderly at Home*. London: HMSO/Office of Population Censuses and Surveys.

Jones, G. (1986) 'Stratification in youth'. PhD thesis, University of Surrey.

Levin, E., Sinclair, I. and Gorbach, P. (1983) *The Supporters of Confused Elderly Persons at Home*. London: National Institute for Social Work.

McKee, L. (1987) 'Households during unemployment: the resourcefulness of the unemployed', in J. Brannen and G. Wilson (eds), *Give and Take in Families*. London: Allen & Unwin. pp. 96–116.

Nissel, M. (1984) 'The family costs of looking after handicapped elderly relatives', *Ageing and Society*, 4 (2): 185–205.

Nissel, M and Bonnerjea, L. (1982) *Family Care of the Handicapped Elderly: Who Pays?* London: Policy Studies Institute.

Office of Population Censuses and Surveys (1982) *General Household Survey 1980*. London: HMSO.

Parker, G. (1985) *With Due Care and Attention: A Review of Research on Informal Care*. London: Family Policy Studies Centre.

Phillipson, C. and Walker, A. (eds) (1986) *Ageing and Social Policy: A Critical Assessment*. Aldershot: Gower.

Qureshi, H. and Simons, K. (1987) 'Resources within families: caring for elderly people', in J. Brannen and G. Wilson (eds), *Give and Take in Families*, London: Allen & Unwin. pp. 117–35.

Rossiter, C. and Wicks, M. (1982) *Crisis or Challenge? Family Care, Elderly People and Social Policy*. London: Study Commission on the Family.

Townsend, P. and Wedderburn, D. (1965) *The Aged in the Welfare State*. London: G. Bell & Sons.

Ungerson, C. (1983) 'Women and caring: skills, tasks and taboos', in E. Gamarnikow, D. Morgan, J. Purvis and D. Taylorson (eds), *The Public and the Private*. London: Heinemann. pp. 62–77.

Ungerson, C. (1987a) 'The life course and informal caring: towards a typology', in G. Cohen (ed.), *Social Change and the Life Course*. London: Tavistock.

Ungerson, C. (1987b) *Policy is Personal: Sex, Gender and Informal Care*. London: Tavistock.

Walker, A. (1981) 'Community care and the elderly in Great Britain: theory and practice', *International Journal of Health Services*, 11, (4): 541–57.

Walker, A. (ed.) (1982) *Community Care: The Family, the State and Social Policy*. Oxford: Blackwell/Martin Robertson.

Wright, F. (1983) 'Single carers: employment, housework and caring', in Finch and Groves, *op. cit.*, pp. 89–105.

6

Poverty, Care and Age: a Case Study

Bill Bytheway

The main focus of a study[1] of informal care in the families of older redundant South Wales steelworkers was the informal care system. In constructing a typology of such systems, I characterised six (out of a sample of fifty-nine) as 'increasingly impoverished' (Bytheway, 1987). The case study presented in this chapter represents this small but significant group and raises a number of issues about poverty, disability, gender and the production of family care. What it also does is point to certain less apparent questions about age and ageing. In addition, it is included in this volume because it amplifies some of the points raised in other chapters about work-ending, gender, care and household structure.

The two households and four key people I first met in April 1985 are:

● Tom, the redundant steelworker, born in 1929, and his son, Gwyn, born in 1960;
● Doris, Tom's sister, born in 1926, and their father, Martin, born in 1901.

These two households occupy similar three-bedroom terraced council housing on an isolated estate near a large valley community.

1985

Tom is widowed and lives with his son, Gwyn, who suffers from epilepsy. Gwyn needs constant attention, and for this reason Tom receives an Attendance Allowance from Social Security. It was a doctor who suggested applying for this, seven years after it had been diagnosed. At first he was refused, the examining doctor saying Gwyn was 'a fine looking lad'. Gwyn is in his mid-twenties and weighs sixteen stone. Tom's appeal was successful, but he remains bitter that he was 'cheated' out of seven years of the benefit.

He was not very happy about the redundancy agreement when he finished work in 1980. The Steel Corporation was not as generous as some people imagine, he said. He was under 55 years of age when he finished but is now in receipt of his works pension because of his own disability – due to childhood polio. However, he has been refused Invalidity Benefit from Social Security.

Four years ago, after redundancy from the steelworks, Tom was offered a job in a park. At £70 per week, it meant £28 in the pocket, he said, after taking out tax and travel costs. He was getting £25 on the dole. The clerk at the Job Centre said there would be plenty of overtime, but Tom replied he wanted a job, not to live there. Now, in 1985, Tom is 56, living on Social Security, and anxious because he can no longer afford to run his car (an old three-wheeler van).

When I interviewed Tom, I asked about the older generation, and Tom mentioned that his father, Martin, was living nine doors down the road. Tom takes Martin in the car to the local club two or three times a week, but Martin is rapidly losing his sight now. Living with and looking after Martin is his daughter, Tom's sister, Doris. Tom told me that she had had rheumatic fever as a child and now has a 'dicky heart'. Sometimes she spends all day sitting in the corner, he said. At that time she and Martin were with her daughter in Neath, because Doris had been unwell.

A week or so later, I was able to interview Doris and Martin back in their own home. As I arrived, Martin was sitting outside his front door enjoying the sunshine. Doris has lived in her house for thirty-three years. She had been widowed eleven years, her husband, a miner, having died of pneumoconiosis. He had told her to insist on a post-mortem if he should die so that she could make a claim, but unfortunately, she said, he had died in hospital, and the death certificate made no mention of the disease. As a result she had had no compensation.

She told me that Tom's wife had died of TB in the 1960s when Gwyn was young. Doris had then done much to raise both Gwyn and Tom's daughter (now married and living in Neath) as well as her own son and daughter.

Martin has been with her for fourteen years. He is 84 years old and had been a miner for forty-three years. He came out with nothing, so at the age of 65 he had got a job as a janitor in the steelworks. He told a sad tale of his second marriage – 'She robbed me clean off my feet.' When it came to a head, he walked out to come to live with his daughter and son-in-law. Doris said she was glad he came – he wouldn't be alive today if he hadn't – and Martin agreed it was the best thing he'd ever done. At that time he had been fit and active although suffering from bronchitis and arthritis. He had looked after the garden for Doris.

I was able to record my interview with Doris and Martin, and the following is a transcription of parts of this:

B.B.: [to Martin]: Your health was OK up until about five years ago?

M. : Yes, it was a pleasure to see my garden and somebody else's garden, and doing two jobs a day.

B.B.: What sort of help have you needed over the last five years, then?

M. : Well, my eyes have gone. They can't do nothing about that. Specialist told me: we can operate on you, he said, but you won't gain nothing. Fair enough, I said. Go see the optician, he said. I told him, I went to see him. He tried all the gadgets he had, but I couldn't see nothing out of this eye. I could see a spot with that eye. I'm very sorry, he said, you've got to live with it.

D. : He's got cataracts. They can remove the cataracts, but it's pointless putting him through that operation because he's got scars on the eyes underneath them. Well, that's through working underground, but can you get a certificate? By gosh! They won't admit it.

M. : I can't put sugar in my tea without putting sugar on my saucer. That's how bad they are. People think because you've got glasses, you can see. 'How are you, Martin?' I don't know who they are. They must think, there's a toffee-nose he is.

D. : On times, he goes down on his knee as well. At one time, one summer, that's all he had was scars on the shin. Well, he's got a dressing now on one knee. So he has to be just so careful walking – but the doctor wants him to walk to keep his knees going.

. . .

B.B.: So who helps you get down to the club, and things like that . . .?

M. : I goes down to the club in town every Sunday night. My boy [Tom] takes me to the door and back to this door.

D. : He comes home then because of Gwyn, but more often than not Gwyn is by here, because when his father goes out, he comes over by here, see.

M. : He's lucky – he's got two homes.

D. : My husband and I more or less reared him, because his mother was in hospital with TB when he was a baby. My husband ruined him. My boy is so much older than him. He was ruined.

M. : And he gets these bouts, you know. He gets no warning. Sometimes he falls on the pavement and . . . oh. I've seen him coming in here and I've a good look to see who he was. He's had one or two by here, sitting by here. I've had to catch him without him hurting himself, see.

D. : The armchair I had by there before I got that one. He used to sit in that if he was in. Of course, he was a bit better then. He could go out oftener then, like, see, and he'd go . . . [Demonstrating] That's how he goes without warning in the middle of a conversation, you know. And he was in that chair by there, between his sixteen stone, me on my own . . . I had to hold his head one side with one hand. You know, so as not to swallow his tongue, and hold the chair up because the chair was going with him, see. He was such a big boy. His legs could be up here . . . Oh, good God!

M. : He was like a horse.

. . .

B.B.: I'm interested to know what the effects of looking after Gwyn are upon Tom and whether it's stopping him . . .

M. : Oh, he couldn't work. He couldn't go to work in the morning and come home in the night.

D. : No, he couldn't.

B.B.: Some people can't go out working because they're tied to looking after somebody . . .

D. : Well, he's got to be . . . Well, sometimes now, perhaps, Gwyn will go to raise his money on the Monday . . . at the post office. Oh, he's had many up there. A phone call will come then, and Tom will go with that little van, the three-wheeler – he can't afford a better one – but he goes up there and brings him down, see. Because when he's coming out of them, he doesn't know where he is or what . . . he's done, been doing. It's on his mind, see.

M. : He had one last week. Listen to this. He came round. He was going home. In the house he was. 'You are home', and Tom tried to put him right. 'I'm going home!' Down the steps. Tom had to watch him now. Go after him down the road. Gwyn! He was in the house, man, but going the wrong way, you know.

D. : He followed him. He shouted after him: 'Gwyn there's a cup of tea ready for you.' He turned back, went straight to his bed. Went out of his own house to go . . . That's all he wants – to go home to go to bed.

M. : It's all trouble.

. . .

B.B.: When your health isn't too good, you go to stay with your daughter in Neath?

D. : No. I did this once, because I've had a rough winter – pulls with bronchitis – and I can't stay in bed because I've got to see to fires etcetera for my father. I was really ill one Monday. I got up early because the rentman comes about ten. He said: 'Have you phoned for a doctor?' I said: 'No, because I can't go to bed if he tells me to.' Rentman said: 'If you're not going to phone, I'm going to.' So I did phone, and of course I suffer with my nerves and my heart. They've cut down on these tablets – they're not as strong. I rang the receptionist, and once I heard her voice, I broke down on the phone. She said: 'Make yourself a cup of tea, doctor will be there now.' He came, examined me: 'Bad infection.' Daughter came up, packed my case and said: 'No arguments – the two of you are coming over our house.'

M. : She's got five bedrooms.

D. : She's got three children. She said: 'I can't come back and fore to look after you', because of the children and her husband. I remember her taking me up the stairs, and I don't remember anything for four days.

B.B.: Feeling better now?

D. : Now I'm starting to pick up because I've been lazy.

. . .

B.B.: If your brother's health wasn't too good, what do you think he'd do?

D. : Our Gwyn. When he's alright, he's pretty handy.

B.B.: So Gwyn would look after him?

D. : He'd have to. I couldn't.

B.B.: They wouldn't go off to stay with someone else?

D. : There isn't anyone else. We're a small family.

. . .

B.B.: Getting any help from Social Security?

D. : I've started having it now – having 55p. I'll be 60 now.

M. : May 21st.

D. : On my pension, I'll be having . . . On my husband – because I've never been able to work. I think my Social Security will go up a bit then.

B.B.: Any Heating Allowance?

D. : Coal Allowance – that's included. That's why I'm only having 55p.

B.B.: Your father's not getting Attendance Allowance?

D. : Care and Attention – yes.

B.B.: Getting an allowance for that?

D. : Yes. We only had that last year.

M. : I've had nothing. Worked all my life. I was 81 when I finished – had nothing from nowhere.

D. : It's been a struggle. I wasn't 50 when my husband died. I was only having nine pounds a week.

B.B.: Now, is your weekly income sufficient to meet your requirements?

D. : Yes, because this [cigarettes] is my only vice. I don't go out, don't drink. Never been in a bingo hall, nothing else around here.

M. : Before you go from here, you got to have ten bob in your hand for the bus fare – 33p from here down to Dyffryn.

. . .

B.B.: You say your brother's leg is bad – how long has it been bad?

D. : He was back and fore, Cardiff Infirmary.

M. : What do they call it when . . .

D. : Some doctors were saying it was polio. He fell over a short stone wall and he was complaining about his leg after that.

M. : Complaining of other leg now.

B.B.: So it's been a bit of a handicap all his life?

M. : Yes.

D. : I remember when we were in school, he'd lose the use of it. They couldn't do anything till he was 7. Teachers would fetch me then – there's five years between us – 'What shift's your father working?' If he was in work, I'd have to carry him home. Or they'd send me home for Father, who'd bring him home on the crossbar of his bike.

Later she told me of her attempts to get the council to convert the upstairs so that the door of the toilet did not open on to the top of the stairs. She was fearful that Martin would fall in the middle of the night.

Two months later, on a Friday in July 1985, I visited the Age Concern West Glamorgan Advice and Information Office and found that there had been a call for help from Doris. I offered to go round myself, and when I arrived in the mid-afteroon I found Doris looking very tired and weak. Martin had been ill in bed for three days. She was no longer interested in getting the council to alter the bathroom but asked me if I could get a urine bottle for Martin from the health centre. She told me that the doctor had been that morning and had said he would arrange for a consultant to come to see Martin. She thought I might have been him.

It was not appropriate to press her with questions, but I was prepared to sit there whilst she talked. She described with some exasperation how the doctor had called, had asked Martin how he was doing. Martin had answered 'not too bad', the doctor had said 'that's all right then', and that had been about it. Typical of men, she said. In the course of this, a car drew up, and she suggested this might be the consultant. I looked out of the window and saw a man getting out of his car with an open-necked shirt and large medallion round his neck. Not the consultant, he was George, the secretary of the club that Tom would take Martin to two or three times a week. George sat down opposite Doris and did what he could to raise her spirits.

She had said, in passing, that Martin's bedding needed changing because he had spilt his coffee. As George talked, it occurred to me that this was probably the best chance of the bedding being changed that week. It might be that others would be calling in, but it might also be that Martin would be left in damp sheets for several days, Doris growing more and more depressed. I had the time whilst George talked to savour what I was about to propose: two virtually strange men going upstairs to strip and change the old man's bed. When I put it to Doris, she thought long, looking at the two of us, doubting I suspect our competence, but realising that this might indeed be the only opportunity. She and George went upstairs to see Martin. She then called down that it was all right. So the three of us, in a crowded bedroom with precious little leg-room, managed to strip and remake the bed, Martin rolling from one side to another to save him having to get up. George remained upstairs to do what he could to cheer up Martin, and, assured that there was no more to be done, I set off to get a bottle from the health centre. Unfortunately, by that time it was 4.30 and the centre had closed. I left a message asking the nurse to call round as soon as possible.

1987

In August 1987, a little over two years later, I returned to deliver to Tom a copy of a summary report on the study. Gwyn answered the door and called his father. Tom was decorating and couldn't stop to talk. From half-way down the stairs he told me that Doris was still living up the road, but his father, Martin, had died two years ago. I handed over the report and left.

Doris recognised me with some difficulty but then remembered well my visit on the Friday afternoon in July 1985. She invited me in and readily recounted the events of her father's death.

Their GP had always explained Martin's condition as being due to old age. 'Everything was old age to him,' she said. Initially he had told her father to stop gardening. Martin had been keen on gardening but he always said that if you don't do what the doctor says you might as well not bother him. As Martin's condition didn't improve, the doctor next told him to throw away the hatchet that Martin used to chop wood. He diagnosed lumbago even though he hadn't examined Martin. According to Doris, he'd come and in two shakes he was gone.

She was up day and night with Martin after that. She would bath him down to his waist and up to his knees. He'd do the rest. He was an old collier who believed in a daily bath and a clean change of clothing.

Eventually Martin said: 'You pack a case for me to go into hospital.' He knew that he wasn't well. He would fancy food and then wouldn't eat it. Tinned fruit: he'd never like tinned fruit before. A lot was thrown away.

The week in July that I had called, Martin had stayed in bed since the Tuesday. For the previous twelve weeks she hadn't been able to shop, being so run down herself. She thought they should get another opinion, and so the doctor had arranged for the specialist to call on the Friday or the Saturday. She had thought both I and then George were the specialist when we called on the Friday afternoon. In fact he came on the Saturday morning at 11.50. He went upstairs to examine Martin. He came down and said he thought there was a cancerous growth on the kidneys. He asked if there had been a blood test done and was shocked to hear that there had not. He asked if he could phone the GP there and then. You can, she said, but you'll only get the answering machine now – he leaves at 12 noon on Saturday because he's the doctor that attends the rugby game. Right enough, he was not available. He was disgusted because her father was so bad.

It was a terrible weekend for Doris. Martin was 'losing his mind' and he told people who called that Doris never used to go out but now she was out all the time. She didn't undress the whole time, just sat in her bedroom through the night. At one point Martin called to her in Welsh asking where she was. Then he went back years and began to talk about a close friend who had been killed in the colliery. All night he was going through this.

On the Monday morning the nurse called with a bottle (as a result of my request on the Friday afternoon). Then the GP called. He was surprised to see the nurse there and asked why. She explained about the bottle and said she should have been informed earlier so that she could have arranged a sitter. 'There are two patients here at their wits' end,' she said.

The doctor hadn't been in touch with the specialist before calling. He said that he would try to get Martin into Aberneath Hospital. Her father was booked to go in on the Tuesday and to have a blood test on the Wednesday.

She went to visit him on the Wednesday but on the Thursday Doris had a call to say that Martin had been transferred to Pentyn for further tests. When she visited him that evening she 'had never seen such a look on him'. She'll never forget the look, she said. On the Friday he was worse and also on the Saturday. She was told it was not a cancerous growth but that the kidneys had collapsed. Again she was asked when he had last had a blood test and she said that to her knowledge he'd never had one.

On the Sunday, Martin 'was dying' and didn't recognise anyone. That night Doris visited him with Tom and Gwyn. He was reaching up with his arms. 'We looked at him. We couldn't see his tongue, but he was trying to say something to me. He couldn't see but knew his son was there by the cough. The last thing he said was: "(mumble, mumble) . . . Gwyn". He was asking how his grandson was.'

She didn't want him to suffer any more and prayed that he might die that night. It had been the first day that her daughter had not been to visit her grandfather, so she phoned her. She had had visitors. Doris said that she was glad that she had not been able to visit: she herself had had to leave the ward – he was dying. At 11.45 p.m. she had a call from the hospital, a nurse, who told her he had died. The nurse was very concerned; she asked Doris if she was on her own. 'Don't upset yourself,' the nurse said. 'Don't worry. I'll go straight round to my brother.' She knew Tom sat up to watch the late films on TV and asked a neighbour to go to get him. He brought his van round and they went to the hospital. Her daughter came too. A neighbour had gone to stay with the children, so her daughter was able to come home with her.

In the morning Doris told her daughter there was no need to stay, to go back to her children. 'I've got no work now,' she said. Her daughter went but returned at teatime. They fixed the funeral for the Wednesday. Her son went to the hospital to collect his belongings and phoned her to say they had asked if they could do a post-mortem. She was confused but said right-o, if it would help other patients in the future – that would be what Martin would have wanted. But they still didn't tell her what they found. They put something about the collapsed kidney on the death certificate. The post-mortem meant that they had to postpone the funeral after having informed all the family.

Doris went to stay with her brother in Bournemouth for a month. It was difficult coming back to her own home. She had never lived on her own. Her husband had died when he was only 49; but, although it had been a shock, she had to keep going because of her father. He would keep her busy with his baths and so on. Now she was on her own and found it difficult to know why she should struggle on.

The month following her return, her daughter started teacher training in Swansea, and so she did not see so much of her after that.

Gwyn calls often and will just sit with her. He stayed with her all evening last Saturday. But he won't eat there because he knows that she has a bad heart.

Last September (1986), Gwyn and her daughter had been round on a Sunday. After they had gone she went upstairs and then found herself feeling very funny. It must have been another 'pull'. She went to bed and was unable to get downstairs again until the Tuesday morning. Once she tried but found that her legs wouldn't take her. The phone is downstairs, and so she couldn't phone anyone. She has a very good neighbour three doors up, but she has her hands full. Eventually on the Tuesday she got downstairs to phone her daughter, who told her that if she didn't phone the doctor she'd phone him herself. Both called, and as a result she went to stay with her daughter for a month.

She gets on well with her son-in-law, but he works in North Africa, and they only see him when he's home on leave. She feels she would turn to him if she needed someone to rely on. She had upset her daughter when she had said something to this effect.

She is fond of her neighbour three doors up, but she has a daughter 'with a mental age of 5'. One day recently the daughter turned up on Doris's doorstep. Her mother was down in Port Talbot visiting her own mother. Doris phoned, but she had just left, so the daughter waited with Doris. It turned out that she had been on a shopping trip into Swansea and, without telling anyone had decided that she'd like to go home.

Finally Doris told me of her contacts with the home help department of the Social Services. The home help wouldn't lift the rugs on the carpet and had complained about Doris's hoover. As a result Doris had removed the rugs herself before the help called, but then she didn't turn up, and so Doris had had to put the rugs back down herself. She had been having a help since she was 52, ten years before, but after her stay with her daughter the help had stopped coming.

Eventually she was told that since it was so long since she'd had the help she'd have to be classed as a new applicant and that as such her age – 'only 62' – was against her. She was advised to see if Social Security would make a payment for a private help. She hadn't bothered.

She did however tell the tale of presenting herself at the Social Security office about help with payment for Martin's spectacles. She was told that they needed some medical certification. She explained that she couldn't afford to return with it. Eventually she said that she would go down to the opticians and pay for it herself with the housekeeping. With that she left but then arrived at the opticians to learn that the Social Security officer had phoned to say that the bill should be sent to the DHSS office.

Discussion

It is clear that, for Tom, Doris and Martin, becoming old is primarily about matters other than their sixty-fifth birthdays, retirement, becoming widowed and grandparenthood; that chronological age is of major significance in their dealings with Social Security and with the social services; and that old age is a familiar explanation that is used by the GP and undoubtedly by others to account for Martin's health problems.

This case study is, of course, based almost entirely upon my exchanges with them, and in particular upon what I was told. It may be that a clinical or more triangulated approach would have uncovered a different account and that the distinctive processes of becoming and being old might have been more apparent. I doubt it, however. It would seem that, for all three, later life has been characterised by a continuing struggle to cope with chronic disabilities and to maintain the supply of basic resources. Over the years income has come from health-damaging work; and when income-generating employment was no longer available, financial compensation for unemployment and disability has come in a way that is complicated, inadequate and subject to delay. To cope with this and with the consequences of premature mortality, they have to some significant extent pooled the resources of their two households. There is much to be said for the study of later life being based upon the network (Pruchno *et al.*, 1984) or care system (Daatland, 1983) rather than the abstracted ageing individual.

This family was selected (a) because it represents a small but significant minority within a larger sample and (b) because I was in contact with them at a time of significant change. There is of course a major question about the extent to which it represents the experience of a significant group of families within the general population. It might be thought, for example, that they were exceptional people caught up in exceptional circumstances. It is the kind of 'story' that an experienced social worker may bring before a discussion of some of the issues raised in this book.

I would argue that it does 'statistically' represent a significant group in the following senses: first, it typifies a number of families within those I studied (proportionately about 10 per cent); and second, while the sample, based upon older redundant Welsh steelworkers, is hardly typical in regard to such variables as occupation and recent income histories, nevertheless, in regard to the generation of post-war industrial workers who 'enjoyed' full employment for most of their working lives, they and their families are appropriate representatives who, if anything, will be biased against those in poverty. Thus I would suggest that one can conclude that this case does represent a minority of between 5 and 20 per cent of the population and the kind of experiences they will have when the eldest come to die.

Is the process of becoming old, then, anything other than life's long struggle? The study suggests two conclusions: first, that chronological age is important at all times in the regulation and expectation of state provision; second, that it is the deaths of others that lead people into a sense of being old. Doris in 1987 is living alone, feeling incapable, unneeded and vulnerable and wondering why she should struggle on.

Note

1 The study was funded by the Joseph Rowntree Memorial Trust.

References

Bytheway, B. (1987) 'Care in the families of redundant Welsh steelworkers', in S. di Gregorio (ed.), *Social Gerontology: New Directions.* London: Croom Helm. pp. 177–87.

Daatland, S.O. (1983) 'Care systems', *Ageing and Society*, 3 (1): 1–22.

Pruchno, R.A., Blow, F.C. and Smyer, M.A. (1984) 'Life events and interdependent lives', *Human Development*, 27 (1): 31–41.

7

Differentiation in Later Life: Social Class and Housing Tenure Cleavages

Maria Evandrou and Christina R. Victor

> Far too often, 'the elderly' are still treated as a homogeneous, classless, and largely dependent group that can be 'shunted off' for investigation by a limited number of enthusiasts. (Means, 1987: 96)

In this chapter we extend our analysis of social class in differentiating life-styles in later life and begin to examine housing tenure as an alternative tool for analysing cleavages within the elderly population. The objective is not to assess the relative usefulness of each approach, but to employ a variety of indicators which encompass aspects of people's past and current life experiences.

Recently, efforts to demonstrate the presence of heterogeneity amongst older people and their life-styles have become more explicit (Means, 1987; Thane, 1987; Victor and Evandrou, 1987), although not necessarily more frequent. Yet the impact has been somewhat limited. Consequently much research and public debate still treats individuals in later life as a unitary category, which maintains the assumption that these individuals share common experiences and life-styles. This approach serves to perpetuate the stereotypical view of older people as a distinct and uniform social group, detached from the wider social context. For example, the age categories often employed in research, such as '65 years and over', reflect this collapsing together. In contrast, adults below retirement age are automatically differentiated with the use of finer age categories. Similarly, with respect to household structure, the most popular typology consists of distinguishing between elderly people living alone, those living with their spouse and a miscellaneous 'all other elderly people' category.

The heterogeneity of older people is reflected in a variety of ways, including health, consumption patterns, financial resources, leisure pursuits, physical mobility and psychological disposition, where they live and who they live with. Over three-quarters (78 per cent) of all non-institutionalised elderly people live either alone or with their spouse, yet it is important to demonstrate the many other household units in which individuals reside in later life. Dale *et al.* (1987) show the complexity of taking into account the various household structures in which elderly people reside, requiring a 25-category typology to classify them all. In researching socio-economic issues in old age, the use of general terms, such as 'the elderly', as a convenient shorthand term may be unavoidable at times. However, analysing and interpreting social reality in terms of such 'conceptual flags of convenience' can still be avoided (Sayer, 1984).

Research in social gerontology has, as Marshall (1986) observes, concentrated upon examining ageing at an individual as opposed to a societal level. Where the perspective has been widened, the tendency has been to examine the adjustment of the older person to the social context, as in, for example, disengagement theory. It is still less common for gerontologists to examine how the structural organisation of society influences and constrains the experience of ageing. Thus only recently have gerontologists considered how systems of stratification influence the quality of life of older people, and made distinctions in terms of gender, household composition, ethnicity and social class. For example, Phillipson (1982) suggests that one cannot develop a complete understanding of the experience of later life without incorporating social class in the analysis.

This relative neglect seems to stem from a rather naive view that the profound inequalities based around social class, identified in earlier phases of the life cycle (Reid, 1977), are not maintained into old age. This reflects the view that class-based differences in life-style decrease in old age because the exclusion of older people from the labour market results both in a decrease in their economic power, and in power differentials within the elderly population. Thus social class is viewed as of little importance in differentiating the elderly population and irrelevant to the experience of old age.

The validity of the assumption of later life as a classless experience has been addressed in an earlier paper (Victor and Evandrou, 1987). This work demonstrated the relevance of an occupationally based social class typology for the analysis of differentiation amongst older individuals. Social class emerged as a useful analytical tool with which to deconstruct 'the elderly' population and highlight inequalities in later life, characteristic of earlier stages of the life cycle. Using secondary analysis of the 1980 General Household Survey, it emerged that the income and health status of older people were strongly related to an occupational measure of social class. Consistently, older individuals from manual occupational backgrounds experienced poorer health than their contemporaries from professional and managerial occupational groups. Furthermore, elderly people from classes IV and V were found to be significantly more materially disadvantaged than those from classes I and II; that is, fewer of them reported income from occupational pensions and savings/investments, and of those who did, they reported lower median income levels from these sources. However, the class-based variations in the use of health and personal social services were not consistent.

Similar findings have also been reported in a study of 600 people aged 60 years and over living in Aberdeen (Taylor and Ford, 1983). The distribution of personal resources (financial, health and social contacts) was examined, and attention was given as to whether gender and class differences persisted in old age. The main findings documented were: a fall in such resources with increasing old age; and individuals from higher social class backgrounds had higher levels of these resources (with the exception of social support) than those persons from lower social class groups. Regarding income, earlier class differences widened for women. However, with respect to health and social support, evidence of 'social levelling' was found.

There are different approaches to the definition of social class. 'Gradational' and 'relational' theories of social class have been discussed in Victor and Evandrou (1987). The measurement of social class in both the above pieces of research was in terms of previous occupational status – that is, a gradational approach. However, it has long been argued that there are many other dimensions to social inequality than social class. More recently, it has been suggested by Saunders and others that a new division has emerged within British society which cannot be reduced to any of these more 'traditional' sociological concerns. This new dimension is located within the sphere of consumption, and as such requires the development of a 'new' sociology of consumption (Saunders, 1984, 1986: 289–351; Saunders and Harris, 1987). This work is complex and has recently received detailed discussion elsewhere (Burrows and Butler, 1988). However, within the context of the present chapter, key elements of the debate will be noted.

In simple terms, Saunders argues that a new social cleavage is opening up around the axis of ownership and non-ownership of the means of consumption: that is, between those people who can meet the majority of their consumption needs through personal ownership of goods and services, and those who cannot and are thus reliant upon state provision. For example, owner-occupiers as opposed to local authority tenants, those with private medical insurance as opposed to those reliant upon the National Health Service and those who privately educate their children as opposed to those using state schools.

Saunders views the cleavage within housing tenure as the most salient in present times, whereas the latter two examples he sees as taking on greater importance in the future. This development is resulting in the creation of an inverted social pyramid composed of the 'middle mass', who are able to purchase social benefits (such as housing) in a modified market (or 'privatised') mode of consumption, and a 'residualised minority', who are reliant upon a state-provided (or 'socialised') mode of consumption.

Saunders argues that the cleavage between 'privatised' and 'socialised' housing provision has developed its own 'specificity' which is not reducible to class, gender or ethnic divisions – the tripartite dimensions which have hitherto dominated sociological analyses of heterogeneity amongst social groups. He argues that this cleavage 'may actually come to outweigh class location' (Saunders, 1986: 323) in the determination of many spheres of people's existence. It is our intention in this chapter to begin to explore the viability of identifying such a consumption sector cleavage as an analytical tool, within the context of an analysis of older people in Britain.

Fox and Goldblatt (1982) have empirically examined the use of tenure as a class measure in the analysis of mortality differentials amongst employed males. This study showed that there was a clear differential in mortality experience between males in the different tenure sectors. Those resident in owner-occupied housing had a substantially lower mortality than those renting dwellings from either the local authority or a private landlord. Murphy and Sullivan (1985) have examined the relationship between housing tenure and patterns of family formation, and have found the former to be an important discriminatory variable. Indeed, they argue that it is not only an alternative, but a more powerful indicator of the socio-economic status of individuals than occupationally-based measures.

Whilst the debates about the existence of discrete housing classes continue, it is clear that, within the broader sphere of housing studies, older people tend not to figure prominently as an important group for analysis in housing debates (Means, 1987). When they do, it is often in terms of a 'special needs' category such as the concern about sheltered housing or a 'housing problem'. Housing tenure cleavage analysis cannot really develop and progress as long as individuals in old age are primarily treated as a unitary 'special needs' group within mainstream housing debates. Such treatment encourages stereotypical views of older people as 'dependent' and 'marginalised' individuals (Forrest and Murie, 1983). Means (1987) calls for a re-evaluation of the manner in which elderly people have been treated within housing studies and, moreover, for the development of a gerontological perspective within mainstream theoretical housing debates.

In this chapter we examine aspects of the standard of living of older people, as defined by income and ownership of consumer durables, in relation to social class, thus extending earlier work. We also consider the relationship between social class and housing tenure. We examine the extent to which housing tenure characteristics enable us to further this analysis in differentiating between the life-styles of elderly people.

Moreover, we consider its relationship with income, health status, use of services and ownership of consumer durables, and comment on the usefulness of housing tenure as an alternative measure of social cleavage.

Data and method

To consider the usefulness of measures of social class and housing tenure in differentiating life-styles in later life, this chapter employs secondary analysis of the 1980 General Household Survey (GHS). Ideally, large-scale longitudinal survey data would be more appropriate for our research purposes. However, in its absence, the GHS offers rich data of high quality for 4,500 people aged 65 years and over, extracted from a random sample of over 30,000 individuals in Great Britain (resident in private households). The analysis makes use of the Registrar-General's typology of social class, which is far from ideal yet widely used. The Office of Population Censuses and Surveys (OPCS) is currently considering alternative measures to such an occupationally based categorisation for the 1991 census, due to the lack of grounded social theory upon which this measure is based (Turney, 1987). Here, social class has been operationalised in terms of the previous occupation of the elderly person. Occupational socio-economic groups (SEGs) were collapsed into four categories: I and II (professional, technical and managerial), IIIN (intermediate non-manual), IIIM (skilled manual), and IV and V (semi-skilled and unskilled).

Information on housing tenure characteristics was grouped into six categories: owner-occupiers; local authority tenants; private sector furnished; and private sector unfurnished accommodation tenants. Persons resident in housing association dwellings or housing co-operatives, and those renting from relatives, were also kept distinct. However, inferences drawn from the characteristics of those renting from relatives and persons living in privately rented furnished accommodation should be made cautiously due to the small numbers involved.

Social class and standards of living

Income is a basic element influencing the quality of life of older people. There are profound class-based differences in the receipt of different sources of income in later life. Older people from the manual occupational groups are much less likely to receive an occupational pension or unearned income than their counterparts from the professional groups (Victor and Evandrou, 1987: 258–61). Consequently older people classified in classes IV and V have a much lower median income than those in classes I and II and are much more likely to experience poverty in old age. Consistently women, irrespective of social class, reported lower median incomes and were more likely to be dependent upon state benefits for their income than men.

Another dimenson of living standards is the ownership of consumer goods such as a washing machine, freezer and colour television or having central heating. The ownership (or access to) these goods varies significantly across social class; for example, 73 per cent of those in classes I and II reported having central heating in their home as compared with 37 per cent in classes IV and V – see Table 7.1. This trend is repeated with respect to other consumer durable goods, although the gradient is least regarding ownership of a vacuum cleaner. Possession of these goods is also related to the age of the elderly person and to the type of household in which they live. 'Young' elderly people (65 to 74 years) are more likely to own these items than 'old' elderly individuals (75 years plus). Sole elderly persons living with a young couple, or elderly people resident in three-generational households, are most likely to have access to these domestic goods. In contrast, elderly people living alone are least likely to own these items. This association between ownership of consumer durables and social class is maintained irrespective of age or household structure; that is, within each age group the likelihood of having central heating, washing machine, freezer or colour TV decreases as one moves from higher to lower classes – see Table 7.2. Furthermore, we found that within each type of household in which the elderly person resides, a significantly higher proportion of those from professional and managerial backgrounds (I and II) reported having central heating than those in classes III, IV and V – see Table 7.3.

Table 7.1   *Ownership of consumer durables of persons aged 65 years or over by social class (percentages)*

	Social class				All elderly
	I and II	IIIN	IIIM	IV and V	
Central heating	73	56	42	37	48
Washing machine	68	62	66	57	62
Freezer	46	31	28	20	28
Colour TV	79	66	60	50	60
Vacuum cleaner	96	94	95	90	93
Total (N)	512	1,057	959	1,669	4,186

Key: I and II—professional, technical and managerial; IIIN—intermediate non-manual; IIIM—skilled manual; IV and V—semi-skilled and unskilled manual.

Source: GHS, 1980

Table 7.2   *Ownership of consumer durables of persons by social class for selected age groups (percentages)*

	65–9 years				80 years or over			
	I and II	IIIN	IIIM	IV and V	I and II	IIIN	IIIM	IV and V
Central heating	75	61	45	38	70	45	39	34
Washing machine	82	72	74	67	37	41	52	41
Freezer	61	39	41	28	25	18	17	11
Colour TV	85	71	70	55	71	53	50	40
Vacuum cleaner	99	96	98	95	93	85	89	81

Source: GHS, 1980

Table 7.3   *Ownership of central heating by persons aged 65 years or over by household structure and social class (percentages)*

	Social class				Row total
	I and II	IIIN	IIIM	IV and V	
Lone elderly	71	50	39	38	(1,441)
Elderly couple	76	61	44	37	(1,931)
Two or more sole elderly	52	46	37	33	(143)
Two or three generations	70	61	43	35	(711)

Source: GHS, 1980

In Britain, housing quality is commonly defined in two ways: access to standard amenities and overcrowding. Evidence shows variation in the quality of housing amongst the elderly population. Individuals in later life living alone are more likely to experience poor housing conditions than those living in other types of household (Henwood and Wicks, 1985). Research based in Wales found that overcrowding, as measured by the standard census definition of 1.5 people per room, was not a housing problem which significantly affected older people (Victor *et al.*, 1984). However, elderly people in general are much more likely to live in dwellings which lack the standard amenities of a fixed bath/shower and inside toilet (OPCS, 1984).

There is a social class differential in the quality of housing occupied by elderly individuals, although very slight; for example, 1 per cent of those grouped in social classes I and II did not have access to a bath/shower compared with 6 per cent from classes IV and V. Similarly 1 per cent of classes I and II do not have an inside toilet compared with 8 per cent of those in classes IV and V.

Housing tenure and household amenities constitute important

indicators of quality of life. Conceptually it is important to distinguish between those who own their own home and those who rent their accommodation from landlords, either private or public. A steep social class gradient in housing tenure is evident in Table 7.4. Seventy-six per cent of those older people from professional and managerial occupations, classes I and II, are owner-occupiers compared to 32 per cent of those from classes IV and V, the semi-skilled and unskilled occupational groups. An equally steep gradient is identified in the opposite direction, when examining the proportion of old people living in the local authority housing sector: 13 per cent of those in classes I and II compared to 52 per cent of classes IV and V. This differential is maintained after having standardised upon age and degree of disability of the elderly person. A similar trend is evident for those living in unfurnished privately rented dwellings. Below we consider to what extent similar trends are found using mode of housing tenure.

Table 7.4 *Housing tenure of persons aged 65 years or over by social class (percentages)*

	Social class				All elderly
	I and II	IIIN	IIIM	IV and V	
Owner-occupier	76	60	46	32	49
Rented:					
From local authority	13	25	40	52	36
From housing association (or co-operative)	2	2	3	3	3
From relative	2	2	1	1	2
Privately—furnished	0	0	0	0	0
Privately—unfurnished	6	10	10	11	10
Total (= 100%)	512	1,057	959	1,669	4,197

Source: GHS, 1980

Housing tenure in later life

Before examining the extent to which housing acts as a discriminating variable amongst elderly people themselves, it is important to document trends in their housing tenure as compared to the population as a whole. This is followed by an analysis of the issues surrounding health, service use, income and ownership of consumer durables.

General trends
Owner-occupation is the main tenure group in the general population. However, older people resident in this mode of tenure are under-represented when compared with the total population; that is, 49 per

cent of people aged 65 years and over in the GHS sample were home owners compared to 55 per cent of the general population. These figures are comparable to the 1981 census data. In contrast, older people are more likely to live in privately rented unfurnished accommodation, or in local authority housing, when compared with the population as a whole. It is of particular interest that 10 per cent of older people live in private rented unfurnished accommodation, nearly twice the proportion for the total sample population (6 per cent).

Table 7.5 *Housing tenure of persons aged 65 years or over by region and age group (percentages)*

	Region			Age			
	Met. counties	Other urban	Rural counties	65–9	70–4	75–9	80+
Owner-occupier	39	53	57	49	49	49	47
Rented:							
From local authority	46	33	28	39	37	35	34
From housing association (or co-operative)	4	2	2	2	2	3	3
From relative	1	1	2	1	2	2	3
Privately—furnished	0	1	0	1	0	0	0
Privately—unfurnished	10	10	10	8	10	11	13
Total (= 100%)	1,695	1,775	1,071	1,668	1,267	892	714

Source: GHS, 1980

Overall, older people constitute nearly a quarter (23 per cent) of the privately rented unfurnished sector, and a fifth (20 per cent) of the local authority sector, whilst they make up only 12 per cent of all owner-occupiers. This distribution is important to note because it is in those sectors where elderly people tend to be concentrated, especially in the private unfurnished rented sector, where one finds consistently lower-quality housing standards.

The percentage of elderly people in owner-occupied accommodation remains fairly constant across different age groups. However, the proportion of local authority tenants falls slightly with increasing age from 39 per cent of 65- to 69-year olds to 34 per cent of those aged 80 years and over – see Table 7.5. There is also an increase with age in the fraction of individuals living in private rented unfurnished dwellings: from 8 per cent of 65- to 69-year olds to 13 per cent of those aged 80 years and over. The trend for very elderly people to be disproportionately represented in certain housing sectors may be explained by the 'cohort effect'. That is, 'older' elderly individuals entered the housing market at a time when private rented accommodation was still a major housing sector, and local authority housing and home ownership was less widespread.

The distribution of housing tenure amongst elderly people varies between and within regions. Inter-regional variation reflects general economic differences and also the skewed geographical distribution of the elderly themselves (Falkingham, 1987). The GHS data suggest that elderly owner-occupiers are under-represented in metropolitan counties (39 per cent) compared with the proportion of owner-occupiers amongst all elderly people (49 per cent). Table 7.5 shows that the opposite trend is evident for those renting from the local authority.

Health status

This section deals with health differentials and how they vary with mode of tenure. The GHS distinguishes between several different measures of health status: long-standing limiting illness, acute illness, sight and hearing difficulties, and perceived health status. In addition, a disability measure which takes into account ability to perform activities of daily living, based on an index of 'personal incapacity', has been constructed (Townsend and Wedderburn, 1965; Bebbington, 1982).

Housing tenure characteristics in relation to the level of disability of the elderly person are described in Table 7.6. First, we consider the housing tenure distribution of those elderly without any impairment. Some 32 per cent of those elderly people who have no disabilities live in local authority accommodation compared with 34 per cent of the elderly population. The opposite is the case for owner-occupiers; that is, 53 per cent of elderly with no incapacities are resident in this type of housing compared to 49 per cent of all the over-65s.

Given this overall distribution, Table 7.7 shows that the highest proportions of elderly people with at least some degree of physical impairment are found to be renting from the following four sources: local authorities; housing associations; relatives; the (unfurnished) private sector. Between 50 and 58 per cent of elderly people living in these four sectors reported physical incapacities. Consistently, older people who are home owners are less likely to be disabled than older people in other tenure groups. This trend is repeated with respect to the other health measures; for example, 20 per cent of elderly people living in council housing report acute ill health, compared with 15 per cent of those in owner occupation, however, individuals resident in housing association co-op dwellings report the lowest level of acute ill health (11 per cent) amongst all tenure groups – see Table 7.7. With regard to self-perceived general health status, local authority tenants report higher levels of 'poor health' at 29 per cent compared to 20 per cent of owner/occupiers and 22 per cent of housing association/co-op tenants.

Table 7.6   *Housing tenure of persons aged 65 years or over by degree of disability (percentages)*

	Degree of disability[1]			
	None	Slight	Moderate	Severe
Owner-occupier	53	47	40	45
Rented:				
From local authority	32	38	46	42
From housing association (or co-operative)	2	3	3	2
From relative	1	2	2	2
Privately—furnished	1	0	0	0
Privately—unfurnished	11	10	9	9
Total (= 100%)	2,139	1,124	762	337

[1] Using the index of 'personal incapacity' of Townsend and Wedderburn (1965).

Source: GHS, 1980

Use of services

Housing tenure is examined in relation to the use of at least one domiciliary or personal health service (that is, home help, meals on wheels, lunch clubs, elderly day centres, district nurse, health visitor and chiropody visits). Elderly users of these services are more likely to live in local authority housing and less likely to be owners than the general population. Thus 42 per cent of elderly service users live in local authority dwellings compared with 36 per cent of all elderly people who are local authority tenants.

The highest fraction reported to have used domiciliary or personal health services can be located amongst those living in housing associations or housing co-ops (46 per cent), those resident with relatives (35 per cent) and those living in local authority housing – see Table 7.7. Similar proportions of elderly living in owner-occupied accommodation (26 per cent) and in private rented unfurnished homes (26 per cent) use such statutory services. The higher concentration of service users amongst housing association and local authority tenants may reflect the higher prevalence of ill health amongst older people living in these types of housing. However, it may also reflect the fact that within these sectors of the housing market there are often concentrations of older people living, for example, in sheltered housing developments. Thus the high use of services amongst these groups of elderly may, in part, reflect the fact that they represent visible concentrations of need.

Specific domiciliary and personal health services were also considered in relation to housing tenure characteristics. It was found that elderly people resident in housing association or housing co-op accommodation reported the highest level of home help visits (in the previous month) with 17 per cent, compared to 9 per cent of all elderly in the GHS sample. Furthermore, 12 per cent of old people living in local authority housing and 8 per cent of those in owner-occupied accommodation received such home help support. This trend was broadly repeated with respect to use of other services such as meals on wheels, seeing a district nurse or health visitor and attending an elderly lunch club.

Table 7.7 *Housing tenure of persons aged 65 years or over by various health indicators (percentages)*

	Housing tenure					
	OO	LA	HA	RR	PRF	PRU
Acute illness	15	20	11	16	15	17
Service user[1]	26	34	46	35	12	26
Non-service user	74	66	54	65	88	74
General Health (in last year)						
Good	43	29	28	43	50	35
Fair	37	42	50	35	35	40
Poor	20	29	22	22	15	25
Disability						
None	53	43	48	42	75	50
Mild	25	26	27	30	20	26
Moderate	15	22	19	18	5	17
Severe	7	9	6	10	—	7
Total[2] (N)	1,930	1,442	103	65	17	408

[1] Used at least one of the following domiciliary or personal health services: (a) home help, meals on wheels, lunch club, day centre for the elderly, district nurse in *the last month*; and (b) chiropodist (home and surgery visit) and health visitor in *the last year*.
[2] There is some small variation between the sections in the table in totals; these are the lowest numbers.

Key: OO—owner-occupier; rented: LA—from local authority; HA—from housing association (or co-operative); RR—from relative; PRF—privately—furnished; PRU—privately—unfurnished.

Source: GHS, 1980

Income sources and levels

The variation in median income between the different sectors of the housing market is complex, reflecting the age, health and employment status of the older people within these sectors. However, what is evident is that elderly owner-occupiers are the most financially advantaged in terms of being most likely to have an occupational pension or receive unearned income. For example, 37 per cent of all elderly home owners were reported to be in receipt of an occupational pension, compared to 34 per cent of those in housing association and housing co-operative schemes, and 29 per cent of those elderly in local authority dwellings – see Table 7.8. Our analysis also shows that 8 per cent of elderly home owners were reported to be in receipt of a supplementary pension, compared to 32 per cent of those in local authority housing and 22 per cent of those living in housing association dwellings – see Table 7.8. The income status of older people in the private rented unfurnished sector seems to be bimodal. This segment contains not only a high proportion (31 per cent) of older people with an occupational pension, a strong indicator of a higher income in later life, but also a significant number (21 per cent) of people claiming supplementary pension, which is indicative of a very low income.

Table 7.8   *Housing tenure of persons aged 65 years or over by income from different sources and employment status (percentages)*

	In paid employment	In receipt of occupational pension	In receipt of supplementary pension/ allowance	Row Total
Owner-occupier	8	37	8	(2,204)
Rented:				
From local authority	6	29	32	(1,680)
From housing association (or co-operative)	5	34	22	(112)
From relative	4	28	18	(74)
Privately—furnished	30	20	35	(20)
Privately—unfurnished	12	31	24	(451)
All elderly	8	31	19	(4,541)

Source: GHS, 1980

This general trend is reproduced when examining gross median income levels for the family unit; elderly in owner-occupied housing reported the highest median family income with £46.14, compared to the lowest figure of £33.01 reported by elderly people renting from relatives. The second highest median family income figure (£43.70) was reported by those living in privately rented unfurnished housing, and the second lowest figure (£38.21) was reported by those individuals in housing association or co-operative housing schemes.

Ownership of consumer durables

It is evident from Table 7.9 that extreme variation in ownership of (or access to) consumer durables exists among elderly individuals across different housing tenure sectors. For example, 64 per cent of elderly people in housing association/co-operative dwellings reported having central heating, compared to 45 per cent of local authority tenants, and 15 per cent of those resident in privately rented unfurnished accommodation. There is a consistent difference between owner-occupiers and local authority tenants in the ownership of goods such as washing machine, freezer, colour TV and central heating. Elderly people renting from relatives will automatically have access to the consumer durable goods within the household – such as colour TV and freezer – which they may or may not have had access to otherwise. Ownership of these items is related to age, social class and household structure. However, our analysis suggests that elderly owner-occupiers are more likely to own or have access to such goods than elderly persons in any other tenure sectors.

Table 7.9   *Ownership of consumer durables of persons aged 65 years or over by housing tenure (percentages)*

	Housing tenure					
	OO	LA	HA	RR	PRF	PRU
Central heating	55	45	64	51	40	15
Washing machine	70	58	42	47	5	45
Freezer	39	16	12	35	10	20
Colour TV	71	51	52	69	25	46
Vacuum cleaner	97	91	89	88	55	87
Total (N)	2,204	1,680	112	74	20	451

Key: see Table 7.7.

Source: GHS, 1980

Discussion

In this chapter we have extended our analysis of the relationship between social class and quality of life in old age. Secondary analysis of data from the 1980 GHS has shown that for factors such as income, tenure, housing quality and ownership of consumer durables social class is an important factor differentiating the elderly population. These relationships are largely independent of age and household circumstances of the older person. The consistent way in which social class differentiates the experience of old age challenges the assumption of the elderly as a classless group. Indeed, these data indicate that later life may be conceptualised as representing the continuance and culmination of the inequalities characteristic of earlier phases of the life cycle. This provides support for the hypothesis of Bertaux (1977) that occupational measures of social class identify a lifetime trajectory.

However, it is recognised that occupationally based measures of social class have substantial disadvantages, especially for the analysis of later life. The limitations of this type of analysis for older women are a source of special concern when it is remembered that old age is a disproportionately female experience. Gerontologists should consider the merits of alternative modes of class analysis, such as Saunders' approach to 'consumpton cleavages'. This chapter attempts to examine the relevance of tenure cleavages as another axis of differentiation within the elderly population.

At the most basic level of analysis it has been shown that there is a strong relationship between class, as defined by occupation, and tenure. Home ownership was the preserve of the professional classes and renting the province of those from manual backgrounds.

When the analysis was extended it was found that tenure was an important discriminatory variable within old age. For variables such as health status, service use and income there were clear variations between tenure groups. Although we employed a sixfold housing class typology, it is clear that the most fundamental cleavage is that between older people who are owners and all others. Consistently home owners were the most materially advantaged and experienced better health than those who rented their home regardless of the identity of the landlord. When using the sixfold tenure grouping the position is very complex, and the use of tenure as the unit of analysis does not result in the production of a neat hierarchical structure as is produced with the conventional occupationally based measures of class.

The analysis demonstrates that there is a clear relationship between tenure position and aspects of life-style, especially health and service use. Consistently, older people resident in local authority or housing association dwellings or living with relatives experienced the worst health status. This interrelationship is important when reforming and integrating social policy within health services, community care and housing, rather than attempting to improve the quality of life of people in old age through reforms of policy and public services in isolation of each other, which are not coherently integrated from the outset. The Family Policy Studies Centre advocates such a policy approach.

We have not attempted to show whether tenure class is more important than occupational social class with respect to the study of elderly persons. Examining intra- and inter-housing sector variations is complex and would benefit from the use of sophisticated modelling techniques. This approach would enable us to disentangle what proportion of the variation is explained by social class and which by tenure. It is hoped to adopt such an approach in future work using both the 1980 and the 1985 GHS.

Note

We would like to thank OPCS for permission to use the GHS data and the ESRC data archives for supplying them. The analysis employed the SIR/DBMS data files constructed at Surrey University, Department of Sociology.

References

Bebbington, A.C. (1982) *Using the GHS as a Basis for Territorial Indicators of Need amongst the Elderly*. Canterbury: Personal Social Services Research Unit, University of Kent.

Bertaux, D. (1977) *Destins Personnels et Structure de Classes*. Paris: Presse Universitaires de France.

Burrows, R. and Butler, T. (1988) *Middle Mass and the Pit: Notes on the New Sociology of Consumption*. North-East London Polytechnic, Department of Sociology Working Paper No. 2.

Dale, A., Evandrou, M. and Arber, S. (1987) 'The household structure of the elderly', *Ageing and Society*, 7 (1): 37–56.

Falkingham, J. (1987) 'The demographic characteristics of Britain's aged population – a survey', London: Suntory Toyota International Centre for Economic and Related Disciplines, Welfare State Programme Research Note No. 7.

Forrest, R. and Murie, A, (1983) 'Residualisation and council housing: aspects of the changing social relations of housing tenure', *Journal of Social Policy*, 12: 153 – 68.

Fox, J. and Goldblatt, P. (1982) *Longitudinal Study: Socio-Demographic Mortality Differentials*. London: HMSO/OPCS.

Henwood, M. and Wicks, M. (1985) 'Community care, family trends and social change', *Quarterly Journal of Social Affairs*, 1 (4): 357–71.

Marshall, V.W. (1986) 'Dominant and emerging paradigms in the social psychology of ageing', in V.W. Marshall (ed.), *Later Life: The Social Psychology of Ageing*. Beverly Hills, CA: Sage.

Means, R. (1987) 'Older people in British housing studies: rediscovery and emerging issues for research', *Housing Studies*, 2 (2): 82–98.

Murphy, M. and Sullivan, O. (1985), 'Housing tenure and family formation in post-war Britain', *European Sociological Review*, 1 (3): 230–43.

Office of Population Censuses and Surveys (1984) *Britain's Elderly Population*. London: HMSO/OPCS, Census Guide No. 1.

Phillipson, C. (1982) *Capitalism and the Construction of Old Age*. London: Macmillan.

Reid, I. (1977) *Social Class Differences in Britain*. London: Fontana.

Saunders, P (1984) 'Beyond housing classes: the sociological significance of private property rights in means of consumption', *International Journal of Urban and Regional Research*, 8 (2): 202–27.

Saunders, P. (1986) *Social Theory and the Urban Question*, 2nd ed. London: Hutchinson.

Saunders, P. and Harris, C. (1987) 'Biting the nipple? State welfare and consumer preferences'. Paper presented to the Sixth Urban Change and Conflict Conference, University of Kent at Canterbury.

Sayer, A. (1984) *Method in Social Science: A Realist Approach*. London: Hutchinson.

Taylor, R. and Ford, G. (1983) 'Inequalities in old age', *Ageing and Society*, 3 (2): 183–208.

Thane, P. (1987) *Economic Burden or Benefit? A Positive View of Old Age*. London: Centre for Economic Policy Research, Discussion Paper No. 197.

Townsend, P. and Wedderburn, D. (1965) *The Aged in the Welfare State*. London: G. Bell & Sons.

Turney, J. (1987) 'Stroke of the pen abolishes class war', *The Times Higher Educational Supplement*, 782, 30 October.

Victor, C.R. (1987) *Old Age in Modern Society: A Textbook of Social Gerontology*. London: Croom Helm.

Victor, C.R. and Evandrou, M. (1987) 'Does social class matter in later life?' in S. di Gregorio (ed.), *Social Gerontology: New Directions*. London: Croom Helm. pp. 252–67.

Victor, C.R., Jones, D.A. and Vetter, N.J. (1984) 'The housing of the disabled and non-disabled elderly in Wales', *Archives of Gerontology and Geriatrics*, 3: 109–13.

8

The Living Arrangements of the Elderly in Europe in the 1980s

Richard Wall

Households and censuses

Tracking developments in the composition of the European household since the end of the Second World War is by no means straightforward. Authorities responsible for censuses are less concerned with charting the evolving form of the household than with providing information required by other departments of government. It is more likely that tabulations will be encountered of migration across local authority boundaries than of movements between households, and of tabulations of pensioners than of the elderly. The measurement of change is additionally thwarted by the adoption by the census authorities of new definitions of such basic concepts as household, household head and family, in response variously to calls for the standardisation of definitions and to perceived modifications in societal norms and structure. Nevertheless, the trends over recent decades towards smaller households and more people living alone are so strong that they shine through any number of tabulations of family and household, regardless of definition.[1]

By the 1980s most European countries were including in their census publications some account of the household patterns of the population over the age of 65. The amount of information generated can on occasion be impressive. Unfortunately, the ingenuity that has gone into the design of sometimes very detailed tabulations has not been matched by equal attention to developments in other countries, with the result that appropriate comparisons are not always available for some of the more interesting tabulations. For example, information on the number of elderly people living alone can be assembled for sixteen countries (see Table 8.6), but an account of the generational span of households for only one, West Germany (see Table 8.12). A further limitation to the available data is their cross-sectional nature, as the exploitation of various longitudinal surveys is still in its early stages. Where the residence patterns of the very elderly can be seen to differ from those of the 'young old', as below in Table 8.11, it is impossible to know what proportion of the difference is due to a cohort effect (temporal change) and what to a life cycle effect (ageing).

Residence patterns of the elderly: lines of inquiry

The selection for detailed investigation of particular aspects of the residence pattern of the elderly was governed principally by the desire to provide comparative data to those generated by earlier census rounds. The range of information available in the 1970s on British households containing elderly persons suggested a table on the number of elderly persons living in one-family or two-family households or outside families altogether (either as solitaries or with other persons related or not related, none of them however being members of a family),[2] as well as a more simple table showing the numbers of elderly persons in households according to the number of non-elderly persons also present. Alternatively, major inquiries by sociologists in the 1960s into the residential patterns of the elderly suggested a tabulation according to frequency of co-residence with, in order of priority, spouse alone, married child, unmarried child, other relative or non-relative (Shanas, 1968; Sündstrom, 1983).

In practice, however, neither of these precedents proved a good guide to the range of tables provided by the various census authorities of the 1980s.[3] The ordering of residence patterns in terms of a set of pre-determined priorities remains the preserve of the sociologist. The tabulations of elderly persons in households against the number of non-elderly persons was encountered only once outside Britain, in Cyprus, a legacy perhaps from a fading imperial past (see Table 8.13). Even with the classification of the elderly into one-family, two-family and no-family households, Britain seems to be joined only by Ireland (see Table 8.10).

The authorities, faced with a variety of options regarding the detailed tabulations of household structure, appear in the event to have departed in a number of different directions. It is possible to identify four different approaches to this problem:

1 examination of the composition of households headed by elderly persons;
2 examination of elderly persons in terms of the number and type of person or persons with whom they co-reside;
3 examination of the relationship between elderly persons and the head of the household; and finally
4 examination of elderly persons on the basis of the closeness of the

relationship with other people in the same household (that is, couple, one parent, outside a family).

Exploration of the first of these options is not considered in the present chapter. The need to determine to what extent that part of the elderly population who are household heads can be taken as representative of the residence patterns of all elderly persons results in all sorts of difficulties.[4] The second, third and fourth options were taken up respectively by Ireland and England (see Table 8.10), by Poland and Switzerland (see Table 8.8) and by Ireland and Finland (see Table 8.9).

A fifth option, represented by Table 8.12, details the generational span of households containing elderly persons. This was taken up in West Germany in 1982 and follows a similar table in the 1976 West German census, but appears otherwise to be unique. Indeed, the identification of households with grandchildren is virtually impossible in many European censuses. This is because they are counted as the children of the head if no parent is present or if no parent can be identified from among the members of the intervening generation.[5] For the moment, however, it is better to leave the household structure tables on one side and to concentrate first on a series of more basic tables.

The elderly as members of institutions

Table 8.1 shows that nowhere in Europe does more than one in ten of the population live outside private households in institutions of one sort or another.[6] The percentage of the elderly population in institutions is lower in southern Europe than in western Europe and conceivably lower still in eastern Europe and the USSR. Contrary to expectations that a Communist state would intervene effectively to care for the elderly, neither the extent of institutional provision nor the quality of socio-medical services in general suggests that this has in fact occurred (Yvert-Jalu, 1985). To some extent this may reflect the lack of resources, or a decison that any available resources should be directed towards other groups such as the working population or children on whom the prosperity of the state might more obviously appear to depend. It would be as well to remember, however, the long tradition dating back to pre-industrial times, of more complex households in eastern than in western Europe and the concomitant absence of direct community support of the elderly (Wall *et al.*, 1983).

Within western Europe, some of the variation in the proportion of the elderly population to be found in institutions simply reflects different definitions of the institutional population. For example, the

Table 8.1   *Elderly people not living in private households*
(percentages)

	Date	Elderly persons outside private households
Western Europe		
Belgium	1970	5
France	1982	6
Great Britain	1981	5
Ireland	1979	8
Luxembourg	1981	6
Netherlands	1981	10
Switzerland	1970	7
West Germany	1980	3
Scandinavia		
Denmark	1974	6
Finland	1980	7
Norway	1974	7
Sweden	1980	4
Southern Europe		
Cyprus	1982	2
Greece	1971	2
Spain	1970	2
Central and eastern Europe		
Czechoslovakia	1980	2
Poland	1978	<1
USSR	1970	1

reclassification in West Germany of certain inmates of institutions according to their household of usual residence undoubtedly lowers the registered institutional population relative to that recorded for other countries, such as France where a more *de facto* definition of the institutional population prevails. It is also to be expected that variations in the age structure and marital status of the elderly population between countries will have some effect on the proportion lodged in institutions. In both historical and present-day populations, those lacking close relatives were and are particularly likely to find themselves in institutions (with the unmarried the most likely). The impact, however, on the differences between countries in the proportions of the elderly sheltering in institutions appears surprisingly slight (Grundy and Arie, 1984).

An attempt to measure the variation in the frequency of living outside private households according to the age and sex of the individual sharply reduces the number of countries providing appropriate data – see Table 8.2. Not surprisingly, the older the individual the greater his or her chance of residing in an institution, the rise being steeper for women than for men. Elderly men (even those over the age of 85) are more likely to remain within the household. For women, because of the different survival chances of the sexes (and differences in age at first marriage), such an option is less often available. Nevertheless, at any one time only just over a quarter of French women aged 90 and over were not enumerated in private households in 1982.

Table 8.2   *Elderly people not living in private households by age and sex (percentages)*

	Age group	(a)	(b)	(c)	(d)	(e)	(f)	(g)	(h)	(i)	(j)
Males	65–9	<1	2	2	2	4	2	1	<1	<1	<1
	70–4	1	4	3	3	6	3	2 ⎫	⎫	1 ⎫	1
	75–9	2 ⎫		4	4	8	5	⎪	⎪	⎪	
	80–4	⎬4	⎫	7	8	11	7	⎪	⎬<1	⎪	
	85–9	⎭	⎬10	11 ⎫	⎫	⎫	⎫	⎬14	⎪	⎬6	⎬6
	≥90		⎭	15 ⎬16	16	15	16	⎭	⎭	⎭	
Females	65–9	1	2	2	2	5	4	1	<1	<1	1
	70–4	2	4	3	3	7	5	5 ⎫	⎫	1 ⎫	2
	75–9	3 ⎫		6	6	11	9	⎪	⎪	⎪	
	80–4	⎬7	⎫	10	10	15	16	⎬25	⎬2	⎬9	⎬6
	85–9	⎭	⎬16	18 ⎫	⎫	⎫	⎫	⎪	⎪	⎪	
	≥90		⎭	27 ⎬24	23	27		⎭	⎭	⎭	

Key to column headings: (a) Czechoslovakia; (b)Finland; (c) France; (d) Great Britain; (e) Ireland; (f) Luxembourg; (g) Netherlands; (h) Poland; (i) Sweden; (j) West Germany.

The elderly as household heads

With Table 8.3 the focus shifts to a consideration of the headship rate: the proportions of elderly men and women heading households. Headship rates provide a measure, albeit very crude, of the extent to which the elderly retain the various responsibilities usually associated with the running of a distinct residential and consumption unit. Unfortunately, a number of difficulties arise, some stemming from the inconsistencies in the definition of the household, and others from the fact that married women whose spouses are also present (together with any others whose work, however defined, might be critical for the well-being of the household) are not included as household heads. The significance of varying definitions of the household for the differences between countries in the level of the headship rate is particularly unclear. The lower proportions of elderly persons who are heads of households in Poland, Cyprus and Portugal than in most western European countries are in broad agreement with expectations based on the greater prevalence of more complex households in eastern and southern Europe (Wall *et al.*, 1983: chapters 1, 3 and 17). On the other hand, where the use of the 'housing' concept of the household (all persons in a dwelling considered to form a household) is in force – as in France, Finland and Sweden – rather than the 'housekeeping' concept of the household (the provisioning of a household from a common budget), the recorded headship rates and the proportion of elderly persons identified as solitaries may be depressed relative to the proportions in other countries.[7]

Table 8.3   *Headship rates*

	Elderly men heading households (percentages)				
	Date	Married	Single	Widowed	Divorced	All
Western Europe						
England and Wales	1981					92
France	1975	95	72	75	76	90
Ireland	1979					83
Netherlands	1981	96	54	74		88
West Germany	1982	97	77	82	85	95
Scandinavia						
Finland	1980[1]	70	62	64		68
Southern Europe						
Cyprus	1982	92	53	61	65	85[2]
Portugal	1981					86
Central and eastern Europe						
Poland	1978	85	56	63		80
	Elderly women heading households (percentages)					
Western Europe						
England and Wales	1981					53
France	1975	3	70	74	78	47
Ireland	1979					47
Netherlands	1981	1	58	76		45
West Germany	1982	2	78	86	92	59
Scandinavia						
Finland	1980[1]	3	63	60		44
Southern Europe						
Cyprus	1982	2	46	53	62	28[2]
Portugal	1981					34
Central and eastern Europe						
Poland	1978	7	55	54		39

[1] Subtenants not considered as forming separate households.
[2] Separated persons not separately shown but included in totals.

Rather fewer problems surround the interpretation of variation in the headship rate with marital status when each country is considered separately. For men it is invariably the case that the headship rates of the married exceed those of the divorced, while those of the divorced exceed those of the widowed. The least likely to head a household are never-married men. Similarly, fewer never-married than widowed and fewer widowed than divorced women in France, West Germany and Cyprus head households, but the pattern is broken in Finland and Poland where the headship rates of never-married women are higher relative to those of divorced and widowed women. Finally, once the married population is excluded, it is remarkable how small the differences are between the headship rates of elderly men and elderly women (Wall, 1984).

Table 8.4 extends the analysis of headship rates to take account of the variation that occurs after an individual has reached the age of 65. There is a general rise with age in the proportion of women heading households, continued into the age group 75 and over in Germany and Cyprus. Male headship rates, on the other hand, fall with age. The explanation lies with the increasing likelihood of widowhood and accompanying registration as a household head as women age. Generally speaking, however, when marital status is controlled, headship rates fall with age. Both in Cyprus and in West Germany the decline with age is steeper in the case of the widowed than it is for the never-married. This might imply that the former are more likely than the latter to retire from the headship of the household. However, given that the data draw on a cross-section of age groups rather than cohorts, an alternative explanation that there has been a change in the residence patterns of recent cohorts of widowed cannot be excluded. In either case it is interesting to note that headship rates of the widowed remain above those of the never-married even after the age of 75.

Marital status and living alone

Table 8.5 measures the age at which widowers first exceed the numbers of married men, and widows the number of married women. This very summary measure of the marital status[8] of a population will be referred to hereafter as the age of majority widowhood. Previous research on the elderly in contemporary Europe has shown the critical importance of the marital status of the elderly person in determining the number and type of co-residents,[9] and the purpose behind Table 8.5 is to discover whether differences across Europe in the relative numbers of widowed and married men and women might be a potential source for variation in the residence patterns of elderly people.

Table 8.4 *Elderly people heading households by age, sex and marital status (percentages)*

Marital status	Cyprus 1982 Age group			West Germany 1982 Age group		
	65–9	70–4	≥75	65–9	70–4	≥75
Males						
Single	60	59	42	81	76	74
Married[1]	94	92	88	98	97	95
Widowed	73	65	57	90	87	78
Divorced	73	79	57	90	86	79
Separated[1]	86	76	71			
Females						
Single	51	45	41	78	81	77
Married[1]	2	1	2	2	2	3
Widowed	63	59	45	91	89	81
Divorced	64	64	61	94	91	90
Separated[1]	67	55	61			

Age group	Males			Females		
	Cyprus 1982	Ireland 1979	W. Germany 1982	Cyprus 1982	Ireland 1979	W. Germany 1982
65–9	92	87	97	23	18	50
70–4	88	84	95	28	24	58
≥75	78	77	90	32	23	66

[1] Separated included with married in the case of West Germany.

Table 8.5 *Age at which widowed people constitute a majority of the ever married*

	Date	Widowers	Widows
Western Europe			
Austria	1982	85	68
England and Wales	1981	86	72
France	1982	88	72
Scotland	1981	84	70
West Germany	1982	85	67
Scandinavia			
Finland	1980	85	69
Iceland	1980	87	74
Sweden	1983	87	74
Central and eastern Europe			
Czechoslovakia	1980	84	69
East Germany	1981		68
Hungary	1980	85	69
Poland	1978		68

The principal inference to be drawn from Table 8.5 is that throughout Europe higher proportions of elderly women than of elderly men will reside as solitaries (as indeed proves to be the case – see Table 8.6). There is also evidence of some variation in the age of majority widowhood for women. In central and eastern Europe and in West Germany this occurs when women reach their late sixties, whereas in a number of western European countries the same point is reached only in the early or even the mid-seventies, presumably delaying and curtailing the possible period of residing on one's own.[10]

Table 8.6 *Elderly people living alone (percentages)*

	Date	Males	Females	Both
Western Europe				
Belgium	1981	17	32	26
France	1982	16	43	32
Great Britain	1983	20	45	35
Ireland	1979	14	22	18
Netherlands	1981	14	37	27
Switzerland	1980	14	39	29
West Germany	1982	16	53	39
Scandinavia				
Denmark	1977			35
Finland	1980	17	44	34
Norway	1981			35
Sweden	1980	21	44	34
Southern Europe				
Cyprus[1]	1982			25
Portugal	1981	10	23	18
Central and eastern Europe				
Hungary	1980			20
Poland	1978	10	28	21
USSR[1] urban	1970	5	20	
rural	1970	5	24	

[1] Percentage of population aged $\geqslant 60$.

Information on the proportion of persons over the age of 65 who live on their own is now available in most European countries – see Table 8.6. In some more than 40 per cent of the female population aged 65 and over is now in this position.[11] Such high proportions of solitaries can create a dilemma for the authorities providing formal care for the elderly who remain in their homes, since those in need cannot always be easily identified amongst the mass of elderly solitaries. By contrast, little more than a quarter of elderly women in Poland live on their own, while even lower proportions were recorded for Portugal and Ireland.[12] There can be little surprise, however, given that elderly men are so much more likely than elderly women still to be married (see Table 8.5), that fewer elderly men than elderly women are living on their own. As was the case with elderly women, there is variation from country to country in the proportion residing as solitaries, with two of the three countries that recorded the lowest proportion of female solitaries also registering the lowest proportions of male solitaries. The exception is Ireland, where the proportion of males living on their own is little lower than the levels reached elsewhere in western Europe, in sharp contrast to the situation of elderly females. Conversely, the high solitary rate of elderly females in West Germany is not paralleled by a similar high rate of elderly males. Both these features of the social structure require further investigation, although it is clear from Table 8.5 that in West Germany it is at a relatively early age that widows first come to exceed the number of married women. It is also West Germany that records the largest difference (eighteen years) between the ages at which widows outnumber married women and widowers outnumber married men.

More generally, however, there would appear to be no consistent relationship between the age of majority widowhood and the proportion of the elderly population who reside as solitaries. This is interesting because whether one is or is not married is clearly critical in determining both the frequency with which persons head households and the type of household in which they reside.[13] Comparison of Tables 8.5 and 8.6 reveals that Sweden has both an advanced age of majority widowhood and a high proportion of solitaries. West Germany, on the other hand, shares the high proportion of elderly female solitaries but has an early age of majority widowhood. The impact of marital status on differences between countries in the living arrangements of the elderly might be somewhat greater than appears from the analysis of a crude measure such as the age of majority widowhood. Against this, though, is the fact that applying a correction factor for the different age and marital status distributions explains little of the variation in the proportion of the elderly population residing in institutions (Grundy and Arie, 1984: 131).

Variation in the frequency of residence as a solitary over the age of 65 is measured in Table 8.7. For Great Britain the rates rise much more steeply for both males and females than is the case in either Ireland or Poland or even France. In Poland and Ireland the rates stabilise and even fall back slightly after the age of 75, indicating that in these two countries other alternatives to that of becoming a solitary householder exist to cope with the increasing likelihood of widowhood in extreme old age.[14]

Table 8.7   *Elderly people living alone by age and sex (percentages)*

	Males						Females					
	(a)	(b)	(c)	(d)	(e)	(f)	(a)	(b)	(c)	(d)	(e)	(f)
65–9	12	13	13	11	9	8	32	18	37	31	30	26
70–4	19	15	17	14	12	12	42	24	46	39	40	30
75–9	25 ⎱	⎱	⎱	18 ⎱	⎱	⎱	53 ⎱	⎱	⎱	48 ⎱	⎱	⎱
80–4	⎰ 33 ⎱ 15 ⎱ 24	23 ⎱ 21 ⎱ 10					⎰ 60 ⎱ 23 ⎱ 51	53 ⎱ 40 ⎱ 28				
≥85	29 ⎰						51 ⎰					

Key to column headings: (a) Great Britain 1983; (b) Ireland 1979; (c) Finland 1980; (d) France 1982; (e) Netherlands 1981; (f) Poland 1978.

Composition of households with elderly people

The nature of these alternatives to solitary households can be explored through a more detailed analysis of the composition of households containing elderly persons (see Tables 8.8 – 8.11). Table 8.8 sets out the relationships between elderly persons and the head of the household in Poland and Switzerland. In Poland, where one in ten men and nearly three in ten females were enumerated in 1978 as parents of the head of the household, the extended family still features prominently in the lives of the elderly. In Switzerland it is virtually non-existent as a residential group and conversely a large number of elderly persons head their own households, many of these as solitaries – see Table 8.6.

Table 8.8   *Elderly people: relationship to head of household (percentages)*

	Poland 1978			Switzerland 1982
Relationship to household head	Males	Females	Both sexes	Both sexes
Heads: solitary	10	28	21	⎱ 68
other	71	11	34	⎰
Spouse	5	27	18	23
Parents[1]	12	28	22	5
Other relatives[1]	⎱ 2	⎱ 5	⎱ 4	2
Inmates	⎰	⎰	⎰	1
All	100	100	100	100

[1] Parents-in-law included with parents for Poland; with other relatives for Switzerland.

For a breakdown of relationships of elderly persons which takes account of the age of the elderly person, it is necessary to turn to a different pair of countries (Finland and Ireland) and to a different tabulation which measures the closeness of the relationship of the elderly person with other persons residing in the household – see Table 8.9. In both countries the proportions of persons not residing in families rise steeply with age, while the proportion of couples falls. The influence here of the changing balance during the course of old age in the numbers of married and widowed is clear. The differential likelihood of widowhood in the male and female experience is likewise reflected in the fact that fewer elderly females than elderly males are married. Of much greater interest are the differences between the two countries: the greater prominence of lone parents, particularly among the very old in Ireland; the higher proportions of elderly males in Ireland not being members of families; and, conversely, the lower proportions of married males. Proportions of females not being members of families in Ireland are, on the other hand, slightly lower than those in Finland. These differences may be due to such factors as past rates of out-migration and the nuptuality levels of the non-migrating population in both countries. The fact that in Ireland many of the males who are not members of families are single is certainly suggestive of a link with the low level of male nuptuality in the Irish past.[15]

Table 8.9   *Family status of elderly people (percentages)*

	Age group	Finland 1980 Family status			Ireland 1979 Family status		
		(a)	(b)	(c)	(a)	(b)	(c)
Males	65–9	19	78	2	32	64	4
	70–4	24	73	2	37	58	5
	75–9				42	52	6
	80–4	36	59	4	45	45	10
	≥85				51	35	14
Females	65–9	50	42	8	45	42	13
	70–4	62	31	7	57	29	14
	75–9				65	19	17
	80–4	76	15	8	66	11	22
	≥85				68	6	26

Key to column headings: (a) not in family; (b) couple; (c) lone parent.

In the English census of 1981 the residence patterns of the elderly are investigated on the basis not of family status but of the family structure of the household in which the elderly person resides. These data are presented in Table 8.10 and show that more than three-quarters of the elderly were solitaries or lived in households where there were no unmarried children. Fortunately, an extended version of the same tabulation was also included in the 1979 census of Ireland. Compared with the situation in England and Wales, there is a much greater incidence both of elderly persons living in no-family households consisting of two or more persons, and of elderly persons living in households containing children. Five per cent of the Irish elderly live in two-family households against one per cent of the English and Welsh elderly.

Table 8.10 *Elderly people and their co-residents by household type (percentages)*

| Household type | England and Wales 1981 | | | Ireland 1979 |
	M[1]	F[1]	Both[1]	Both
No family				
Solitary	17	37	30	18
Other no family	5	7	7	14
One family				
Couple alone	} 63	} 40	} 48	19
Couple + others				5
Couple + child	} 11	} 8	} 9	14
Couple + child + others				12
Lone parent + child	} 3	} 6	} 5	9
Lone parent + child + others				3
Two family	} 1	} 1	} 1	5
Three family				0
All	100	100	100	100

| Household type | England and Wales 1981 | | | | | |
| | Single | | Married | | Widowed | |
	M[1]	F[1]	M[1]	F[1]	M[1]	F[1]
No family						
Solitary	54	59	1	2	67	70
Other no family	32	32	1	1	9	8
One family						
Couple	6	3	83	83	4	3
Couple + child	3	2	13	12	7	5
Lone parent + child	4	4	0	1	12	13
Two family	0	0	2	2	0	0
All	100	100	100	100	100	100

[1] These figures are for males aged 65 and over and females aged 60 and over.

For Ireland, it is also possible to measure the variation of residence in a no-family or family household with age, and this information is presented in Table 8.11. A composite picture of the residence patterns of the Irish elderly now emerges. The low and relatively unvarying proportions of solitaries over the later stages of the life cycle in Ireland that were noted earlier (Table 8.7), despite the fact that low proportions of the elderly were married, can be accounted for by the frequency with which elderly persons, particularly the never-married, lived with others not being members of families, and by the frequency with which older never-marrieds, along with the older widowed, were accepted into family households.[16] It is noticeable, too, that once marital status and age are controlled there is little difference between the family status of elderly men and women, as indeed proved to be the case with the headship rate – see Table 8.4 and panel 2 of Table 8.10.

Table 8.11   *Membership of no-family and family households, Ireland, 1979 (percentages)*

	Single people									
	Not in family households				Members of family households					
Age group	Solitary		Other		Children		Others		All	
	M	F	M	F	M	F	M	F	M	F
65–9	37	30	47	56	1	1	15	13	100	100
70–4	37	33	46	54	0	0	17	14	100	100
75–9	37	34	44	50	0	0	19	16	100	100
80–4	33	36	43	46	0	0	24	18	100	100
≥85	30	28	38	44	0	0	32	28	100	100

	Married people											
	Not in family households				Members of family households							
Age group	Solitary		Others		Couples		Lone parents		Others		All	
	M	F	M	F	M	F	M	F	M	F	M	F
65–9	1	2	1	1	97	94	1	2	0	1	100	100
70–4	2	2	1	1	96	93	1	2	1	2	100	100
75–9	2	3	1	2	95	89	1	3	1	4	100	100
80–4	1	3	1	2	94	84	2	5	2	5	100	100
≥85	1	3	1	4	92	75	3	9	3	10	100	100

	Widowed people									
	Not in family households				Members of family households					
Age group	Solitary		Others		Lone parents		Others		All	
	M	F	M	F	M	F	M	F	M	F
65–9	33	33	7	10	38	35	22	21	100	100
70–4	34	35	8	11	29	28	28	26	100	100
75–9	31	30	9	10	26	28	34	31	100	100
80–4	24	23	7	10	28	31	40	36	100	100
≥85	16	15	8	10	29	35	47	40	100	100

The last two tables of the series can be discussed more summarily. Table 8.12 shows how very rare it is for the elderly in West Germany to live in a full three-generation household. Some arrangements of this type are without doubt included in the count of the elderly in England and Ireland living in two-family households – see Table 8.10 – but the comparison is not exact; and, as was intimated above, many members of the grandchild generation escape detection through their classification as offspring. Finally, Table 8.13 throws a little further light on the residence patterns of the elderly in Cyprus. Relative to the situation that prevails in Britain, the elderly in Cyprus are less likely to live on their own or in a household consisting entirely of elderly people.

Table 8.12 *Elderly people and their co-residents by generational span of household, West Germany, 1982 (percentages)*

Generational span of household	Males	Females	Both sexes
Solitary	16	53	39
One generation	65	28	42
Two generation	13	10	12
Three generation	4	5	5
Other relative + non relatives only	2	3	3
All	100	100	100

Table 8.13 *Households containing elderly people by number of elderly and non elderly persons in household (percentages)*

Households containing	Cyprus[1] 1982	Great Britain[2] 1981
Solitary elderly people	32	41
≥ 2 elderly people, no others	3	28
≥ 1 elderly person, 1 other	16	20
≥ 1 elderly person, 2 others	14	} 11
≥ 1 elderly person, 3 others	35	
All households with elderly persons	100	100

[1] Households containing elderly people aged ≥ 60.
[2] Households containing males aged ≥ 65, or females aged ≥ 60.

Discussion

Accounts of the changes in the composition of European households over recent decades indicate the move towards smaller and less complex households. The trend for elderly people to live as solitaries is strongly represented throughout western Europe, and is visible, if less marked, in eastern and southern Europe.[17] The focus of the present survey of the living arrangements of the elderly in the 1980s has rather been on the diversity of these arrangements across Europe, a diversity that would undoubtedly seem all the greater if one were able to disaggregate the patterns according to region and social class.[18]

Some important issues, however, remain unresolved. First, there is the question whether the differences *between countries* in the proportion of the elderly living alone or sharing with others, married or unmarried, should be considered large or small. Secondly, it needs to be established whether these differences can be identified far back in Europe's past and whether they have lessened in recent times. This historical perspective is unfortunately not yet available in a suitably detailed form, but it does at least suffice to show that there is a long-standing association both of complex households with eastern and southern Europe and of nuclear households with north-western Europe and no sign as yet of a convergence of European countries around a high level of one-person households.[19] The comparative perspective would indicate, therefore, that the variation across present-day Europe in the overall shape of the household is indeed significant, if not as significant or as large as that prevailing in pre-industrial times, and that, given the proportion of elderly householders in the numbers living alone, the same will hold specifically in regard to the living arrangements of the elderly. In addition, it could be argued that the fact that the Europe-wide differences in living arrangements have survived the strong impetus towards smaller households is itself evidence enough that such differences have to be taken seriously.

Interpretation of these patterns is considerably more hazardous as the census remains silent as to why people move towards particular types of household. Scholars who have monitored the recent changes in household forms have attempted to distinguish, not always very convincingly, changes resulting from economic, cultural and demographic factors.[20] This might be caricatured as an attempt to measure whether there are more people able to live alone, more people wanting to live alone or more people of an age where they will live alone. Clearly there has been a change, both in the willingness and in the ability of people to establish particular households, and the difficulty has been to decide which type of factor ought to be considered dominant.

The same sort of problem arises when trying to 'explain' variations in the living arrangements of the elderly. The impact of the state is most obvious in the amount of institutional accommodation made available to elderly people, but the state's action (or inaction) is largely determined by value judgements as to what is 'appropriate' in particular circumstances, and by the extent of its susceptibility to pressure from interested parties.[21] Table 8.1 would suggest that, in relation to other western European and Scandinavian countries,

Britain has a relatively small institutionalised elderly population. There would appear to be no peculiarity in the age structure or marital status of the elderly population of Britain which would lead one to expect fewer institutionalised elderly. Such comparisons are bedevilled, however, by inconsistencies in the definition of the institutional population. Similarly it would not seem likely that demographic factors could account for the varying proportions of elderly people living on their own, despite the clear association between an individual's age and marital status and the likelihood of solitary living.

Assessment of the impact of cultural and economic factors is considerably more difficult because much vital information is either not readily accessible or simply not available. In particular, it would be useful to be able to offer a comparative perspective on the state services made available to the frail elderly who wish to maintain their own homes, and on the range of housing schemes open to them that fall short of institutionalisation. A comparative survey of attitudes towards the care of the elderly would also be valuable in order to see, for example, whether there is any variation by country in the strength of the desire to maintain independence in old age, which might in turn be reflected in varying proportions of the elderly living alone.

Studies such as this traditionally end with a call for further research. In the present case the need is clear, but it is hoped that more has been achieved here than just a redefinition of research objectives and an illustration of the variety of approaches to the analysis of household composition. Some of the recent attempts to conceptualise the new forms of the domestic group have come close to implying that Western society is rapidly fragmenting towards its basic unit, the individual. There remains, however, a considerable diversity that has survived the tumultuous changes to family forms in recent years and may indeed be enduring.

Notes

This is a revised and extended version of a paper originally presented to an IUSSP seminar in Berlin in September 1984.

1 See, for example, the series of studies of trends in household composition in various European countries published in the journal *Population* and, in particular, Nilsson (1985) and Blanc (1985). On some of the major definitional problems, see note 7 below and Wall *et al.* (1983), Roussel (1983) and Le Bras (1979).

2 The definition of a family for this purpose is that of married couple with or without unmarried child(ren) or lone parent with unmarried child(ren). This definition, extended to cover cohabiting couples where they can be identified, has been adopted by most European census authorities, although Sweden and France employ a more restrictive definition under which children over the age of 25 are not considered to be family members.

3 I am indebted to the members of the various statistical offices for responding in such positive ways to my circular requesting information on the residence patterns of elderly persons. The present chapter is very largely based on the data they supplied, supplemented on occasion by reference to the most recent statistical yearbook of the appropriate country and a few specialist studies. A full list of the tabulations consulted is given in the Appendix.

4 At the same time it has to be said that it is not without interest who or how many people the elderly reference person or household head can call on in the household. See Parant (1981). 'Reference person' has now replaced 'household head' as the favoured term where one individual in the household rather than its composition needs to be identified, as, for example, in an examination of the relationship between members of the household. The term 'household head' is retained in the present chapter.

5 The Office of Population Censuses and Surveys estimates on the basis of the birth records of some of these children that approximately 50,000 households of the two-family type were misclassified for this reason in the 1981 census of England and Wales. See OPCS (1981).

6 Only Cyprus provided an explicit definition of the institutional population. Included were persons who had been or were planning to stay in the following institutions for at least a year: old people's homes, hospitals, convents, prisons and psychiatric clinics. The institutional population of the Soviet Union is those resident in retirement homes. See Yvert-Jalu (1985).

7 According to the United Nations *Demographic Yearbook 1976* (1977: 53), the housing definition of the household was in force in 1970 only in Sweden and Switzerland, but changes since the 1970s have complicated the picture. In Switzerland, the reclassification in 1980 of subtenants as independent householders (Blanc, 1985: 659) would seem to remove much of the difference between the housing and housekeeping definitions of the household. Conversely, the authorities in Finland adopted in 1980 the housing concept of the household, having previously favoured the housekeeping one (Central Statistical Office of Finland, 1980). There has also been a definitional change in the British census, with persons sharing a common living room in 1981 being considered as forming one household whether or not they took at least one meal together, but the impact on the measurement of household size appears to be marginal (OPCS, 1981, 1982). Another caveat concerns France. Le Bras (1979: 75) claims that the definition of the household used in the French census is not in conformity with the housekeeping concept recommended by the United Nations, and its wording seems to imply rather approximation to the housing concept.

8 English data show that older men are more likely than older women to be in a second or subsequent union and that, for example, more than a third of the married men aged 95 and over in 1981 had remarried. Nevertheless, the overall effect of remarriage on the proportion widowed was simply to postpone by a single year the point at which the number of widowers would exceed the number of married men.

9 See Wall (1984) and also Table 8.11 where the family status of elderly men and women in Ireland in 1979 is examined, distinguishing the never-married from the married and widowed.

10 No curtailment would occur if, in countries where widowhood occurred in the mid-seventies, widows survived as long as widows in countries where the age of majority widowhood occurred in the late sixties. This seems unlikely, but, according to the United Nations *Demographic Yearbook 1982* (table 21), women in Iceland and Sweden (with an age of majority widowhood of 74) might expect at age 75 to live 11.80 and 10.63 years respectively; whereas in those countries with an age of majority widowhood of 68 or 69, only between 11.47 and 12.80 years could be expected at age 70.

11 Relative to other countries, the proportion of solitaries in West Germany is undoubtedly overstated because of the double counting of people occupying more than one house and the reclassification of many residents in institutions to their households of normal residence.

12 Yvert-Jalu (1985) reports that the proportion of solitaries amongst the elderly in the Soviet Union had increased to 25 per cent by 1980.

13 Table 8.3 details headship rates. Table 8.11 demonstrates for Ireland the impact of marital status on the proportion of elderly persons who are not members of a family (see also Wall, 1984: 489).

14 Even for England, survey data indicate that the trend in the proportions of the very elderly (aged 75 or over) living on their own falls considerably short of the rise in the proportion of the elderly lacking a spouse (Wall, 1984: 486).

15 For example, just over three-quarters of all Irish males aged 65 to 69 who were not members of families had never married. Their share of older age groups was naturally somewhat less, but they still constituted more than half of non-family members aged 75 to 79.

16 Table 8.11 differs from Table 8.9 in that, for the purposes of Table 8.9 on the *family status* of elderly people, members of family households not themselves being couples or lone parents were included in the category 'no family'. However, when these persons were members of a household which included a family, they have been counted in Table 8.11 as belonging to a family household.

17 See, for example, Roussel (1983: 995–1013). A general survey of the changes in the European household since 1945 is provided in Wall (1984).

18 Wall (1982) sets out for Great Britain the variation by region in the kin composition of the household and at national level the variation by social class and socio-economic group.

19 On the historical perspectives, see Wall *et al.* (1983: chapters 1 and 3). Trends in one-person households since the Second World War are surveyed in Roussel (1983) and Wall (1984).

20 See contrasting interpretations offered for the rise in the proportion of solitaries of Schwarz (1983) and Pampel (1983).

21 This argument has developed from the account of Johnson (1986) of the *malaise* of the welfare state.

Appendix

A full list appears below of the sources consulted in connection with Tables 8.1 to 8.13. Some census authorities were prepared to fill in a table to my specification. Others forwarded published or previously prepared tabulations (as numbered in the list). In some cases however, further computation was necessary to produce the figures in the tables, which should not be regarded as having any 'official' weight.

Austria
Statistisches Handbuch für die Republik Österreich 1983: 24 and table 2.10.

Belgium
Grundy and Arie, 1984: 131 (population not in private households).
Annuaire Statistique de la Belgique 1984: 104, table 11 (elderly persons living alone).

Cyprus

Unpublished tables received from Department of Statistics and Research, Nicosia, on the Greek-Cypriot population.

Czechoslovakia

Unpublished tables received from International Statistics Division, Federalni Statisticky Urad, Prague, and cf. *Statistická ročenka Ceskoslovenske Socialistické Repubiky 1982*: 96.

Denmark

Sündstrom, 1983: 28 (population not in private households).

Sündstrom, '100 years of co-residence between the generations', unpublished paper in the library of the Cambridge Group.: table 6 (elderly persons living alone).

Finland

Central Statistical Office of Finland, *Population and Housing Census 1980*, VII: tables 1 and 5 (population not in private households; family status of elderly persons; elderly persons living alone).

Central Statistical Office of Finland, *Population 1981*, I: table 5 (age of majority widowhood).

Central Statistical Office of Finland, unpublished table (headship rates).

France

Institut National de la Statistique et des Etudes Economiques, unpublished table (population in non-private households).

Annuaire Statistique de la France 1984: 46 (age of majority widowhood) and 59 (elderly persons living alone).

Parant, 1981: 581 (headship rates).

Germany, East

Statistisches Jahrbuch der Deutschen Demokratischen Republik 1983: 347.

Germany, West

Statistisches Bundesamt, Wiesbaden, unpublished tables, unnumbered, B14, 3a – b, 1.33 (population not in private households, age of majority widowhood, headship rates, elderly persons living alone, generational span).

Great Britain

Office of Population Censuses and Surveys (OPCS), *Census 1981: Communal Establishments*: table 2 (population not in private households).

OPCS, *Census 1981: Persons of Pensionable Age*: tables 1 and 2 (age of majority widowhood) and table 6 (elderly and non-elderly persons in household).

OPCS, *Census 1981: Household and Family Composition*: table 7 (headship rates) and table 9 (elderly persons and their co-residents by household type).

OPCS, *General Household Survey 1983*: table 3A (elderly persons living alone).

Greece

Statistical Yearbook 1982: table 24.

Hungary
Tables received from Central Statistical Office, Budapest: 2.6 (age of majority widowhood) and 1.4 (elderly persons living alone).

Iceland
Statistical Bureau of Iceland, Reykjavik, unpublished table.

Ireland
Central Statistics Office, *Census of Population of Ireland 1979*, Vol. III. *Household Composition and Family Units*: II. table 8 (population in non-private households, family status of elderly persons, membership of no family and family households), I. table 11 (headship rates, elderly persons living alone) and I. table 14 (elderly person and their co-residents by household type).

Luxembourg
Annuaire Statistique 1983/4: 27,77.

Netherlands
Personal communication from J. T. M. van Laanen, referencing Netherlands Central Bureau of Statistics, *Woningbehoeftenonderzoek 1981* (population not in private households; headship rates; elderly persons living alone).

Norway
Sündstrom, 1983: 28 (population in non-private households).
Sündstrom, no date '100 years co-residence between the generations': table 6 and personal communication (elderly persons living alone).

Poland
Central Statistical Office, Warsaw, unpublished tables.

Portugal
National Statistical Institute, Lisbon, tables 4.03 (headship rate) and 4.01 (elderly living alone).
Annuairio Estastico 1982: 16 – 17 (total population aged 65 or over).

Spain
Grundy and Arie, 1984: 131.

Sweden
Sveriges Officiella Statistik, *Folk-ochbostadsräkningen 1980*, Vol. 5: table 1 (population in non-private households).
Statistical Abstract of Sweden 1984: 26 (age of majority widowhood).
Nilsson, 1985: 235 (elderly persons living alone).

Switzerland
Grundy and Arie, 1984: 131 (population in non-private households).
Blanc, 1985: 664 (elderly persons living alone).
Statistisches Jahrbuch der Schweiz 1983: (relationship to household head).
Statistisches Jahrbuch der Schweiz 1984: 20 (total population aged 65 or over).

USSR

Yvert-Jalu, 1985: 848 and 851 (elderly living alone; in retirement homes).

References

Blanc, O. (1985) 'Les ménages en Suisse: quelques aspects de leur évolution de 1960 à 1980 à travers les statistiques de recensement', *Population*, 4–5: 657–74.

Grundy, E. and Arie, T. (1984) 'Institutionalisation and the elderly: international comparisons', *Age and Ageing*, 13: 129–37.

Johnson, P. (1986) 'Some historical dimensions of the welfare state crisis', *Journal of Socoal Policy*.

Le Bras, H. (1979) *Child and Family*. Paris: OECD.

Nilsson, T. (1985) 'Les ménages en Suede, 1960–80', *Population*, 2: 223–48.

OPCS (1981) *Census 1981: Definitions*: 3.

OPCS (1982) *General Household Survey:* 10, 255.

Pampel, F.C. (1983) 'Changes in the propensity to live alone; evidence from consecutive cross-sectional survey 1960–76', *Demography*, 20 (4): 433–48.

Parant, A. (1981) 'Les personnes âgées en France et leurs conditions d'habitat', *Population*, 3: 577–608.

Roussel, L. (1983) 'Les ménages d'une personne: l'évolution récente', *Population*, 6: 995–1016.

Schwarz, K. (1983) 'Die Alleinlebenden', *Zeitschrift für Bevölkerungswissenshaft*.

Shanas, E. (1968) *Old People in Three Industrial Societies*. London: Routledge & Kegan Paul.

Sündstrom, G. (1983) *Caring for the Aged in Welfare Society*. Stockholm Studies in Social Work, Vol. 1.

United Nations (1977) *Demographic Yearbook 1976*. New York: United Nations.

United Nations (1982) *Demographic Yearbook 1982*. New York: United Nations.

Wall, R. (1982) 'Regional and temporal variations in the structure of the British household since 1851', in T. Barker and M. Drake (eds), *Population and Society in Britain 1850–1980*.

Wall R. (1984) 'Residential isolation of the elderly: a comparison over time', *Ageing and Society*, 4.4: 483–504.

Wall, R., Robin, J. and Laslett, P. (1983) *Family Forms in Historical Europe*, 8.

Yvert-Jalu, H. (1985) 'Les personnes âgées en Union Sovietique', *Population*, 6: 829–54.

PART THREE

OLD AGE

9

Ageing and Old Age: Reflections on the Postmodern Life Course

Mike Featherstone and Mike Hepworth

Postmodernity and the life course

During recent years there has been a good deal of sociological interest in the deconstruction of the life course. The term 'deconstruction' has been used by Derrida (1988) to point to the way in which the structure or 'architecture' of the life course is built up in order to reveal the underlying principles of its construction (Kohli and Meyer, 1986). According to this mode of analysis the assumptions which underpin psychological models of universal stages of life development can be shown to be flawed. These weaknesses have been revealed partly by methodological criticisms of the interrelationship between the research and the researcher in the narrative framing of events and the retrospective construction of an ordered sequence of stages through which all individuals allegedly move during the course of their lives (Freeman, 1984). In addition, there has been a strong dissatisfaction with the absence of concepts of social structure from developmental psychological models which have a tendency to reduce complex notions of 'environment' and 'context' into simple 'variables' (Kohli and Meyer, 1986). The result is that individual development is artificially isolated from its social context, and the life course is not fully taken into account as a social institution in its own right interconnected with other parts of the social structure.

In contrast, it is argued, sociological analysis of the life course as a social institution makes it possible to demonstrate the ways in which this institution changes alongside other changes in social institutions associated with the process of Western modernisation. In particular, it can be shown that during the course of this historical process a life form in which chronological age was much less relevant was replaced by an increasingly age-relevant one. As Ariès (1973), Elias (1978) and others have shown, the status of the family in pre-modern European societies was much more important than chronological age in determining questions of maturity, independence of action and power than in our present-day society where these elements tend to be firmly coded according to chronological age in socially constructed stages which include childhood, adulthood, middle age and old age. With the growth of the state, industrialisation and the 'panopticon society' described by Foucault (1979), the life course was subjected to greater surveillance, control and normalisation, with the result that we now see a much more extensive institutionalisation of the life course socially structured into orderly sequences of psycho-social 'growth' and development.

The notion of the deconstruction of the life course, therefore, arises not merely from a heightened theoretical sensitivity but also in response to perceived social changes which are seen by sociologists of postmodernity to be producing a reversal in those processes of industrialisation and modernisation which brought about the institutionalisation of life stages to which we have referred (the prescription of, for example, rules concerning childhood and development, schooling, careers, marriage, retirement). Theorists of the movement towards a postmodern society point to an emerging de-institutionalisation and a de-differentiation of the life course, with less emphasis than in the past being placed upon age-specific role transitions and scheduled identity development. Postmodern change, it is argued, will lead to some blurring of what appeared previously to be relatively clearly marked stages and the experiences and characteristic behaviour which were associated with those stages. Meyrowitz (1984), for example, argues that in contemporary Western society children are becoming more adult-like and adults more childlike. There is an increasing similarity in modes of presentation of self, gestures and postures, fashions and leisure-time pursuits adopted by both parents and their children, and some movement can be seen towards a more informal uni-age style. The so-called 'private sphere' of family life, especially in the middle classes, is becoming correspondingly less private and less authoritarian. Children are granted access through television to previously concealed aspects of adult life and experience such as sex, death, money and the problems besetting adults who are anxious about the roles and selves they present to children. Meyrowitz sees this movement towards a uni-age behavioural style as influenced by the advent of media imagery which as a major form of communication bypasses the controls which adults had previously established over the kinds of information formerly believed to be suitable for children and the institutionalised processes of socialisation and education.

This sociological perspective on social change (which we must stress is seen as largely experienced by the middle classes) is increasingly evident in the body of postmodern theorising currently making an impact on a wide range of academic disciplines. It indicates a move away from universalism towards the tolerance of local knowledge (Lyotard, 1984) and the need to admit the 'other' as co-equal speaker in human dialogues. The de-hierarchisation and pluralism advocated by postmodern theorists, and detected as an emergent aspect of contemporary culture, point to the need to deconstruct development, to spatialise out and admit a multiplicity of variations under conditions of co-equality. Thus Friedman (1987), writing as an anthropologist who has to work in a context in which his subject matter, the other, demands the right to reply and contest his interpretation, typically observes: 'Ultimately the life cycle can be understood as a panorama of cultures. What we are witnessing here is the collapse of an authority structure, one that defines the superiority of adulthood, of rational discourse, of standard linguistic usage' p. 35.

It must not be forgotten that such postmodern theorising is as yet far from being an everyday reality. At best these theories draw our attention to *emergent cultural tendencies*. At the same time it is also possible to show that they do gather some support from gerontological research which records evidence of the declining significance of age grades in contemporary social life in the West. One interesting example can be found in the increasing awareness of resistance to the notion of 'middle age' and the current social exchange value of phrases such as 'mid-life', which normally refers to a very loosely defined age stage covering the wide chronological range 35 to 60, if not beyond. In addition, much of our contemporary cultural imagery of ageing is enlivened by heroes and heroines who vigorously deny the relevance of age-graded statuses. 'I don't think of myself as old-aged,' the film star Bette Davis recently observed; 'I don't feel old at all. Later years would be a more polite term from you' (*Sunday Times*, 20 September 1987). Politicians such as President Reagan and Prime Minister Thatcher present themselves and are presented as anything but stereotypical 'grandad' or 'grandma' figures. Near or past conventional retirement ages, they continue to deny the need to slow down, to rest, to take the back seat – responses traditionally associated with old age. It has, of course, often been pointed out that one's capacities to avoid retirement, or early retirement, depend upon the power resources one can muster; those at the bottom of the social class hierarchy have few resources to facilitate the choice of a positive old age in terms of continued career/work, or a positive and active retirement. Yet for those in the middle classes with the prospect of generous pension incomes and who have planned for retirement, old age holds out the prospect of a prolongation of the plateau-like phase of adult life, with continued relatively high consumption and the pursuit of consumer culture life-styles, body maintenance and styles of self-presentation (Featherstone and Hepworth, 1988).

As far as body maintenance is concerned, an array of evidence continues to accrue which disproves the necessary decline of mental, sexual and physiological capacities in old age. Chronological age continues to be discredited as an indicator of inevitable age norms and life-styles, and a new breed of body maintenance experts optimistically prescribe health foods, vitamins, dieting, fitness techniques and other regimens to control *biological* age, which, it is argued, is the true index of how a person should feel. In effect, they hold out the promise of turning the clock back and clearly have a strong appeal in the new middle-class markets for middle-aged and older people (Walmsley and Margolis, 1987).

In addition, therefore, to state intervention to promote an active, positive old age as a response to the demand to spread resources more thinly in the face of the old age population boom, there has been considerable impetus from the cultural sphere, where, as we have seen, the question of the deconstruction of the life course has been raised. Amongst the most significant features of 'postmodern culture', therefore, we must include:

1 the emphasis upon the cultivation of life-styles or designer lives in which life and the consumer accoutrements which make it possible are styled to achieve a pleasing effect;
2 a playful, youthful approach to culture in which mass spectacles (Disneyworld), the media (MTV, videos), theme parks and post-tourism are paramount, and the knowledge that they *are* simulations does not interfere with their public acceptance or in any way reduce their pleasurable effect (Urry, 1988);
3 the emergence in the new social movements of post-scarcity values where women, nature, Third and Fourth World 'otherness', formerly excluded, are now admitted as valid partners.

Clearly, a strong generational factor can be detected underlying these values. They can be seen to represent cultural attitudes generated in the large post-Second World War cohort in Western countries – the 'baby-boomer' generation which explored counter-cultural life-styles in the 1960s and are now entering what used to be called 'middle age'. As they do so they are taking with them many of the values and cultural tastes of their youth (Hepworth, 1987), and to speak of the 'new middle age' (Hepworth and Featherstone, 1982) is in part to refer to a generational shift implicated in the emergence of a new cohort. As they work their way through into retirement and old age, new generations will continue to take with them many of their cultural tastes, values, preferences and sensibilities, and for any adequate analysis and understanding of these processes the life course must be firmly situated in this historical process and considered as a continual reconstruction as we move forward through historical and lived time.

Adult life, then, is a process – a process, we must emphasise, which need *not* involve development and stages of growth. The stages or hurdles which are placed in front of people and the barriers through which they have to pass (age-specific transitions) can be shifted around and even discarded. Yet having said this we must be careful not to adopt a view of the life course in which culture is granted the over-arching power to mould nature in any form it chooses. Human beings share with other species an embodied existence inevitably involving birth, growth, maturation and death. Our naturally endowed capacity to learn, to speak, to produce signs and symbols and to communicate knowledge through them should not make us neglect the unavoidable biological aspects of existence. To be an embodied person and to become a fully fledged member of society necessarily involves a developmental sequence of biological growth; the body has to grow to produce the physiological co-ordination necessary to facilitate move-ment, facial and bodily gestures and other interpersonal responses. There is also the need for a certain amount of cognitive development and the acquisition of language, memory and communicative compet-ence, as well as emotional development or the capacity to control and regulate the emotions. All are essential to becoming a person; yet the point at which it is assumed that development is complete will show considerable cultural variation. Different societies, for example, may require much lower levels of emotional and cognitive development, which require less than full biological maturation to grant quasi-adult status. An interesting example can be found in Ariès' (1973) research on childhood where he suggests that in pre-modern times the child was allowed to participate as an adult after the age of 7. In contrast, our present-day society formally demands a relatively high level of cognitive, emotional and biological development before human beings are treated as accredited persons. Yet as critics such as John Holt (1969) have pointed out, the chronological age at which we grant citizen rights to the child and make him or her an adult contains many contradictory and arbitrary assumptions. (Few would want to follow Holt and grant full citizen rights to all children, although we can point to some legal erosion of the formerly protected statuses of childhood.)

If the process of becoming an acceptable human being is dependent upon those developments, the loss of cognitive and other skills produces the danger of social unacceptability, unemployability and being labelled as less than fully human. Loss of bodily controls carries similar penalties of stigmatisation and ultimately physical exclusion. Deep old age is personally and socially disturbing because it holds out the prospect of the loss of some or all of these controls. Degrees of loss impair the capacity to be counted as a competent adult. Indeed, the failure of bodily controls can point to a more general loss of self-image; to be ascribed the status of a competent adult person depends upon the capacity to control urine and faeces. The sense of shame at the loss of control, Elias (1978) argues, varies historically with a greater sensitivity to the improprieties of bodily betrayals in our society. It can also be argued that it varies with social class. Individuals who have been brought up in an upper-class milieu may be more easily able to distance themselves from bodily betrayals and adopt a detached attitude towards them and experience less shame at the 'indignity' of being 'cleaned up' by lower-class persons. Members of the new middle class, whose class background and trajectory through life encourage many of the anxieties of the autodidact who is unsure of the appropriate behaviour in various contexts, may experience extreme shame and loss of self-image through their failure to live up to the perceived standards of others (Featherstone and Hepworth, 1988). The loss of bodily controls also impairs other interactional skills, and the loss of real social power through decline in these competences may induce others to feel confident in treating the individual as less than a full adult. Carers may, for example, feel secure in the belief that the 'person inside' will not be able to return and wreak any vengeance on them whatever their former social status or class background.

The mask of old age

In Gubrium's (1975) sociological analysis of the discovery and conceptual elaboration of Alzheimer's disease in the United States and the establishment of boundaries between 'normal' and pathological ageing, old age is seen to be characteristically defined as a mask which conceals the essential identity of the person beneath. This view of the ageing process as a mask or disguise concealing the essentially youthful self beneath is one which appears to be increasingly popular (Featherstone and Hepworth, 1988). When asked at the age of 79 to describe what it felt like to be old, the celebrated author J.B. Priestley replied:

> It is as though, walking down Shaftesbury Avenue as a fairly young man, I was suddenly kidnapped, rushed into a theatre and made to don the grey hair, the wrinkles and the other attributes of age, then wheeled on stage. Behind the appearance of age I am the same person, with the same thoughts, as when I was younger. (Puner, 1978: 7)

In these examples it is the ageing mask which is pathological or deviant and the inner essential self which remains – even beneath or 'inside' Alzheimer's disease – as normal. Such a conceptualisation of ageing seeks for hope in the belief that ageing is a potentially curable *disease*, although several enormously expensive decades may pass before the desperately desired cure is discovered.

Other forms of traditionally age-related camouflage are also seen as barriers to person-perception. In her book *The Language of Clothes*, Lurie (1981) shows how conceptions of age-appropriate clothing confirm the association between physical ageing and decline. Lurie notes that the tradition of marking the transition from maturity to old age by a change of costume is well established. Certain garments such as the shawl come to be associated with old age partly because they may be worn for extra warmth. Other garments become associated with old age for reasons which are less obvious and linked to movements of fashion. Lurie observes a generational variation in fashion take-up:

> Even after pyjamas were widely available and had been popularised by such Hollywood films as *'It Happened One Night'* (1934), long nightshirts of white cotton or red flannel continued to be worn by conservative elderly men, especially in rural areas. (Until very recently they could be ordered from the Sears catalogue.) The wearing of somewhat outmoded daytime fashions is another recognised sign of age – and of the possession of aged opinions and beliefs. (1981: 49)

Lurie also suggests, as a general principle, that if a garment is available in different lengths the longer version will be worn by older people. This applies to both men and women:

> At the height of the miniskirt boom . . . an American magazine published a guide to the proper hem length for women of different ages. A photograph showed three generations of smiling middle-class housewives in identical dresses. Grandmother's skirt clears her knees; Mother's is about four inches shorter; and Daughter's four inches above that. (50)

Clothes therefore transmit age-related messages, and when men or women do not dress to their age society may be offended. The source of offence or deviation here is not the fact of being old but the refusal to accept the state ('mutton dressed as lamb'). 'Extreme disparity of age and costume . . . is seen as disgusting or even frightening.' Some strong taboo, Lurie argues, is being broken – 'something forbidden is being said in the language of clothes' (1981: 57):

> The older woman who makes this error is especially apt to be castigated as 'mutton dressed as lamb'; but men are by no means immune. Cousin Feenix, the elderly beau in *Dombey and Son*, 'so juvenile in figure and in manner, and so well got up', is just as much a figure of fun as his relative the Hon. Mrs Skewton, though he does not inspire the same horror – perhaps

because it is only she that we are allowed to see in private at her toilet: 'The painted object shrivelled under her hand; the form collapsed, the hair dropped off, the arched dark eyebrows changed to scanty tufts of grey; the lips shrunk, the skin became cadaverous and loose; an old, worn, yellow nodding woman, with red eyes, alone remained in Cleopatra's place, huddled up, like a slovenly bundle, in a greasy flannel gown.' (56)

Such images are considered ageist because they portray old age as an inevitable period of decline and, what is more, a period of decline which is at best laughable and at worst disgusting. Feminist writers have detected a strong sexist element in this theme. Fairhurst (1982) identifies the theme of decay as a socially constructed sexist stigma particularly limiting to women and adding terror to the menopause. The process here is a reflexive one where women (and men) evaluate the ageing processes of their bodies according to culturally validated ideas of physical attractiveness and age-appropriate behaviour. Fairhurst shows that, although physical attractiveness is 'not the exclusive concern of women', and both men and women 'believe they should make the "best of themselves" ' (1982: 14), the ways in which they handle the problem vary according to the meanings they give to growing older. Significantly, the women she interviewed worried more about the images conjured up by the term 'old age' than about any supposed loss of physical attractiveness. Her interviews with a sample of middle-aged men and women in a northern English city reveal an important distinction between the physical body and the self. Changes in outward physical appearance are seen as separate from the self, which is considered to be more enduring. One man said: 'I think you'll find yourself that you reach a stage where you don't grow any older inside. Outside you do but you're perpetually 28 or something or whatever it may be – wherever you stop' (p. 11).

This finding is not dissimilar to that reported by Kastenbaum *et al.*, (1981), who show that most people have conceptions of ages other than their chronological one, and who distinguish between personal age as revealed in self-reports of age status, and interpersonal age or the age status of an individual as evaluated by others. 'Consensual age' is the relation between the two. On the basis of a structured interview schedule given to a sample of gerontological students aged 20 to 60, and a matched sample of men and women following studies and careers involving personal interactions but not gerontology, they discovered that personal age appeared to be a separate concept from chrono-logical age, and there was 'an increasing personalisation of personal age with advancing chronological age' (p. 59). Personal age, moreover, tended to be younger than chronological age and to decrease with advancing years. Observers were more likely to rate age in terms of external appearance ('look age' compared with 'feel age'), and 'the present data imply that how old people *look* and *feel* (both from their own frame of reference) represent appreciably different aspects of their total personal age' (p. 65). The age a person 'believes that she or he *looks* tends to be that aspect of personal age which is closest to chronological age' (p. 61). Interestingly the authors observed that 'gerontologists do not appear to be immune to the challenge of age-oriented inquiry. Several gerontologists were among those who expressed the greatest amount of perturbation during and after the interview.' They also note that this confirms their impression that training in gerontology 'does not invariably prepare specialists to cope with age-related problems on a personal basis' (p.58).

It is instructive to compare concern over the stigmatisation of ageing and the 'age segregation' it can undoubtedly produce with the image of ageing as a mask which it is hard to remove. In the context of a postmodernist deconstruction of the life course, the image of the mask is a further sign of attempts to undermine traditional age-related categories. Beneath this imagery it is possible to detect three underlying issues and a closer look at these should provide a further indication of the possible direction of cultural change with regard to ageing.

First, the image of the mask alerts us to the possibility that a distance or tension exists between the external appearance of the face and body and their functional capacities, and the internal or subjective sense or experience of personal identity which is likely to become more prominent in our consciousness as we grow older.

Secondly, it indicates that an important deficiency of the vocabulary of ageing in its present forms is its limited potential for giving elderly people sufficient scope to express their personal feelings as distinct from stereotyped responses to inquiries about 'how you feel'. It seems to be very often the case that we fix elderly people – usually those without resources – in roles which do not do justice to the richness of their individual experiences and multi-facets of their personalities. The sanitised one-dimensional benign stereotypes 'granny' and 'grandpa' are good examples of this ageist trap. The classic granny celebrity in the UK is of course the Queen Mother, typically described in tabloid newspapers as 'Our Super-Gran'.

The contrast between this stereotype and the reality as far as many of today's grandparents are concerned has been revealed by Cunningham-Burley (1985), who carried out intensive research on the ways in which people relate to the role of grandparents in Aberdeen. She points out that although the stereotype of grandparents is one of men and women who are chronologically elderly, the reality is that most people become grandparents in middle age, and would in fact be great-grandparents by the time they are old. But there is little sociological research which looks at the 'middle-aged nature' of grandparenthood.

In other words, the reality of grandparenthood is ignored, as the stereotype of the Queen Mother in the role of everyone's idealised super-gran testifies. The problem is, therefore, that because we *imagine* grandparents are old we don't *feel* 'like' them when in middle life we become grandparents ourselves. However, postmodern times are changing, and the publication of the magazine *Grandparents* is one move towards the destabilisation of traditional stereotypes.

The third issue is the matter of generational change, to which we have already referred. Whilst the image of the mask seems to remain the most appropriate as far as the present generation of the elderly are concerned, there *are* signs that, for certain sections of the population in or entering *middle age* (in particular the middle classes), images and expectations are gradually beginning to change: a new language of ageing with a much greater expressive range has been gradually emerging. And the quest for a new public language to challenge and destabilise traditional cultural images of middle age for both women and men is a significant feature of the culture of mid-life as it has emerged in the West since the Second World War.

Positive ageing and the social reconstruction of middle age

To put mid-life culture into a nutshell, during the last twenty to thirty years middle age has increasingly become a cause for concern. The public stereotype of middle age as a kind of 'mature' interlude with relatively unambiguous physical and psychological boundaries between young adulthood and declining old age has been replaced by an ideal of active, prolonged mid-life which has more in common with youth than age. For the sake of convenience these changes can be broadly periodised as follows:

First, the closing decades of the nineteenth century through to the outbreak of the Second World War. These years saw an increasing concern with the elderly as a problem but, more particularly, the expansion of the concept of retirement both in Britain and in the United States. As, for example, William Graebner (1980) shows in his history of retirement in the USA, the ostensible meliorative institution of retirement is itself the product of the desire to redeploy older workers. As such it is part of a process of age discrimination which has the effect of increasing age consciousness amongst both men and women.

Secondly, the post-Second World War period through to the 1970s. Both periods reveal the growing influence of *consumer culture*, but it is in the late 1950s and early 1960s in the USA where the elderly (or certain sections of the elderly population) are defined as a new market for consumer goods. As Calhoun (1978) puts it in his unwaveringly optimistic study of the 'emergence of the senior citizen between 1945 – 1970': there was 'an upgrading of the image and status of the elderly in American society' (p. 33). There was also the first outcrop of popular books redefining middle age as a positive period of growth and development, though in the context of a movement through relatively fixed life stages. These books drew heavily, albeit selectively, on the increasing academic interest in middle age in the USA. Research into the menopause, for example, was highlighted, and tentative scientific speculations on the 'male menopause' received an airing.

Thirdly, the mid-1970s through to the present day. In the UK, as in the USA, the concept of the 'mid-life crisis' is by now taken much more seriously, and the popularity of such terminology alongside the word 'menopause', and even 'male menopause', reflects the legitimation of *a new vocabulary of motives* which places an emphasis on the positive value of greater flexibility and openness and a willingness to discard 'chronological bonds'. Such a view is confirmed by Stoddard (1983) in her study of the portrayal of women and ageing in American popular film, where she describes how the 1950s saw important changes in attitudes to women on the cinema screen. These were, she says, 'the years in which old age became part of a woman's life cycle to be avoided, physically and mentally, and the time that middle age began to turn in a period of crisis' (p. 117). During the 1960s and 1970s, 'as the movie audience of the early sixties moved into an awareness of their own march towards early middle age in the late seventies, the film images became more and more sympathetic'. And by the early 1970s, middle age had become a crisis period for men as well as women and 'measured more in terms of self-fulfilment than terms of traditional social expectations' (p. 121).

The use of the term 'mid-life' should not be taken to imply a complete break with the past on the part of a new generation of 'mid-lifers' but is a rather loosely arranged collection of ideals which intersect around the concept of youthfulness and its capacity for personal and social change and the irrelevance of chronologically determined age-related statuses. The significant reference point of the ideal imagery of the new middle age is the conception of the 'generation gap' which is expressed on two levels:

1 a sense of breaking with conventional images of age and what is sometimes described as 'loosening the chronological bonds' (Featherstone and Hepworth, 1984);
2 an appeal for the shared experiences of particular generations of men and women who are urged to discover a common identity and cause – the generation, born 1928–38, for example, who Rayner (1980) has described as the 'buffer generation' .

In this emerging and transforming context the culture of mid-life can be seen as one strand in the broader process, often described as the 'modernisation of ageing', which involves a distancing from deep old age – a distancing which is achieved through flexible adjustments to the gradually blurring boundaries of adult life. And this process of transformation has three significant characteristics:

1 Attempts to disconnect the cultural links that have been established since the latter decades of the nineteenth century between retirement and old age: this process involves appropriate changes in the imaging of retirement in terms which are positively youthful.
2 The social reconstruction of middle age, which becomes more fluidly defined as 'mid-life', or the 'middle years': there is a clear dissociation here from the dependence and powerlessness of deep old age. In 1894 Gardner defined the boundaries between middle and old age as follows: 'Some have said a man is old at forty-five; others have considered seventy the normal standard. Long observation has convinced me that *sixty-three* is an age at which the majority of persons may be termed old; and, as a rule, we may adopt this as the epoch of the commencng decline of life. Exceptions, of course, there are; but in a mixed company, few would fail to discern those who may fairly be pronounced old people, as distinguished from the middle-aged; and, we venture to say, most of them would be found, on enquiry, to have reached or passed sixty-three' (p. 13).
3 The elaboration of the contemporary period of extended mid-life into a complex of states of 'being', 'development' and personal growth mediated by *transitional* states or crisis: this elaboration of mid-life increasingly implies a flexible, individualised, biographical approach which takes into account human diversity.

As we stated in our discussion of postmodern deconstruction, this flexible biographical approach is neatly accommodated by the conceptual shift in gerontology from life *cycle* to life *course* analysis. Unlike the term 'life cycle', which implies fixed categories in the life of the individual and assumes a stable system, the term 'life course' suggests more flexible biographical patterns within a continually changing social system. It permits a more dynamic approach to relations between the individual, the family, work and others, and highlights the capacities of members of differing generations to sustain reciprocal relationships over time. In his essay 'Ageing, Dying and Death', Turner (1987) argues that we can theorise the stigma of both youth and the aged with reference to a disengagement from the community expressed as a relative absence of reciprocity. Turner has devised a 'reciprocity-maturation curve' to demonstrate an increase in social prestige as one moves into mid-life and reciprocity and social integration increase. The community grants esteem to such people for their services and for the value it has for them. In line with disengagement theory, as people become elderly and unable to reciprocate and perform responsibilities they are forced to withdraw from powerful social roles and lose prestige. Likewise young people score low on reciprocity because it takes time to build up the skills and 'capital' that make this possible – they are unable to reciprocate and to become involved in the community. This model may go some way towards explaining the low status of the old and children.

We would, however, like to supplement this in terms of our previous discussion of postmodernity and ageing. First, it is possible for different groups and classes to manage the decline of reciprocity in different ways. While we agree with Bourdieu's (1984) statement that ageing involves an accumulation of capital (economic, cultural, social and symbolic), and a shedding of all types of capital as one moves towards old age (in a similar manner to Turner, 1987), the differential possession of different amounts of capital in old age will allow varying classes to manage the loss of status in different ways. With regard to our previous discussion of the life course, and adult life as a process, Turner's account should also be supplemented by adding an analysis of the three types of control (cognitive, emotional and bodily) to which we have also referred. Clearly the timing and degree of the loss of these controls would result in a decline or ultimate loss of confirmation of full adult status. The decline of these competences could also produce a curve which is identical to Turner's reciprocity curve. However, it is possible, even likely, that these curves will *not* coincide, which will add a further series of combinations to our understanding of old age. We could, for example, have an inverted horseshoe reciprocity curve accompanied by incline and plateau shaped competence curves, and of course a range of combinations.

It is therefore important to have some sociological understanding and theorisation of the social construction of the life course in order to address the question of old age. Old age can only be understood in relational terms to (a) a discussion of the grounds for accounting for other stages of life; (b) a discussion of the previous life of the old people which acts as a background and context for their expectations and experience of old age; and (c) the relation of old people to the other generations following behind who may have their own cultural priorities which point towards either a 'caring' or a 'stigmatising' attitude towards the old. The cultural factors influencing generational experience are, of course, variable: the post-war 'baby-boomers', for example, will take into old age quite different values and resources from those who preceded them and from those who follow. And for the immediate future it looks as if it is this generation (particularly the articulate middle classes) which is at the forefront in the elaboration and expression of a public vocabulary of ageing in direct opposition to the traditional static model with which we have until recent times been more familiar.

References

Ariès, P. (1973) *Centuries of Childhood*. Harmondsworth: Penguin.

Bourdieu, P. (1984) *Distinction*. London: Routledge & Kegan Paul.

Calhoun, R. (1978) *In Search of the New Old: Redefining Old Age in America 1945–1970*. New York: Elsevier.

Cunningham-Burley, S. (1985) 'Constructing grandparenthood: anticipating appropriate action', *Sociology*, 19 (3): 421–36.

Derrida, J. quoted in G. Rose (1988) 'Architecture to philosophy – the post-modern complicity', *Theory, Culture and Society*, 5 (2/3): 357–71.

Elias, N. (1978) *The Civilising Process: The History of Manners*. Oxford: Blackwell.

Fairhurst, E. (1982) ' "Growing old gracefully", as opposed to "mutton dressed as lamb": the social construction of recognising older women'. Paper presented to The British Sociological Association Conference, University of Manchester.

Featherstone, M. and Hepworth, M. (1984) 'Changing images of retirement: an analysis of representations of ageing in the popular magazine *Retirement Choice*', in D.B. Bromley (ed), *Gerontology: Social and Behavioural Perspectives*. London: BSG/Croom Helm. pp. 219–24.

Featherstone, M. and Hepworth, M. (1986) 'New lifestyles in old age?', in C. Phillipson, M. Bernard and P. Strang (eds), *Dependency and Interdependency in Old Age: Theoretical Perspectives and Policy Alternatives*. London: BSG/Croom Helm. pp. 85–94.

Featherstone M. and Hepworth, M. (1988) 'Images of ageing', in J. Bond and P.G. Coleman (eds), *Ageing in Britain: An Introduction to Social Gerontology*. Forthcoming.

Foucault, F. (1979) *Discipline and Punish: The Birth of the Prison*. Harmondsworth: Penguin.

Freeman, M. (1984) 'History, narrative and lifespan developmental knowledge', *Human Development*, 27 (1): 1–19.

Friedman, J. (1987) 'Prolegomena to the adventures of Phallus in Blunderland: an anti-anti-discourse', *Culture and History*, 1 (1): 31–49.

Gardner, J. (1894) *Longevity: The Means of Prolonging Life after Middle Age*. London: Henry J. King.

Graebner, W. (1980) *A History of Retirement*. New Haven: Yale University Press.

Gubrium, J. (1986) *Old Timers and Alzheimer's: The Descriptive Organisation of Senility*. Greenwich, Connecticut and London: JAI Press.

Hepworth, M. (1987) 'The mid life phase', in G. Cohen (ed.), *Social Change and the Life Course*. London: Tavistock. pp. 134–55.

Hepworth, M. and Featherstone, M. (1982) *Surviving Middle Age*: Oxford: Blackwell.

Holt, J. (1969) *Escape to Childhood*. Harmondsworth: Penguin.

Kastenbaum, R., Derkin, V., Sabatini, P. and Artt, S. (1981) ' "The ages of me": toward personal and interpersonal definitions of functional ageing', in R. Kastenbaum (ed.), *Ageing in the New Scene*. New York: Springer.

Kohli, M. and Meyer, J.W. (1986) 'Social structure and the social construction of life stages', *Human Development*, 29.

Lurie, A. (1981) *The Language of Clothes*. London: Heinemann.

Lyotard, J.F. (1984) *The Postmodern Condition*. Manchester: Manchester University Press.

Meyrowitz, J. (1984) 'The adult child and the childlike adult', *Daedalus*, 113 (3): 19–48.

Meyrowitz, J. (1985) *No Sense of Place*. New York: Oxford University Press.

Puner, M. (1978) *To the Good Long Life: What We Know about Growing Old*. London: Macmillan.

Rayner, C. (1980) *Lifeguide*. London: New English Library.

Stoddard, K.M. (1983) *Saints and Shrews: Women and Ageing in American Popular Film*. Connecticut: Greenwood Press.

Turner, B.S. (1987) 'Ageing, dying and death', in Bryan S. Turner (ed.), *Medical Power and Social Knowledge*. London: Sage. pp. 111–30.

Urry, J. (1988) 'Culture change and contemporary holiday making', *Theory, Culture and Society*, 5 (1): 35–56.

Walmsley, J. and Margolis, J. (1987) *Hothouse People: Can They Create Super Human Beings?*. London: Pan.

10

Does Age Matter? The Case of Old Age in Minority Ethnic Groups

Ken Blakemore

In arguing for a recognition of the role of ethnicity in ageing, it is important to state at the outset that the object is not to reduce everything to differences or inequalities between ethnic groups, nor to argue that in view of such differences age itself is of no consequence. A drama in which Ethnicity unthinkingly elbows the character Age to one side, or refuses to take a bow with Class and Gender, would be an unconvincing performance. To conceptualise the role of ethnicity in this way would lead to a reductionist view of social reality.

Unless we attempt to integrate the study of age and ageing with various other areas of sociological discourse, we will lose sight of the complex interactive influences which age, ethnicity, social class, gender and other variables have upon one another over time. There is a danger that ageism and the disadvantages which many elderly people face could come to be seen as having a peculiar force or logic of their own. In the author's view this could lead to an over-abstract or one-dimensional view of the problems older people face, much as some studies of gender and race relations have the undesirable effect of divorcing sexist and racist patterns of discrimination from their antecedents and economic or social contexts.

The accent of this discussion will be on the significance of ethnicity, on the contribution of the experiences of minority ethnic groups to understanding general aspects of the ageing process and on how we might begin to integrate studies of ethnic differentiation with those of age differences. Thus minority ethnic groups should not be seen as exotic specimens of ageing but rather should help underline the point that all members of society possess ethnic and racial identity. Reference to 'elderly ethnics', in addition to stigmatising minorities as deviant from supposed majority norms, betrays a failure to realise that all people are 'ethnics'. All life courses and the transitions within them are affected by ethnicity, whether through self-conceptions and attitudes arising out of distinct cultural values or through the impact of outsiders' definitions of, perhaps hostility to, one's ethnic identity.

The meaning of ethnicity

Any attempt to search for those elements of an individual's or group's identity which may be called 'ethnic' is rather like wading into a muddy pool. There are three sources of confusion. First, there is no neat distinction between race and ethnicity, even though they are not the same kind of concept or classification. Second, individual and collective strategies for coping with the effects of disadvantage are frequently confused with ethnic identity. As Holzberg shows (1982: 250–1), if research concentrates solely on indicators of social deprivation, little or no light is thrown on the issue of how culture and ethnicity influence people's response to problems, or how ethnic identity might in some circumstances prove to be a resource for people as they age. The third complication is due to the addition of the concept of 'a minority' to that of 'an ethnic group'. The idea of a minority group is often used unthinkingly, and as if there is a homogeneous majority against which that minority can be contrasted. But though Britain may appear to be a relatively homogeneous country when compared to the United States, British society includes a wide variety of ethnic identities resulting from recent immigration and from the settlement of other ethnic groups at earlier times.

The focus of this chapter will be on issues of ethnicity and ageing as they affect Afro-Caribbean and South Asian elderly people. This is not meant to imply that study of ageing among white ethnic groups is less important (see, for example, Hazan, 1980; Holmes, 1983); nor is a focus on black elderly people meant to suggest that they should always be seen as a special case. The study of the experience of black elderly people in British society can establish some general points about being old. First, it can highlight the central significance of cultural values, ethnic traditions and a sense of belonging to a group with shared experiences in which the individual may ground his or her identity. Second, the experience of black elderly people of being a minority within a minority is important. An examination of the minority concept raises questions about the validity of supposed majority norms. Third, the experiences of minority ethnic groups in trying to obtain fair treatment from the health and social services expose the ethnocentric nature of much welfare provision and raise a question of central significance: how far should institutionalised provision for elderly people strive to meet individual needs? It can be argued that, by voicing their requirements, minority ethnic groups reveal the tendency of providers and the middle-class policy-makers responsible for services to override individual needs and sensitivities.

Against all these arguments for seriously considering the impact of ethnicity on ageing is the counter-argument that ethnic differences pale into insignificance when put into the context of old age itself. Whether as a result of inevitable biological processes or dependency-creating social roles, it could be argued that old age is a major social leveller – not levelling to a state of complete uniformity, but at least reducing formerly significant differences between old people, including those of ethnicity. What evidence is there that those in minority groups are being absorbed into a general 'elderly role' in British society? Before answering this kind of question, the general proposition that age is dominant must be examined briefly.

Old age: the great leveller?

As interest in ageing and, in particular, concern about the position of the old have increased, leading questions in gerontology often seem to be 'In what ways does age make a difference?' or 'Why are elderly people disadvantaged?' It is often taken for granted that age itself is of fundamental and causal significance. Yet chronological age can be a rather unpredictable guide to social circumstances or change in individual behaviour. Age, like sex difference, does not signify either biological or social imperatives. It is a useful summarising variable but can mask a variety of social roles or physiological states. Even when chronological age is abandoned as a measure in favour of age-*related* characteristics, such as membership of a particular cohort of people born between specified dates, we may find that our suppositions about the importance of such characteristics rest on shaky foundations. To say that all those born between 1900 and 1910 have been through a common set of experiences, or that there is a great deal in common between those who migrated to Britain between 1950 and 1961, is to exaggerate wildly the significance of cohort effects. As Schaie *et al.* say of differences between elderly black and white people: 'What may be a period of dramatic change for one part of society may be stability or stagnation for another' (1982: 224). Thus race, ethnicity, class and other variables may represent much stronger types of influence on the experience of old age than membership of an age cohort.

Having introduced a note of caution with regard to the significance of age, or of cohort or period effects, is however not the same as saying that age is unimportant. To point out that elderly people can be viewed as many different groups, each with distinct life-styles, levels of satisfaction or access to material resources, does not mean that age has no impact on ethnic, racial, class or gender differences. Rather, age and age-related variables do exert some influence on everyone. The point is that while some – notably the materially better-off – might be able to minimise or almost entirely escape *some* of the effects of old age roles, their chances of experiencing poorer health, loss of physical and mental functioning and the inability to engage in relationships on an equal footing are bound to increase. As Taylor reminds us: 'Our capacity for physical and psychological functioning . . . does diminish with ageing', and we should not, despite the undoubted importance of social influences, 'ignore the ineluctable processes of ageing' (1982: 259).

From a study of elderly people in Scotland, Taylor and Ford recorded 'rather more evidence of social levelling than we have of the amplification of social differences' (1983: 204). Though the gaps between social class groups and the sexes narrowed only slightly overall, it was found that 'all groups experience a loss of nearly all [types of] resources over time' and that 'the decline in health and functioning is particularly marked' (1983: 183), especially among middle-class women.

While many of the economic and social disparities of younger ages continue to divide people in old age, a common and highly significant effect of being old in an industrial society is 'disattachment from the productive process' (Estes *et al.*, 1982: 159). Even wealth does not give protection from loss of involvement in work, with consequent loss of work-related friendships, social status, leisure activities and sense of purpose. In old age, control over production or business investment is lost, and most of the wealthy are usually only involved in 'the juridical relationship of the ownership of property' (Estes *et al.*, 1982: 159). The wealthy apart, most elderly people must face a future on fixed incomes and the likelihood of increasing dependency on health and welfare services.

To the loss of 'productive' roles in paid employment must be added the effects of age on life-satisfaction, morale and psychological well-being, though here the evidence is mixed. Summarising a number of findings, Abrams and Savage (1977) suggest that 'old elderly' people are more likely to be satisfied with their lives than the 'young elderly'. Manuel, reviewing United States research, reports that while some studies reveal a negative relationship between satisfaction and increasing age, others have shown a positive relationship or no relationship at all (1982a: 225). These contradictory findings could partly be explained by cohort effects, as Abrams explains in a later study (1978), and partly by methodological differences and difficulties in measuring life-satisfaction.

In all, however, there is powerful evidence that while increasing age by no means levels everyone to a common social position or physiological state, it does narrow some inequalities and considerably modifies the influences of other variables. The question is, how far are ethnic distinctions modified by age?

One way of trying to resolve the question is to conduct research, as in the United States, to ascertain how far 'double jeopardy' (the combined effects of race and age discrimination) affects black elderly people and how far age acts as a leveller between racial groups. As can be seen, this approach is above all concerned with *racial* inequalities, and, though ethnic influences on well-being might be considered, the tendency in the research has been to downplay ethnography or in-depth studies of the status of elderly people in minority communities (Holzberg, 1982: 251).

As far as Britain is concerned, several problems make it difficult to reach firm conclusions about whether differences between ethnic groups, or between black and white people, are narrowing or widening in old age. Though there is strong evidence that black elderly people do experience sharp disadvantage, and local community surveys make much of this (Berry *et al.*, 1981; Bhalla and Blakemore, 1981; Barker, 1984; Fenton, 1987), there has been little systematic comparison with white elderly control groups matched for age and social class. For the most part, these surveys have been oriented to urgent needs and local concerns with services. This does not mean that the evidence is worthless, only that we must be content with indirect or exploratory findings on double jeopardy.

Another problem is that what little discussion there has been in Britain about age and ethnicity has tended to assume that double jeopardy is simply a way of describing the facts about inequalities. Black elderly people are described as those who experience the heaping of racial disadvantage on to the common disadvantages of being old (Mays, 1983; Norman, 1985). This is all right as far as it goes, but it fails to treat double jeopardy as a hypothesis to be tested and it rules out the possibility of age acting as a leveller. Both hypotheses include a requirement that differences between ethnic groups are measured over time (or cross-sectionally, by reference to different age groups) and are not descriptions of present inequalities. As Bengston explains:

> The relative numbers of ethnic *aged* having good health and adequate income may be less than those of aged whites. If, however, the percentage differences between middle-aged blacks . . . and their white counterparts are greater yet, a characterisation of the minority aged as being in double jeopardy would be an incomplete description. It may be that age exerts a *levelling* influence on the ethnic differences found among younger cohorts. (1979: 20)

Despite methodological flaws and contradictory evidence on some aspects of double jeopardy such as health inequalities (Manuel, 1982b), Jackson concludes that the US evidence tends to confirm the existence of double jeopardy as far as health, income and other aspects of material disadvantage are concerned (1982: 79). However, the evidence on what might be seen as more subjective aspects of ageing – for example, life-satisfaction, levels of anxiety and loneliness, quality of social support – is less clear. Perhaps elderly people in minority ethnic groups are not as disadvantaged as some categories of elderly people in the 'majority' population in these important dimensions of ageing, though as noted above it is possible that some of the research has romanticised minority ethnic cultures; however, it may at least be the case that former advantages among majority whites in terms of social contact, support or psychological well-being are eroded with age.

The British community surveys of the needs of elder Asian and Afro-Caribbean people make it reasonably clear that being old and black has resulted in multiple hazards to health (Blakemore, 1982; Ebrahim *et al.*, 1987) and additional disadvantage in terms of income (Bhalla and Blakemore, 1981; Blakemore, 1985; Boneham, 1987) and non-provision of appropriate social services (Bhalla and Blakemore, 1981; Norman, 1985). For example, while thorough comparative work between ethnic and racial groups has yet to be done, old Asians and Afro-Caribbeans – though on the whole a 'young elderly' group – are already reporting levels of illness comparable with older whites living in the same neighbourhoods (Blakemore, 1982), indicating that racial inequalities in this respect can only widen with age.

Because the broad outlines of double jeopardy have become apparent and as early work in Britain seems to be confirming US conclusions about material disadvantage and health inequalities, this set of issues in the field of age, race and ethnicity will not be pursued here. As already suggested, concern with poverty and deprivation is of urgent importance. But often, in much of the discussion of double jeopardy, ethnic differences and ethnic influences on how people experience and perceive old age can be missed. Though black elderly people may be confronted with racial discrimination whatever their cultural background, religion or history, this does not mean that we should insensitively ignore real ethnic differences among black and white elderly people. For this reason and despite the difficulties involved in gathering reliable evidence, the remainder of this chapter will focus on two main 'subjective' aspects of ageing, namely the nature of the social ties and relationships which surround old people in minority ethnic groups and indications of life-satisfaction or associated aspects of morale and psychological well-being. It is these aspects of ageing which perhaps best illustrate the effects of ethnicity and culture, essential though 'hard' data on racial inequalities in health and living standards may be.

Ethnicity and social networks

Patterns of social interaction, relationships and residence among older Asian and Afro-Caribbean people in Britain do not provide cut-and-dried conclusions about the effects of ethnicity and how these influence the texture of daily life. Residence and the clustering of ethnic communities, for example, are arguably as much the outcomes of the operation of racial discrimination in the housing market as of the exercise of ethnic preference (Rex and Moore, 1967). However, bearing in mind that racial discrimination, class and status factors have all contributed to shaping residence patterns, distinct ethnic differences in social life and the networks surrounding old people in minority groups can be discerned. Another problem is, what should we make of these differences? It is easy to fall into the trap of assuming that minimal social contact is a bad thing, especially when it is found disproportionately in one ethnic group as compared to another, whereas frequent or prolonged contact with relatives, neighbours and friends is always seen as beneficial. But demonstrating the levelling effect of old age is a more complicated business than comparing quantified measures of social contact. A frequency of contact that might be regarded in one ethnic group as virtual ostracism might be seen as satisfactory in another.

Cantor's comparative study of US black, white and Hispanic elderly people illustrates this (1976). The Spanish-speaking elderly group were found to have the most contact with children, grandchildren and other relatives. However, they were significantly more likely than the other two groups to be concerned about being abandoned or neglected by their families. They were also the most worried about a general decline of extended family ties and traditions. Therefore those who appear to be objectively the best-off in terms of familial support can be the most vulnerable to fears of change. Dependence on the family may also be associated with lack of familiarity within the English-speaking world of officialdom and public welfare, making it difficult for most of this group of elderly people to contemplate living alone.

Like Hispanic elderly people in the USA, the overwhelming majority of elderly people in the various Asian communities in Britain live with relatives, usually in large households. In Birmingham, for example, it was found that only 5 per cent of old Asians live alone (Bhalla and Blakemore, 1981: 15); the Age Concern survey of Asians aged over 55 living in London and Manchester found a similar proportion living alone (Barker, 1984: 22), as did a more recent survey in Coventry (City of Coventry, 1986). Both the All Faiths For One Race (AFFOR – Bhalla and Blakemore, 1981) and Age Concern surveys showed that it is a clear majority of old Asians who live in households of six or more people: in Birmingham, 60 per cent; in London and Manchester, 71 per cent. But in Coventry, where over a thousand Asian people over the age of 55 were interviewed, the picture is quite different. There, only 12 per cent live in large households of six or more. Crude distinctions of ethnicity cannot account for this striking difference, because, comparing the Birmingham and Coventry samples, about the same proportions of the major linguistic-religious groups – Punjabi-speaking Sikhs (about half) and Gujarati-speaking Hindus (about a quarter) – were present in both. In the Birmingham sample, however, we find that almost all the Punjabis and Gujaratis had migrated directly from India, whereas in Coventry over a quarter of older Asians have come from East African countries.

We do not yet know exactly why the East African experience may have contributed towards a smaller, possibly more 'Westernised' household structure, and it is also possible that local differences between Birmingham and Coventry – for example, in the nature of the housing market – play a part. But whatever the reasons, findings such as this underline the point that generalised ethnic labels can easily mislead. Migration history and subsequent patterns of adjustment in British society qualify crude ethnic distinctions as different communities develop distinct local identities. As Barker comments:

> Many . . . differences are now . . . between the cities in Britain to which different groups migrated: most of the elderly Asians living in . . . Brent are Hindu Gujarati-speakers who have spent large parts of their lives in East Africa. The Manchester population, by contrast, is made up of a population of what we have called 'pioneers' – mainly early travelling merchants, seamen and professionals who came to Britain for education – and Urdu-speaking Muslims . . . who were recruited . . . to work in the mills and the factories. (1984:14)

It should also be stressed that though most old Asian people live with others it is not necessarily an overwhelming majority who live with *close* relatives. In Birmingham, for example, we found that a quarter of old Asians who lived with others were sharing either with distant relatives or with people who had originated from the same district or region in the old country. And in Coventry, though much the largest proportion live with a spouse and close relatives, a significant minority of widows (12 per cent) live with in-laws only (City of Coventry, 1986), a proportion which will increase sharply in the near future.

This is not to say that in-laws or those counted as distant relatives or as friends and compatriots will fail to provide support or satisfying social interaction when needed; we do not yet know enough about ties in such Asian households to estimate how much of a resource such relationships will prove to be. But stereotypes of all-embracing Asian families which protect all ageing Asian people from loneliness and neglect must be jettisoned.

Questions must also be asked about the quality of care old Asian people might receive from their relatives, however close or distant the ties of blood. The status of elderly people in some traditional Indian societies can be ambivalent, and they are not always accorded the degree of deference and respect one is led to expect (Harlan, 1964). It is therefore perhaps not so surprising to find that, in some Asian households, the status of old people can be low – more commonly for women and especially widows who have no sons or sympathetic male relatives to defend their interests. Boneham (1987) records considerable distress among some elderly Sikh women who are quite oppressed by their position in the family, experience feelings of depression and are sometimes desperate for company outside the house. And though we must be aware of the danger of counter-myths of widespread neglect among old Asian people – many of whom seem to be well regarded by their families – it is perhaps significant that the first cases of physical abuse have begun to be reported.[1]

The evidence on older Asians' residence patterns, while it may not identify quality of interaction or hidden problems between family members, does establish the ethnic distinctiveness of Asian communities when compared with Afro-Caribbean and white groups. The Afro-Caribbeans, like white elderly people, tend to live either as couples or alone. For example, in Birmingham it was found that two-fifths of Afro-Caribbeans lived alone and the same proportion as couples (Bhalla and Blakemore, 1981); in Coventry, the equivalent proportions are 17 and 35 per cent (City of Coventry, 1986) and in Bristol 36 and 32 per cent (Fenton, 1987: 15).

The Birmingham survey also showed that approximately the same proportions of whites as Afro-Caribbeans live singly (two-fifths) and in couples (two-fifths). Yet the Birmingham sample of older whites was a considerably older group than the Afro-Caribbeans; so, as the latter age, we will find higher proportions of black elderly people living alone than among their white counterparts aged over 70. A larger proportion of older black people *begin* retirement as single people, and this is at least in part an ethnic difference, reflecting distinct Caribbean household and family structures (Foner, 1979; Fryer, 1984).

Though a considerable proportion of older Afro-Caribbeans appear to be involved in wide social networks, often involving social clubs or church and community groups, it would be a fair generalisation to say that they are more likely to be at risk of isolation and loneliness than either old Asian or white people. Old whites often lose contact with relatives and friends as people move out of the inner city, but are rooted in the local community and often are people who grew up locally (Blakemore, 1983). But older Afro-Caribbeans seem to form a much less settled population. For example, in one attempt to re-interview Afro-Caribbean respondents to the AFFOR survey,[2] it proved extremely difficult to find more than a handful of people out of over a hundred who two years before had agreed to the idea of being contacted again. As one respondent put it: 'We're mobile people – we don't like to stay in one place too long!' While such mobility may be less common in long-established black communities such as those in Bristol and Cardiff, other community surveys have confirmed impressions that old Afro-Caribbeans after retirement can often find themselves leading lone existences. And unlike Asian people, the majority of whom live either in owner-occupied or privately rented accommodation, quite substantial proportions of Afro-Caribbeans live in rented council accommodation or in housing association property: about a half do so in Birmingham, for example (Bhalla and Blakemore, 1981). So partly as a result of dispersal on council housing estates or in other council accommodation they are less likely than Asians to live in neighbourhood social clusters. This does not mean that there are no well-known or geographically identifiable Afro-Caribbean communities in British cities, but the point is that Afro-Caribbean people over retirement age are more likely than older Asians to live farther away from the centres of their communities. The experience of contacting old Afro-Caribbeans for the Coventry survey (City of Coventry, 1986) showed that almost all were scattered in various inner-city wards.

While ethnic and other factors appear to have led to distinct differences in residence patterns between older Afro-Caribbeans and Asians the influence of ethnicity is also observable in the ways that each group spends time. The Birmingham survey, for example, found that older Afro-Caribbeans and whites are mostly engaged in rather similar activities: cooking, housework, gardening, watching television or performing semi-recreational, semi-work activities such as sewing or home maintenance. The same survey showed that Afro-Caribbean men are the most home-centred of the three main groups of Afro-Caribbean, Asian and white elderly males (Bhalla and Blakemore, 1981). It is old Asian men, on the other hand, who are the most likely to be out of the house during the day.

The recent survey in Coventry (City of Coventry, 1986) confirms these findings about the role of old Asian men, a considerable proportion of whom spend parts of their days 'wandering' rather aimlessly or 'visiting friends'. Perhaps, as some suggest, these patterns of activity are bound up with the lack of a clearly identified role for older Asian men and occur because, when younger males are out of the house, it might be considered improper for them to remain with women at home. However, while there may be something to these explanations, there is a danger in explaining their being 'at a loose end' as a problem arising from some cultural failing in their own ethnic group. The problems both men and women experience in Asian communities are at least in part those posed by the devaluation of old age in an industrial society and by racial disadvantages reflected in a lack of adequate social facilities.

How old Asian men spend their time and indications that some of them are bored and dissatisfied with their lives therefore take away some of the gloss associated with integration in close and supportive family networks; like other old people, some Asians struggle with the existential uncertainties of old age. Yet, allowing for the distortions of quantitative measures of contact, there is no doubt that, in a three-way comparison between elderly Asian, Afro-Caribbean and white people, it is the former who have by far the greatest amount of contact with relatives. Only 14 per cent of Asian elderly people see relatives less than once a week, but the corresponding proportion among Afro-Caribbeans is a third and among elderly whites over two-fifths (AFFOR, 1979).

The information collected by AFFOR on frequency of interaction with friends, neighbours and relatives suggests that, on the face of it, elderly whites in inner-city environments are less well-off than either Asian or Afro-Caribbean elderly people. This differs in one way from the evidence of Dowd and Bengston on US elderly people, whose comparisons of blacks and whites showed that while old whites similarly had the lowest amount of contact with relatives, they reported '*higher* levels of contact with friends and neighbours than Blacks or Mexican Americans at all ages' (1978: 433).

In Birmingham, however, we found that, while about a half of both white and black elderly people reported seeing friends every day, significantly more whites than blacks were likely to go for a week or more without seeing friends (Blakemore, 1985: 98). Differences in amount of contact with relatives were even more pronounced: twice as many Asians and Afro-Caribbeans reported seeing relatives daily as whites.

What appears to be a racial or ethnic difference in social interaction in old age could perhaps be explained by an age difference – since the whites are older and more of them are housebound, does this not account for their lower rate of participation? According to Abrams, however, social contact *increases* with age, partly because of greater dependence (1978: 30). Therefore it is likely that the difference in amounts of social contact between white and black elderly people which we observed in Birmingham is an ethnic rather than an age difference. Though it may be that special factors operate in inner-city neighbourhoods to reduce the amount of social contact white elderly people receive, patterns of daily activity among them – for example, the proportion going out each day to shop or to visit others – are quite similar in the AFFOR sample to the nationally representative samples studied by Abrams.

Before jumping to the conclusion that the case for double jeopardy does not hold water as far as social interaction and social support are concerned, we should however remember the points made above about quantity not equalling quality; for some old Asian women, for example a lot of family interaction might spell oppression. Another point to remember is that, for Afro-Caribbean elderly people in particular, contact with others outside the home might be relatively frequent but refer to only a small, restricted network rather than a rich, extensive one. And finally, as far as Asian people are concerned, Western distinctions between 'friends', 'neighbours' and 'relatives' may either have no meaning or carry different meanings in different Asian communities. The experience of the surveys in Birmingham and Coventry shows that it can be hard to tell whether contact with 'friends' should be counted as a separate category from relatives, but if it is there is a possibility of considerable double-counting of contact with others.

Life-satisfaction and views on old age

Previous work on life-satisfaction and its connection with ageing has revealed major flaws in the positivistic approach (Larson, 1978; Burton and Bengston, 1982; Palmore, 1983). Should we attempt to generalise about inequalities in life-satisfaction between groups which have different languages and cultures?

Despite the danger of creating misunderstanding, it is argued here that it would be a mistake to leave out any consideration of such important aspects of ageing, especially since they throw light on our central concern as to whether ethnic identity can be a psychological resource or can offer some protection against loss of roles and of sense of purpose in old age.

Assessment of life-satisfaction or the views of older people on what it is like to grow old in a minority ethnic community in Britain has not been carried out in the systematic fashion of the US researchers referred to above. However, subjective perceptions of ageing and the effects of ethnic identity on these can be inferred from some common threads running through the various community surveys of Asian and Afro-Caribbean elderly people. But as with ethnic differences in residence patterns and social interaction, it is too early to draw hard-and-fast conclusions about whether being old, black and in a minority ethnic community always leads to increased chances of feeling dissatisfied, stressed or cut off from one's past, or whether membership of a group with a well-defined identity protects older people from these hazards.

What can be said is that late life is a period in which everyone is forced to deal in some way with losses and earlier disjunctive transitions such as retirement or loss of work before that, loss of a spouse or other loved ones or, in the case of international migrants, some loss of contact with significant others in the old country. Dealing with disjunctive transitions need not necessarily be a self-conscious process in which all painful memories are relived, however much those who believe in the 'therapy of reminiscence' might wish this to happen! As Hazan's (1980) study of an elderly Jewish community shows, one strategy is for old people to be selective in eliciting memories and images from the past; attempts by outsiders to recall painful memories may be angrily dismissed.

It is clear from studies of life-satisfaction and psychological well-being in the general population that though health, income and other material factors are very important influences, expectations are perhaps just as important. Thus the ability to balance what one had envisaged late life *would* be with the reality of old age as it is actually experienced is highly significant. If feelings of disappointment arise, they might be described as a kind of relative deprivation – a sense of injustice or loss not in relation to another social group, but relative to one's own anticipated old age.

International migrants are those who have taken the momentous step of leaving their own societies and cultures to live elsewhere; as such, they are perhaps more likely than most to reflect on what they have done and whether old age has turned out to be what they expected. But if this is so, they illustrate in a particular way a general process of coming to terms with old age.

Despite ideas of migration being associated with threats to psychological well-being, we know from large-scale surveys (see, for example, Nagi and Haavio-Mannila, 1980) that migrants are no more likely than non-migrants to be mentally ill; likewise, reviews of research on psychological instability among black migrant groups in Britain (Runnymede Trust, 1980) conclude that there is no evidence that mental health is poorer in minority ethnic groups, though they appear to suffer from racially discriminatory practices in treatment.

Therefore, on the face of it, there is no need to be particularly concerned about low morale, depression or anxiety among elderly people in minority groups. But there are strong reasons to challenge such an assumption. First, the medical evidence referred to is based on surveys of migrants or minority populations of all ages, yet it is only now that significant numbers of Britain's black population are reaching retirement age – new needs and problems in old age have yet to emerge. Second, data on mental health are usually based on use of medical services, a form of measurement which cannot reveal hidden problems of a serious nature or psychological stress not recognised as such. And third, black – white comparisons do not identify differences among ethnic groups and the particular difficulties experienced by subgroups: for example, depression or loneliness among certain groups of older women, or among old migrants who come as dependants to join younger relatives in an unfamiliar society.

Above all, the evidence of the community surveys suggests significant hazards to psychological well-being and to a sense of satisfaction in old age among many, if not all, older people in minority ethnic groups. For example, though very few Afro-Caribbeans – like older Asians – make specific plans to visit the 'home' country or return there, almost two-fifths in the Birmingham sample expressed a preference for living in another country (Bhalla and Blakemore, 1981); the proportion of Asians feeling this (16 per cent) was considerably smaller.

While cultural differences undoubtedly influence results such as these, it is likely that some real differences between old Afro-Caribbeans and Asians do exist as far as views on old age in Britain are concerned. As we have already seen, social networks surrounding older Asians are denser than those of the Afro-Caribbeans, with exceptions in each case. Though these networks can be oppressive sources of constraint and dissatisfaction it is likely, as we suggested in the Birmingham study, that old Asians stand a comparatively greater chance of experiencing some reinforcement of ethnic identity and, with that, some commitment to 'stay, be cared for and die in Britain' (Bhalla and Blakemore, 1981: 46). This is borne out by Bhachu's (1985) study of an Asian community from East Africa in which the myth of return to a country which is 'home' is almost impossible to sustain. As a consequence – and despite problems of adjustment to life in Britain – mental and material resources are not diverted elsewhere; and one has the impression that older people in the Sikh community studied by Bhachu are much more settled than those in other Asian communities which have an ambivalent attitude towards return (Anwar, 1979) or, more particularly, than old Afro-Caribbeans.

A view of older Asians' responses in more detail shows that a considerable proportion of older men are dissatisfied with their *daily lives* in Britain even though they might enjoy considerable advantages over women in determining their own lives and are not so affected by dreams of a return 'home' as Afro-Caribbeans. It will be recalled that the Birmingham survey asked about use of time; in response to one question, a quarter of old Asian men said that they could not occupy their time sufficiently, compared to only small numbers of whites and Afro-Caribbeans (Bhalla and Blakemore, 1981: 24–5). The more recent survey of Asian and Afro-Caribbean people in Coventry (City of Coventry, 1986) lends support to these findings.

Hidden problems and needs among older Asian women should also be remembered. As Boneham (1987) points out, Asian women are particularly disadvantaged by expectations of docility and passivity, so that, if questioned in the presence of men or other senior female relatives, they tend to be discouraged from voicing their true feelings. Boneham is convinced, from participant observational study, that levels of dissatisfaction are seriously underestimated in previous studies of the position of older Asian women.

These pieces of evidence suggest that it is important to keep an open mind about the existence of double jeopardy in life-satisfaction and psychological well-being and the influence of ethnicity in these respects. The US work indicated that it is not a foregone conclusion that older people in minority ethnic groups are worse off. Depending on the ethnic groups in question, life-satisfaction and morale among the minority elderly may even improve with age, relative to the position of the majority of elderly people. Some elements of minority ethnic community life – for example, strong attachment to religious institutions and social activities associated with them – provide continuity through disjunctive life transitions (Hazan, 1980; Holzberg, 1982).

Once we look beyond broad distinctions between black minority and white majority elderly people, however, a complex picture becomes apparent. For example, while migration and the experience of racial disadvantage in Britain may not always threaten life-satisfaction and psychological well-being, they do appear to vary in their effects, in part because of ethnic differences in patterns of migration, residence and social life. This is emphatically not to say either that ethnicity is a cause of problems or that it should be seen separately from leading causes such as racial discrimination; however, ethnic differences have been demonstrated in the ways Afro-Caribbeans and the various Asian communities have begun to respond to the problems which face them in old age.

Conclusion

Does age matter? This chapter on the position of elderly people in minority ethnic groups may have given the impression that it matters very little. Without considering inequalities in income and health, which have been shown elsewhere to increase between racial groups with age and to contradict the notion of age as a leveller, we have seen that distinct ethnic differences in residence patterns and social interaction and in terms of life-satisfaction and views on old age all seem to suggest that as people age they remain ethnically different from each other, or perhaps become more different from each other. There are few signs that older Asian and Afro-Caribbean people, for example, are being integrated into a general elderly role or status. In fact, it was suggested that one of the contributions of the study of such minorities is to highlight the cultural heterogeneity of ageing and to point out that there is no majority norm.

As stated at the beginning, however, it is misleading to think of variables operating as discrete influences, some of which always seem to be of more consequence than others. Some of the US studies, for example, read almost as if they were court-room dramas at the end of which a verdict is proclaimed: double jeopardy upheld here, so race and ethnicity have priority over age: age-as-leveller upheld there, so age is the most important variable!

For at least two major reasons it is concluded that we should try not to think in this way. First, because most of the comparisons that have been made to date across ethnic or racial groups have involved older people who, if not of pensionable age, are approaching it. But an answer to the question 'does age matter more than ethnicity?' might be very different if comparisons are made between generations or cohorts *within* ethnic groups. Because inter-generational relationships between Asian parents and their children can be especially problematic, for example, it is clear that age-related influences are highly significant and do sometimes override ethnic identity. At least one study of old Asians in Britain (Fenton, 1987) has reported that fears about social change and its effects on younger generations undermine satisfaction in old age. Another reason for doubting the validity of clear-cut distinctions between the relative importance of age, ethnicity and other variables is that all such influences must operate through given time periods and in certain contexts. The term 'ethnicity', for example, has been shown, through the various Asian and Afro-Caribbean communities, to be an umbrella term masking a variety of cultural, linguistic and religious identities. Whether someone speaks Punjabi, say, tells us relatively little; we do not know from that one clue about ethnicity: whether he or she is a Sikh or a Muslim, comes from India, Pakistan or an East African country, when arrival in Britain occurred and for what reasons, or where in Britain he or she has lived.

Though all these complexities are difficult to deal with, however, it is concluded that development of research on the contribution of the variety of influences that could be called 'ethnic' would provide much-needed illumination of the cultural content of general assumptions about old age and services for old people. But to achieve this, much more detailed ethnographic study and cross-cultural research (involving white and black communities) than has yet been done in Britain will be needed.

Notes

1 Personal communication with social workers in Coventry and Birmingham.
2 A follow-up survey sponsored by the Nuffield Foundation – see Blakemore (1983).

References

Abrams, M. (1978) *Beyond Three Score and Ten – a First Report on a Survey of the Elderly*. Mitcham: Age Concern.

Abrams, M. and Savage, R.D. (1977) *Personality and Adjustment in the Aged*. London: Academic Press.

All Faiths for One Race (1979) Unpublished survey. Birmingham: AFFOR.

Allen, S. (1982) 'Perhaps a seventh person?', in C. Husband (ed.), *Race in Britain: Continuity and Change*. London: Hutchinson.

Anwar, M. (1979) *The Myth of Return: Pakistanis in Britain*. London: Heinemann.

Barker, J. (1984) *Black and Asian Old People in Britain*. Mitcham: Age Concern.

Bengston, V.L. (1979) 'Ethnicity and aging: problems and issues in current social science enquiry', in D.E. Gelfand and A.J. Kutzik (eds), *Ethnicity and Aging*. New York: Springer.

Berry, S., Lee, M. and Griffiths, S. (1981) *Report on a Survey of West Indian Pensioners in Nottingham*. Nottinghamshire County Council, Department of Social Services.

Bhachu, P. (1985) *Twice Migrants – East African Sikh Settlers in Britain*. London: Tavistock.

Bhalla, A. and Blakemore, K. (1981) *Elders of Minority Ethnic Groups*. Birmingham: All Faiths For One Race.

Blakemore, K. (1982) 'Health and illness among the elderly of ethnic groups living in Birmingham', *Health Trends*, 14: 69–72.

Blakemore, K. (1983) 'Ageing in the inner city: a comparison of old blacks and whites', in D. Jerrome (ed.), *Ageing in Modern Society*. London: Croom Helm. pp. 81–103.

Blakemore, K. (1985) 'Ethnic inequalities in old age: some comparisons between Britain and the United States', *Journal of Applied Gerontology*, 4 (1): 86–101.

Boneham, M. (1987) 'Ethnicity and ageing in Britain: a study of elderly Sikh women in a Midlands town'. PhD thesis, Centre for Urban and Regional Studies, University of Birmingham.

Braham, P., Rhodes E. and Pearn, M. (1981) *Discrimination and Disadvantage in Employment*. London: Harper & Row.

Brown, C. (1984) *Black and White Britain – the Third PSI Survey*. London: Heinemann.

Burton, L. and Bengston, V.L. (1982) 'Research in elderly minority communities: problems and potentials', in R.C. Manuel (ed.), *Minority Aging*. Connecticut: Greenwood Press.

Cantor, M.H. (1976) 'The effect of ethnicity on life-style of the inner-city elderly', in *Community Planning for an Aging Society*. New York: Dowden, Hutchinson & Ross.

City of Coventry (1986) *Coventry's Ethnic Minorities Elderly Survey*. Coventry City Council, Ethnic Minorities Development Unit.

Dowd, J.J. and Bengston, V.L. (1978) 'Aging in minority populations: an examination of the double jeopardy thesis', *Journal of Gerontology*, 33 (3): 427–36.

Ebrahim, S., Smith, C. and Giggs, J. (1987) 'Elderly immigrants – a disadvantaged group?', *Age and Ageing*, 16: 249–55.

Estes, C.L., Swan, J.H. and Gerard, L.E. (1982) 'Dominant and competing paradigms in gerontology: towards a political economy of ageing', *Ageing and Society*, 2 (2): 151–64.

Fenton, S. (1987) *Ageing Minorities – Black People as They Grow Old in Britain*. London: Commission for Racial Equality.

Foner, N. (1979) *Jamaica Farewell*. London: Routledge & Kegan Paul.

Fryer, P. (1984) *Staying Power: A History of Black People in Britain*. London: Pluto Press.

Harlan, W.H. (1964) 'Social status of the aged in three Indian villages', *Vita Humana*, 7: 239–52.

Hazan, H. (1980) *The Limbo People: A Study of the Constitution of the Time Universe among the Aged*. London: Routledge & Kegan Paul.

Holmes, D. (1983) *Other Cultures, Elder Years*. Minneapolis: Burgess Publishing.

Holzberg, C. (1982) 'Ethnicity and ageing: anthropological perspectives on more than just the minority elderly', *The Gerontologist*, 33: 249–57.

Jackson, M. (1982) 'To be old and black: the case for double jeopardy in income and health', in R.C. Manuel (ed.), *Minority Aging*. Connecticut: Greenwood Press.

Larson, R. (1978) 'Thirty years of research on the subjective wellbeing of the older American', *Journal of Gerontology*, 33: 109–29.

Manuel, R.C. (1982a) 'The minority aged: providing a conceptual perspective', in R.C. Manuel (ed.), *Minority Aging*. Connecticut: Greenwood Press.

Manuel, R.C. (1982b) 'The dimensions of ethnic minority identification: an exploratory analysis among elderly black Americans', in R.C. Manuel (ed.), *Minority Aging*. Connecticut: Greenwood Press.

Mays, N. (1983) 'Elderly South Asians in Britain: a survey of the relevant literature and themes for future research', *Ageing and Society*, 3 (1): 71–97.

Nagi, S. and Haavio-Mannila, E. (1980) 'Migration, health status and utilisation of health services', *Sociology of Health and Illness*, 2 (2): 174–93.

Norman, A. (1985) *Triple Jeopardy: Growing Old in a Second Homeland*. London: Centre for Policy on Ageing.

Office of Population Censuses and Surveys (1983) *Census of England, Wales and Scotland 1981*. London: HMSO.

Palmore, E. (1983) 'Cross-cultural research: state of the art', *Research on Ageing*, 5 (1): 45–57.

Rex, J. (1986) *Race and Ethnicity*. Milton Keynes: Open University Press.

Rex, J. and Moore R. (1967) *Race, Community and Conflict*. London: Oxford University Press.

Runnymede Trust and Radical Statistics Race Group (1980) *Britain's Black Population*. London: Heinemann.

Schaie, K.W., Orchowsky, S. and Parham, I.A. (1982) 'Measuring age and sociocultural change: the case of race and life satisfaction', in R.C. Manuel (ed.) *Minority Aging*. Connecticut: Greenwood Press.

Stone, J. (1985) *Racial Conflict in Contemporary Society*. London: Fontana.

Taylor, R. (1982) 'Ageing and illness', *Ageing and Society*, 2 (2): 251–63.

Taylor, R. and Ford, G. (1983) 'Inequalities in old age', *Ageing and Society*, 3 (2): 183–208.

Notes on Contributors

Pat Allatt is Principal Lecturer in the Department of Administrative and Social Studies at Teesside Polytechnic.

Sara Arber is Senior Lecturer in Sociology and a member of the Stratification and Employment Group at the University of Surrey.

Ken Blakemore is Senior Lecturer in Sociology and Social Policy, Coventry Polytechnic.

Alan Bryman is Senior Lecturer in Sociology at Loughborough University of Technology.

Bill Bytheway is Senior Research Fellow in the Centre for Gerontology and Institute for Health Care Studies, University College of Swansea.

Maria Evandrou is a researcher in the Suntory Toyota International Centre for Economics and Related Disciplines, London School of Economics, and previously worked in the Department of Sociology at the University of Surrey.

Mike Featherstone is Senior Lecturer in the Department of Administrative and Social Studies, Teesside Polytechnic.

Nigel Gilbert is Reader in Sociology and a member of the Stratification and Employment Group at the University of Surrey.

Mike Hepworth is Senior Lecturer in Sociology at the University of Aberdeen.

Teresa Keil is Senior Lecturer in Sociology at Loughborough University of Technology.

Frank Laczko is a researcher in the Centre for the Analysis of Social Policy at the University of Bath and was previously a member of the Stratification and Employment Group at the University of Surrey.

Jonathan Long is a Lecturer in the Faculty of Educational and Leisure Studies at Leeds Polytechnic and was previously at the Centre for Leisure Research, Dunfermline College of Physical Education.

Tom Schuller is Director of the Centre for Continuing Education at the University of Edinburgh

Cherrie Stubbs is Senior Lecturer in the Department of Social Sciences, Sunderland Polytechnic.

Christina Victor is Director of Community Medicine and the Nursing Research Unit, St Mary's Hospital, London, and previously worked in the Department of Sociology at the University of Surrey.

Richard Wall is Senior Research Associate at the Cambridge Group for the History of Population and Social Structure, Cambridge University.

Name Index

Abrams, M., 161, 168, 174
Abrams, P., 8, 14, 23
Allan, G., 74, 91
Allatt, P., 5, 176
Allen, S., 174
Anderson, M., 23
Anderson, W. F., 61, 71
Anwar, M., 171, 174
Arber, S., 3, 40, 72, 75, 81, 90, 91-2, 119, 176
Archer, M., 42, 53
Arie, T., 124, 139, 142
Ariès, P., 144, 147, 156
Artt, S., 156

Bakke, E., 53
Ball, M., 22, 23
Barker, J., 162, 164, 165, 174
Bebbington, A. C., 75, 91, 113, 119
Bengston, V. L., 162, 168, 169, 174
Berry, S., 162, 174
Bertaux, D., 4, 118, 119
Bhachu, P., 171, 174
Bhalla, A., 162, 163, 164, 166, 167, 171, 174
Blakemore, K., 5, 158, 162, 163, 164, 166, 167, 168, 171, 173, 174, 176
Blanc, O., 137, 138, 142
Blow, F. C., 103
Bocock, J., 7, 23
Bond, J., 26, 40
Boneham, M., 163, 166, 171, 174
Bonnerjea, L., 73, 74, 82, 90, 92
Bornat, J., 43, 53
Braham, P., 174
Briggs, A., 73, 77, 91
Brown, C., 174
Bourdieu, P., 155, 156
Buckland, S., 88, 91
Burrows, R., 106, 119
Burton, L., 169, 174
Butler, T., 106, 119
Bytheway, B., 4, 5, 74, 91, 93, 103, 176
Bryman, A., 5, 176

Calhoun, R., 153, 156
Campbell, B., 18, 23
Cantor, M. H., 164, 174
Chaney, J., 11, 23
Charlesworth, A., 73, 77, 91
Cheal, D., 1, 5
Child Poverty Action Group, 23, 40
City of Coventry, 164, 165, 166, 167, 171, 174
Cowan, N. R., 61, 71
Crawford, M. P., 56, 71
Cunningham-Burley, S., 150, 156

Daatland, S. O., 102, 103
Dale, A., 40, 92, 104, 119
Davies, B., 75, 91
Davis, Bette, 145
Dennis, N., 15, 23
Department of Health and Social Security, 2, 5, 34, 35, 40
Derkin, V., 156
Derrida, J., 143, 156
Dex, S., 43, 47, 49, 54
Dowd, J. J., 168, 174
Durie, A., 91

Ebrahim, S., 163, 174
Elder, G., 65, 71
Elias, N., 144, 148, 156
Employment Gazette, 26, 28, 40
Equal Opportunities Commission, 73, 77, 90, 91
Estes, C. L., 161, 174
Evandrou, M., 4, 77, 91-2, 104, 105, 106, 109, 119, 120, 176

Fairhurst, E., 150, 156
Falkingham, J., 113, 119
Featherstone, M., 4, 143, 146, 148, 153, 156, 176
Fenton, S., 162, 166, 174
Finch, J., 1, 5, 72, 74, 84, 92
Fogarty, M., 6, 23
Foner, N., 166, 174

Pearn, M., 174
Phillipson, C., 6, 23, 44, 47, 53, 54, 65, 71, 72, 74, 92, 105, 119
Piachaud, D., 33, 40, 50, 54
Popplestone, G., 14, 23
Priestley, J. B., 148
Pruchno, R. A., 102, 103
Puner, M., 148, 157

Qureshi, H., 84, 85, 92

Rayner, C., 153, 157
Reagan, R., 145
Reid, I., 105, 119
Rex, J., 164, 175
Rhodes, E., 174
Ringen, S., 25, 40
Roberts, K., 55, 71
Robin, J., 142
Rossiter, C., 77, 92
Roussel, L., 137, 139, 142
Runnymede Trust, 170, 175

Sabatini, P., 156
Saunders, P., 20, 23, 106, 107, 118, 119
Savage, R. D., 161, 174
Sayer, A., 105, 119
Schaie, K. W., 160, 175
Schuller, T., 3, 41, 44, 54, 55, 71, 176
Schwarz, K., 139, 142
Seltzer, M., 44, 54
Shanas, E., 122, 142
Sheldon, J. H. 61, 71
Simons, K., 84, 85, 92
Sinclair, I., 92
Smith, C., 174
Smith, R., 42, 54
Smyer, M. A., 103
Stephens, J., 11, 23
Stockdale, J., 55, 71
Stoddard, K. M., 153, 157
Stone, I., 11, 23
Stone, J., 175
Stubbs, C., 1, 2, 6, 8, 11, 23, 176

Sullivan, O., 107, 119
Sundstrom, G., 122, 140, 141, 142
Swan, J. H., 174

Taylor, R., 106, 120, 161, 175
Thane, P., 43, 54, 104, 120
Thatcher, M., 145
Thompson, E. P., 54
Titmus, R. M., 36, 40
Townsend, P., 47, 54, 61, 71, 75, 92, 113, 120
Troll, L., 44, 54
Turner, B. S., 154, 155, 157
Turner, V., 49, 54
Turney, J., 108, 120

Ungerson, C., 74, 82, 83, 92
United Nations, 138, 142
Urry, J., 146, 157

van Gennep, A., 20, 23
van Laanen, J. T. M., 141
Vetter, N. J., 120
Victor, C. R., 4, 104, 105, 106, 109, 110, 120, 176

Walker, A., 72, 74, 92
Wall, R., 4, 121, 123, 126, 127, 137, 138, 139, 142, 176
Walmsley, J., 146, 157
Ward, S., 53
Watson, S., 7, 23
Wedderburn, D., 75, 92, 113, 120
Wheelock, J., 11, 23
Wicks, M., 77, 92, 110, 119
Wilkin, D., 91
Williams, R., 1, 5
Wimbush, E., 57, 58, 59, 64, 66, 71
Wright, F., 74, 92

Yvert-Jalu, H., 123, 138, 139, 142

Ziesel, H., 54

Subject Index